THE
PERILOUS
CATCH

D1580988

THE PERILOUS CATCH

A HISTORY OF COMMERCIAL FISHING

MIKE SMYLIE

The
History
Press

For Christoffer, Ana and Otis

'However you look at it, fishin's a dangerous occupation. At sea it's the elements; the sea, the cold and the tiredness gets you. On land it's the trudgery. For there's no place like being out at the fishin'. It's in the blood, see. However you look at it, it always gets you one way or other.'

Cruban Stirk

First published 2015

The History Press
The Mill, Brimscombe Port
Stroud, Gloucestershire, GL5 2QG
www.thehistorypress.co.uk

© Mike Smylie, 2015

The right of Mike Smylie to be identified as the Author
of this work has been asserted in accordance with the
Copyright, Designs and Patents Act 1988.

British Library Cataloguing in Publication Data.
A catalogue record for this book is available from the British Library.

ISBN 978 0 7524 9800 3

Typesetting and origination by The History Press
Printed and bound in Great Britain by TJ International Ltd

CONTENTS

INTRODUCTION

Imagine the scenario: being out in the North Sea off the east coast of Scotland in August, with dusk approaching, aboard a small open boat, the coastline a mere blot on the horizon. The sea is calm and there's an oily silence about it, with a slight breeze coming from the southwest. The boat, about 30ft in length, has five people aboard, all fishermen and resting, waiting to haul in the net in a few hours, hopefully full of the silver darlings. The presence of herring in the water is signalled by the gannets diving deep, and they keep a lookout for seals and other predators. As the blue hour comes, clouds build up from the east, hiding the full moon that earlier made its presence known and one of the fishers is alerted when he notices a slight shift in the wind direction. The same man points to a sudden reddening of the sky in the west and the wind again backs a few points to the east. Immediately a strong south-easterly wind picks up strength and the crew quickly start to haul in their net, not able to afford losing such a major piece of gear. The warning is apparent: it is time to seek shelter.

That was exactly the scenario on Friday, 18 August 1848. For all along the stretch of the east coast of Scotland, from Berwick-upon-Tweed right up to Wick in the north, these small boats had set out fishing that afternoon on what promised to be a lovely summer evening. But when an unexpected gale rose up around midnight, these fishers were desperately stranded. For, it being full moon with the spring tides, with the high water at midnight, the tide would be half through its ebb by the time they made the coast and with most of the harbours along this coast drying out, there was no shelter for them to return to. Those boats that did reach the 10 miles to the coast either chanced a landing on a lee shore, assuming they successfully passed through the breaking waves, hoping there might be help on the beach. The approach to any of the drying harbours was exacerbated by the fact that few had any lights to lead the boats in. Even though some boats managed to get home and into shelter not too long after midnight, most did not get away quick enough and the end result was carnage among those fleets from the various harbours and beach landings strung along this coast, numbering almost one hundred. One estimate gave 10,000 fishermen working on this coast. The Wick area alone, the town itself being termed the herring capital of Europe in 1865, had 3,500 fishermen working on 800 boats. In all a hundred lives were lost and 124 boats either wrecked or severely damaged. Although the harbours along the southern shore fared well, being in the lee of the storm, others did not. Peterhead Bay alone saw thirty-seven lives lost. Some boats survived by staying out at sea and a few Wick boats sailed northwards. But destruction littered the exposed coast and onlookers ashore could only stare in horror as the scenes unfolded in front of their eyes, sometimes only yards out to sea.

Of course this wasn't the first time such storms overcame fishing fleets. In 1806, the entire fishing fleet of three boats from the tiny settlement of Stotfield on the Moray Firth, now absorbed into the west side of Lossiemouth, was destroyed on Christmas Day while the boats – open scaffie types – were fishing just offshore. This is often referred to as the first such fishermen's disaster on the east coast of Scotland. The storm took the boats down the Firth and away from home. Each boat had seven crew and they all simply disappeared in the vengeance of the storm that had taken them unawares, even though they had been fishing in sight of their homes in daylight. This tragedy took away every able-bodied man, leaving seventeen widows, forty-seven orphans and two old men behind.

Look around the coast and there are few areas that have not suffered similar fates. But the tragedy of 1848 did rouse the Scottish public's anguish and the government was forced into action when a 1,000-signature petition was delivered to the Lords of the Admiralty, along with a letter from provost, magistrates and town council of Wick. Eventually the Lords Commissioners of the Admiralty decided to instruct a special enquiry 'as to whether the wrecks occurred from the want of a harbour, from the use by the fishermen of a defective class of boats, or otherwise' and Captain John Washington, RN, was chosen to head this.

Washington's thoroughness could not be faulted. He held public meetings in Wick, Banff, Fraserburgh and Peterhead over a week in October 1848, taking oral evidence from fishermen, merchants, Fishery Officers, onlookers and harbour authorities, and later corresponded with a host of people. He also considered the design of vessels all over Britain and Ireland. In his report entitled *Report on the Loss of Life and Damage to Fishing Boats on The East Coast of Scotland* and now commonly referred to as the 'Washington Report',[1] which stretches to over more than a hundred pages and includes drawings of boats and charts of existing harbours and suggested improvements to them, he castigates the British Fisheries Society, the design of the fishing boats and the poor state of the harbours. He also lists all the boats lost with their skippers. In all, the report makes fascinating reading. Fishing boats, in the general opinion of that part of the coast, were best open as this left more space to carry fish. Decks were thought to be superfluous and safety appears to have been low on the list of priorities for these fishermen. However, within ten years fishermen favoured decking over their boats, persuaded by evidence from the report and other authorities.

Following the Douglas Bay fishing disaster[2] was another instance of a change in boat design, which attempted to make fishing a safer labour. This happened at the entrance to Douglas harbour on the night of 20/21 September 1787. A storm the previous year had demolished the old Douglas pier and its lighthouse and no repairs had been made although a temporary lamp had been installed on the ruins of the old quay. Four hundred boats set out that evening for the 'back' fishing in the bay but when a southeasterly gale sprung up the boats were forced to return to the safety of the harbour. The entrance to the harbour was difficult in the dark and the lanterns along the beach were mistaken for the lamp at the end of the pier by many boats. One boat actually stuck the end of the pier and destroyed the post holding up the one lamp, making the situation even more critical. Boats were simply thrown ashore in the confusion and in the morning the enormity of the disaster became apparent: the beach and rocks were covered in wrecks and bodies were floating around the harbour. Some twenty-one fishermen lost their lives with somewhere in the region of fifty boats being wrecked.

Again it was the design of the boat that was partly to blame although common sense suggests the lack of a good light probably accounted more for the loss of boats. The older boats were of a squaresail type of boat imported from Norway ten centuries before. These *scowtes*, as they were called, were open vessels and a fierce debate followed regarding their suitability. The lack of a deck was the main fault and it wasn't long before decked boats, smacks with a cutter rig, appeared. However, within forty years, with the appearance of Cornish luggers, the fishermen turned away from the smacks in favour of the lug-rig.

It was the disaster of 14 October 1881 that must go down in history as the worst such calamity in Scotland. In a storm that sprung up on a Friday afternoon, 189 fishermen from Eyemouth and the surrounding region were drowned.[3] In all ninety-three widows and 267 children were left in the storm's aftermath. All too often it is exactly those left behind – family members and dependents – that suffer the hardship of losing the breadwinner in these disasters. The State itself did not hold any responsibility to care for these victims and it was left to the public to raise money to ensure their survival. The State also chose not to conduct an inquiry into the matter as it had thirty-odd years before.

In Ireland the Cleggan Bay disaster of Friday, 28 October 1927 has left an indelible imprint on the small communities of the west of Ireland but again was not unique.[4] Once more it was a violent storm that had sprung up unexpectedly as the men from the Connemara communities of Inishbofin and Rossadilisk were out fishing. Some were drowned at sea while others were dashed against rocks aboard their vessels trying to reach safety. It devastated the communities and in all forty-six men were lost, leaving 187 dependents.

It is now a familiar story: fishing is a dangerous occupation. As a brief interlude, what exactly is fishing? Fishing, by definition, is the taking of fish, shellfish or any other animals from the sea, river or lake, or the foreshore of, for any means. However, in this book we are only concerned with what could be termed 'commercial fishing' although this, too, is misleading. Is subsistence fishing commercial fishing? Not really, I would argue, although subsistence fishing is very much at the heart of this book. Angling is not included as that is regarded purely as a sport, although some will argue that they are anglers only to gain food. However, in this book we will refrain from the mention of any angling, even if there are those that will complain. We will simply concentrate on fishing as an occupation as well as that, in centuries long gone, at a subsistence level.

Travel around the coast and there are umpteen memorials in unsuspecting places, declaring the names of fishers lost at sea. One that instantly comes to mind is at Portskerra on the very north coast of Scotland, a few miles west of John O'Groats. Here, on a stone plaque by the beach, are the names of folk of the community 'who perished within sight of their homes'. The outcome of three disasters is etched into the stone by way of the names of people: 5 December 1848 when eight men were taken; 25 June 1890 when eleven perished; 22 August 1918 with seven lost. It's a sobering memorial and simply illustrates that fishermen are often lost close to home.

That reminds us of 'Crazy Kate' of Clovelly, north Devon, who saw her husband perish from her house overlooking the harbour. The story goes that Kate Lyall's husband was a fisherman who fished within sight of the house, watched by Kate from the upper window. One day he was overcome by a heavy squall and drowned. She lost her mind without him and eventually walked into the sea, dressed in her wedding dress, to join her husband in a watery grave.

Of course, at the bigger ports where boats used to sail up into the deep Arctic, there resulted in a greater loss of life but that in no way belittles the losses close to our shores. In the northern latitudes stories of vessels overturning because of ice build-up on deck were common and often grabbed headlines whereas local drownings often did not. However, the fact that some 120 large trawlers were lost between 1946 and 1975 illustrates just what the

The plaque at Portskerra in memory of the fishermen from the local community who drowned within sight of their homes while fishing.

risk involved, in working in what were at times extreme conditions. And on top of this there are the unexplained mysteries such as the loss of the trawler *Gaul* off the Norwegian coast in February 1974, the cause of which has never been completely determined.

And of course it never ends. In March 2014, just as the finishing touches were being put to this book, the 35m Portuguese stern trawler *Santa Ana* sank off the Asturian coast of northern Spain, killing eight members of the crew while only the skipper, who was on the helm, was rescued. The crew had all been asleep below. The vessel had run aground after hitting a rock around Erbosa Island at 5 a.m., shortly after leaving the port of Avilés to fish for mackerel. After being submerged and smashed around by the sea, the wreck was later raised in a spectacular fashion and the resultant vessel was not a pretty sight. Part of the port side was missing and the rest was a tangled mess of metal, winches and net, a latent reminder that, wherever fishing boats work, there is danger from many different angles and not always just the weather. Groundings, collisions, nets snagging on the seabed (and submarines) and possible tales of intrigue in the Cold War days all have contributed to the loss of life. In the following pages we tell of the development of the fishing industry, the ways people have fished through two millennia and the perils they faced, and still do even today.

1

EARLY FISHERS

I have a friend who is an archaeologist and he works for the Greek government, the country of his origin. For his doctorate he excavated and studied part of the coastal settlement of Kynos which is situated opposite the island of Eubeoa in the North Eubeoan Gulf, some 100 miles north of Athens. The majority of the site had already been excavated in the 1980s. Several sherds of the same pot (a krater, to be exact) were discovered, dating to the late Helladic IIIC Bronze Age period, approximately 2500 BC, some 4,500 years ago.[1] The illustration on the krater depicts seine-net fishing and is considered to be one of two of the earliest such depictions, the other coming from a vase discovered on the island of Naxos. The position of the settlement just yards from the sea, and given that Homer in the *Iliad* described ships sailing past these waters on their way to Troy, it would seem fairly obvious that the people living in the settlement turned to the sea for much, or at least some, of their diet. According to one source, fish was eaten only by the very impoverished and was considered poor food at the time. In the *Iliad* and the *Odyssey* 'no fish appear at banquets or in the houses of the well-to-do: only in connection with the poorest or starving do they obtain mention'.[2] This has since been countered by scholars who believe fish was eaten by the Mycenaean elite.

Moreover, it is believed that a number of fishing techniques were used at this time. Fishing with spears, traps, hooks and nets both from the coast and aboard small one-man craft, was prevalent. Spears include the trident which was often used to catch octopus although evidence from Kynos suggests that they were using clay pots to trap octopus as well. The same type of pot with a hole in the bottom is used in many Mediterranean countries today and, several years ago, I reported on such techniques seen in Tunisia.[3]

The other fishing evidence from Kynos comes from the bronze hooks, both with and without barbs, and net or line sinkers in the form of perforated sherds. The evidence for the use of nets is backed up by Homer who also mentions net fishing and it has been suggested that these were made from flax.

The depiction on the Naxos vase clearly showing fish inside a seine-net which is being hauled in by fishers on the shore.

In Ancient Egypt, it was thought that a fishing industry of sorts was established much because of the physical appearance of the land, which has little fertile land between desert and coast. It was only the River Nile that gave the country both a surplus of fish and good agricultural land. Fish was eaten widely in prehistoric times, as attested by the amount of fish bones recorded by archaeologists and various depictions of fish related subjects, as well as some implements, have been discovered. One particular sherd shows a hunted animal along with a fish, suggesting a hunter-gatherer environment.[4]

Nevertheless, this evidence doesn't tell us when humans first started fishing and the common belief is that the presence of rock pools on the foreshore that had been left on an ebb tide with fish stuck in them alerted early humans to this fact. In the tidal areas of the world it is assumed that this is how humans discovered how to build fish weirs on the foreshore that created bigger pools once the tide had ebbed. However, this presupposes a significant tidal difference which was lacking in the eastern Mediterranean. Any change in the height of the water from day to day was from weather patterns (high or low pressure) and not only was the difference in height small, it was pretty unreliable.

Evidence in Britain comes mostly from the Mesolithic era when the country had become an island cut off from mainland Europe. We know people were seafaring during this time because the settlement of Ireland can be

Twenty-first-century octopus pots seen in Tunisia. The design hasn't changed much in millennia and the main difference is the line they are attached to and the plastic floats.

dated to *c.* 6000 BC. Later communities started arriving off the west coasts of Scotland, and especially Orkney. Shell middens contain archaeological evidence of human occupation from the seventh to fifth millennia BC. In England middens dating to approximately 4500 BC have been excavated at Westward Ho! in Devon, Culver Well, Isle of Portland in Dorset, and in South Wales at Nanna's Cave, Caldey Island, off Tenby.

The first fishers were undoubtedly hunter-gatherers, living off the land and the sea or rivers. In Britain, the landscape was one of a heavily forested hinterland with prime rivers for catching fish in many parts. In others it was the sea, again rich in all manner of fish and seafood. If one considers what was available before humans started a determined effort to harvest the fruits of the sea, the foreshore alone gave them shellfish – mussels, cockles, oysters, whelks, winkles, limpets and other shellfish – while the rock pools might have contained small fish, crabs and shrimps. The rivers were rich, with their salmon, trout, sea-trout, eels and flounders, while just offshore were all manner of shoaling and bottom-feeding fish and other shellfish such as lobsters. Even the inland lakes produced fish like pike and tench. What a banquet could be collected in a short time.

This may present a false picture that the life of hunter-gatherers was a simple one – the truth is the opposite. It was a strenuous and hard life, with the added conflict between tribes, and roving bandits who were always keen for a free meal and not concerned about the value of human life. History is full of tales of death and destruction, and fishers were not exempt.

The excavations of shell middens on the island of Oronsay, Inner Hebrides produced much information about the gathering of food from the foreshore. Bevel-headed antler, bone and stone tools found in large numbers have been interpreted as 'limpet hammers' or 'limpet scoops'. However, other archaeologists think they were tools for softening skin hides as some show signs of rubbing, polishing and abrasion. Moreover, they also found barbed pots and harpoons which were probably used for the procurement of marine animals and large fish using hand- or long-lining. The most common species of fish found in the middens was wrasse, saithe (coley) and ling which were probably caught using nets or spears.

As time went by, fishing techniques have improved. Fishing without gear – just hands and feet – then led to the development of fishing tools such as knives, spears and long-handled hooks. Divers used such hooks for loosening shells and hooking octopus. There are a number of finds in Scotland that point strongly to the development of deep-sea fishing during the late Mesolithic period. At a midden on the tiny island of Risga, in the mouth of Loch Sunart, bones of various sea fish were found, including skate, conger eel, grey mullet and haddock, indicating the use of a boat for line-fishing or netting.

Over the centuries all manner of methods have been used for catching fish. These include the use of animals such as dogs, otters, cormorants, turtles, octopi and porpoises, using mechanical ways of stupefying fish such as dynamite, toxic plants, clamps and rakes, and electrical fishing. Shooting, spearing and harpooning were ways of capturing fish, especially after it was discovered that light attracted fish.[5] In many parts of the world today bright lights are shone into the water to bring the fish to the surface before they are netted. Few visitors to Southern Europe will have failed to see small open Mediterranean craft sitting on beaches fitted with big lamps.

But we must return to Britain in our discussion with regard to the more common fishing methods and, first and foremost, are fish weirs and traps.

Fish Weirs

Fish weirs are barriers that are referred to as 'fixed engines'. Documented evidence of weirs is scarce though three traps excavated at the Late Kongemose site Agerod V in southern Sweden are said to date back more than 6,000 years. Another, at the Ertebolle site of Jonstorp, still contained a cod and several have relatively recently been excavated in Denmark that date from the Mesolithic and Neolithic times.[6] In Britain various fishing baskets and fish traps at Goldcliff, in the River Severn estuary, have been observed in the minerogenic sediments and date to around 5400–4000 cal BC.[7] Many others have been established for hundreds of years. Indeed, as F.M. Davis recounts, 'the first settlers in Queensland, some of whom lived much among the then Blackfellows, have left very full descriptions of the stone-weirs used by these primitive people who were still in the Stone Age of culture'.[8] The same he says of the Indians of Virginia who developed 'great fish weirs and fish pounds'. Davis also suggests that it is not improbable that the earliest method of fishing in any quantity was by stopping the mouths of narrow tidal creeks with brushwood or stones but when it was discovered that this also blocked the ingress of fish, the weir was developed by forming an opening that could be closed on the ebb. Davis gives the 'Fishponds' of south Devon as an example. In the Outer Hebrides:

> one method of catching fish which was once common was by building yares or stone dykes across a river estuary. The fish that swim in at high tide when the yare was submerged were left stranded when the tide ebbed, and could be collected without much trouble.[9]

As has been mentioned previously, fish weirs are only capable of working effectively in tidal waters and Britain has the remains of many littered around its coast, especially on the western side of Scotland, England and Wales. These weirs were positioned in such a way that they used the natural swimming behaviour of fish that in shallow flowing water tend to swim parallel to the coastline. On the flood many tend to swim towards the shore and away on the ebb. Thus, as the tide recedes, the entrance should be behind the fish. They were generally constructed with stout oak posts bedded into the foreshore with stone walls built up for the first foot or two, and then hazel or willow was used to weave a framework which allowed a flow of seawater to pass. The weave was more tightly woven at the bottom to prevent fish escaping and looser at the top, thus ensuring the greater flow at the higher level of tide passed through without damaging the structure, for the pressure of water can be immense. Some weirs had intricate openings at their mouths with sluices so that these mouths could be opened or shut. The *gorad bach* – literally little weir – on the Menai Strait in North Wales has a 'bass trap' which is a little sluice that could be opened to let whitebait out (a common fish in these parts). Bigger fish such as salmon and bass tended to linger outside awaiting a tasty meal – the owners of the weir, John and Wilf Girling, would wait above with a lap-net to catch the unsuspecting salmon or bass. This weir, along with another larger one a mile to the east called the Trecastell weir, date back several centuries and were very effective at catching all manner of fish: herring, whitebait, salmon, mackerel, bass and even the green-boned garfish. In shape they were the same and consisted of a wall running at right angles to the shore, and out to the low water mark, and then another along the low water mark perpendicular to the first. At the right-hand end, looking from the shore, the end that faces the ebb, a short wall runs back on itself at a sharp angle, thus forming the 'crew' where the fish were unable to escape. The *gorad bach* was in use until the 1960s and the owners then only packed up as it was obvious that the seagulls and bait diggers were having more of the catch than they were! Another weir in this area, called the *lyme-kiln*, was leased to Thomas Norrey in 1438 for twenty years while Thomas Sherwin paid a rent of sixpence a year ten years later for another said to be 'lying between the lyme-kiln fishery and the house of the Friar Minor of Llanfaes'. Given that the *gored bach* is in the vicinity of Llanfaes, it could be assumed that the report refers to this weir.[10]

The Menai Strait had several other fish weirs and one in particular was restored in recent times. Current regulations ban their use so this one has holes in the restored wall that allow any fish to escape. Situated on the small island between the two bridges over the Menai Strait, the weir can be studied from above and if the tide is high, the shape of the weir can clearly be seen. Another used to be worked on the island – the remains are still visible – and the remnants of two others can be found nearby on the Anglesey shore. One of these two uses the method of building a barrier between two islands so

John Girling Snr with a landing net full of whitebait in his fish weir, the *gorad bach*, near Beaumaris, Anglesey. The weir is said to date back to medieval times. (*Courtesy of Bridget Dempsey*)

that the fish can pass around the outside of the island and towards the shore on the flood, but are then are caught when trying to make their way between the islands on the ebb. Further northeast, there is the outline of another at Cadnant clearly visible in the mud at low water. Another used to lie across the Straits on the Bangor side, a vague remnant still visible with the tide out.

Weirs follow various patterns and an attempt has been made to classify them as to whether they are active or passive. Again the shape is important, for a couple on the west coast of Wales are crescent shaped – described by one writer as 'somewhat shaped as a boomerang'.[11] Others are V-shaped often with several side by side and a net of some form across the neck where the fish are caught. But in reality they come in all shapes and sizes. As I write this, the family are watching a programme on television and suddenly there's a mention of fish traps. I stop and listen to hear how dolphins are trapping fish in a manoeuvring technique similar in some ways to these structures. And a very successful technique it is, as fish after fish flop into their jaws. Maybe, then, the development of fish weirs simply came about by watching closely the ways of the creatures that inhabit the seas.

Fish Traps

Various forms of fish traps have been in use since prehistoric times, albeit in a different, possibly updated, form. The best example is perhaps the octopus clay pot mentioned above. Just as lobster, crab, eel and whelk are caught using pots – or creels as they call them in Scotland – today, so were they many years ago. However, throughout the world small-scale fishermen have developed various shaped baskets used as traps, made from an equal variety of material – willow, hazel, bamboo, reeds, rattan and palm leaves. Some are very basic structures while others consist of an intricate weave of materials.

Fish traps do not simply have to be in a basket form and can be man-made structures placed across the current in a river and here, it could be said, there is little difference between a fish weir and a fish trap. However, there is one very important dissimilarity in that weirs are fixed engines while fish traps can be removed and placed elsewhere. One example of this is the Wing trap from the Mekong River in Laos. At the Khone Falls these structures are used between May and July to catch migrating fish moving upstream. When fish reach the falls they are held in the trap by the strong current.[12]

Such structures also occur in Britain, most notably in the River Severn. Putts and putchers are basketwork traps set into frameworks of stakes placed across the flow of the river, the difference between the two being the size. The putcher is the smallest at about 5 or 6ft in length and is a cone-shaped woven basket of willow and hazel. Putchers are mounted in the framework in tiers of three or four, up to thirty or forty along (or more even), giving a total of several hundred. They normally face upstream, thus catching the fish as they swim down on the ebb though occasionally they might face downstream. Once a fish swims into the trap there is no way out. Once the short fishing season is over (June to August), then the putchers have to be removed and taken ashore.

Putts are altogether much bigger and are made up of three integral parts – the kype, butt and forewheel. They work the same way as the putchers and always face upstream. The entrance to the trap, the kype, can be as big as 6ft in diameter and the whole putt up to 14ft in length. They have to be closed to salmon out of season and this is done by driving two lengths of willow crosswise through the rear of the kype where it joins the butt. Salmon cannot then get in but other fish and eels can still be fished. Putts are thought to go back to the fifteenth century and possible even as far as the tenth.[13]

In Greece fish traps were positioned in rivers. Recently I met a fisherman named Kostas Giotis who made one that he called a *silpi* in Greek. Made from local reeds, it is some 6ft long and 2ft wide. It looks a bit like a conical basket that has been split longitudinally so that the mouth is flat, though the tip of the cone is still in place. The trap sits in the river and stones are moved to act as a hedge to lead the fish into it. They get stuck in the tip, unable to swim backwards against the current. This he used when the river was in flood in March, with the snows melting and filling the River Sperheios, in central Greece. Mostly set at night and emptied the next morning, sometimes he would sit by river spearing or stringing fish with worms, the latter used for jigging so that when a fish bites the string is flicked downstream and towards the bank to land the fish. Just after the war, he informed me, they were using grenades to fish with too, as well as poisons. With regard to the latter Aristotle mentions fleabane to make octopi drop off rocks. Mullien was used and continued in use into the twentieth century, as was fleabane. Cyclamen is mentioned by ancient writers as a poison for catching tuna and mullet.

Gorges and Hooks

Although we have mentioned hooks from the Bronze Age, gorges are believed to predate hooks as the method of ensuring a fish doesn't get away after eating the bait on a line and have been in use since the Palaeolithic period. The earliest form of gorge was a straight or slightly curved piece of wood, sharpened at both ends and tied to the line in the middle. It was then inserted lengthways into the bait and is swallowed by that fish so that when the line is tightened it turns transversely inside the belly or throat and cannot be spat out. Gorges are also used for catching birds and similar devices are used for catching crocodiles. Gorges were also made from bone, horn, flint and metal.

Gorges do work, as we once discovered while filming for the BBC for a programme called *The Truth about Food*. I'd made a couple out of thin branches as part of a demonstration on archaeological fishing methods and was fishing with the camera crew and participants a few miles off Dartmouth. On one side we made rods with modern fishing gear and on the other side a gorge and a hook made from a rose thorn. To our surprise a fish took the gorge but, to our dismay, the line broke while pulling it in. However, the rose thorn hook, although I felt one fish having a nibble, didn't catch anything. Meanwhile on the other side of the boat the participants were reeling in the mackerel!

Hooks come in all manner of shapes and sizes, made from a number of materials such as bronze, copper, thorn, bone, antler, ceramic and later iron. Indeed, according to J. Bickerdyke, the thorn hooks mentioned earlier were still in use in parts of the Thames estuary up to 1895.[14] Early hooks didn't have a barb and proved much more ineffectual then those with. Among the fishing collections of the world are beautiful hooks made from mother-of-pearl, tortoiseshell, whalebone and human bones, and these remained treasured artefacts from an era when fishermen took great pride in their gear. Today steel hooks are mass-produced in the same way as their nets, lines and ropes are.

Hooks can be used in a multitude of ways: either singly on hand lines; set on paternosters, again for hand lines; set on feathers for trolling; for multi-line trolling; on spinning hooks for mackerel; fixed into lures for hand lines; and long lines.

Long lines are made up are hundreds of hooks which are tied to 'snoods', short pieces of horsehair, which are in turn tied to the line itself, the snoods being about a foot apart. Long-lining has been described as the simplest method of commercial fishing though its downside was the baiting of the hook which took hours, even after spending time catching the bait. Then, once they were set – another time-consuming labour – they had to be hauled in without getting all the hooks stuck into the side of the boat (or fingers and other parts of the anatomy). In time mechanisation brought about much longer lines that were hauled in with the use of hydraulic winches and, for larger craft, systems were designed for casting lines out. However, we are now in the realms of large-scale commercial fishing, a place we do not want to be in at present.

Nets

Remains of nets have been found at Herculaneum and in Egypt, though because all nets (until recently) were made from organic material, only tiny bits have survived. As we've seen, only implements made from inorganic materials have been discovered on the whole. It is believed that in early times fishing with nets was only from the shore with beach seine-nets, as the Kynos and Naxos depictions suggest.

Nets were made from plant fibre and, according to Oppian, 'very light nets of buoyant flax' were used for tuna fishing. He added that 'they wheel round in a circle round about while they violently strike the surface of the sea with their oars and make a din with the sweeping blow of poles'.[15] The fish are frightened and chased into the net. Also a man used to be positioned in a watchtower to search out and point the boats to a shoal. Part of a net was also found at Nikonion, an ancient (600–300 BC) Greek city on the east bank of the River Dniester estuary in modern-day Ukraine, while a fragment of a net discovered was found to be hemp.

Although various natural fibres could be used – flax, willow, lime, jute, sisal, iris, coir seed, Cretan lily leaf – by far the most common material that would have all the necessary qualities for use as lines and for nets is nettle-hemp. The nettles would be gathered in spring and early summer, the leaves stripped off the stems and the stems immersed in water for several hours. After removal from the water, they would be pulped so that the individual strands would peel away producing long, thin fibres. These fibres would then be spun in the same way as flax and wool, the resulting 'yarn' would then be used for the lines, to make nets and also for the strings of bows. Hemp was considered too rough and used for ropes.

Floats were made from cork, wood, pumice, pieces of bark, goats' wool and sealed containers. Sinkers, as mentioned earlier, were perforated sherds, or stones with natural indentations, lead wrapped around a line, clay wrapped around sticks and fired and terracotta flat discs with two holes at the top. Weights used in weaving were also sometimes used.

2

THE GROWTH OF THE HERRING FISHERY

In terms of fishing, both in the species and the techniques employed, there is a distinct difference between pelagic and demersal fishing. Pelagic refers to fish that live near or on the surface, rarely swimming to a more than a moderate depth while, on the contrary, the latter is said of fish that live in or near the bottom of the sea or ocean. This not to say that pelagic fish do not swim close to the seabed: they can reach depths up to 400m. Generally, though, they live in the top levels of the sea and also feed at the surface.

In Britain the four main pelagic species fished commercially are herring, mackerel, pilchard and sprat, though there are others such as whitebait, anchovy, tuna and blue whiting. Sardines are the same species as pilchard, the latter being a more mature sardine. In Cornwall, where all British pilchards are landed, the name 'Cornish sardines' has been coined in an effort to increase sales. (The word 'pilchard' seems to have unfavourable connotations that 'sardine' doesn't!)

It is the herring fishery that has attracted the attention of writers and historians throughout the last thousand years. Thus much more is known about it and its effect on society than, say, for the mackerel, even if the mackerel is today often regarded as everyone's favourite summer fish.

Herring swim in huge shoals at spawning time and they have done so off almost every part of the British coastline over the last 300 years, even if their numbers are depleted today through overfishing. However, it has always been the fact that the North Sea saw a greater concentration of fish than did the west coast, with the obvious result being a higher concentration in fishing activity. Prior to the mid-eighteenth century, the herring fishery as such didn't really exist and was a resource largely ignored except by the small inshore fishermen who fished mostly for themselves and the locality. Nevertheless, the fishermen realised for themselves that the best time to catch herring at their prime was when they were about to spawn, and that they return year after year to spawn in the same place until something changes their behaviour.

Before we discuss the growth of the business in catching and landing herring into an actual industry, we must go back over a thousand years to the times when the Romans were getting up and departing south from these shores. Yes, of course, they ate herring, understanding the healthy and appetising aspect of the fish, and having learnt what almost sounds like the secrets of the fish from the locals near to their garrison at Garianonum which was a few miles west of what is now Great Yarmouth and thought to have been Burgh Castle. Then the area was a huge estuary with a mass of sandbanks stretching over what we call the Norfolk Broads today.[1]

As the last of the Romans left over the Straits of Dover in the fifth century, a confederation of Germanic tribes migrated towards Britain under Cerdick the Saxon with five ships, although they had been sending incursions over to battle against the Romans for centuries, necessitating the Romans to build their coastal fortifications. Cerdick and his gang found an ideal base upon a sandbank and built a stronghold upon it and discovered an abundance of herring offshore. A century later we find that Felip, Bishop of the East Angles, built a church with 'godly men placed in it to pray for the health and success of fishermen that came to Yarmouth in the herring season'.[2]

The Vikings, who came to Britain in the late tenth century, have been accredited with bringing the techniques of their boatbuilding skills to Britain. This has resulted in influences still being obvious among fishing and other working craft along a huge swathe of coast from the Thames, around the Scottish coast and down the other side as far as the Bristol Channel, and from the southeast of Ireland around to Donegal on the northwest coast. Double-ended in shape, clinker-built in construction, it is now considered that it was the Saxons who first brought these techniques into Britain and which the Vikings only substantiated because they, too, were using similar ways, probably brought about through the same development over the intervening 400 years.[3]

We do not know what life was like for the simple fisherman in these times though presumably they were seamen rather than dedicated fishers. It is probable that the boats were open, propelled by oars, much in the way that Viking boats are today represented. It is, too, unclear exactly how the fish were being caught although we do know that nets were involved. Presumably it was with some form of a drift-net though it is equally possibly that such nets were anchored in specific places and left overnight. Herring tend to rise to the surface after dark, to feed off the plankton that floats there, and this was the best time to catch them, and remained so right up to the development of the mid-water trawling system in the second half of the twentieth century. So, if you don't want to hang about for several hours at night with a train of drift-nets attached to the bow of your boat, given your boat is open and vulnerable to adverse weather, you anchor them, in the same way as Welsh herring fishers did up to the late twentieth century.

The first herring fishery that was under any sort of centralised control was that of the southern Sweden area of Skanor in the late twelfth and thirteenth centuries. This fishery was commanded by the growing Hanseatic League of merchants from the German towns of Lübeck and Hamburg, which later spread its influence across Europe by trading far and wide over the continent. The herring were in these waters a century before when, in a Polish poem recording a victory in Kolberg, famous for its salt herring, in 1105, it was said that 'They brought us herring and stinking fish, and now our sons are bringing them to us fresh and quivering.'[4] The Hanse was greatly helped by the Catholic Church's insistence that fish was eaten on Fridays and other days. Herring largely supplied that market.

Then the herring deserted almost overnight. There they were, year after year after year, and then they were gone. That's been the trouble with investment in herring over the centuries: these fickle fish are capable of changing their migratory patterns overnight, as was mentioned earlier. In this instance it has since been suggested that a combination of high tides and a massive amount of rainfall pouring off the surrounding rivers into the Baltic scared them off and they spawned out in the North Sea. More likely is that other factors were involved in the collapse of the Skanor fishery and the power of the Hanse, such as Danish grappling back the fishing rights in the late sixteenth century.

So what happened next? According to Voltaire, the Dutch 'turned their stinking tons [of fish] into tons of gold' for it was them that harnessed the political power that came with a vibrant herring fishery. In simplistic terms they grasped control of the North Sea herring. But here historical facts can become a bit vague and plagiarised for it would appear that they were already quite well established. Furthermore, Voltaire was writing in the late seventeenth century so he might not be a reliable source. It has been said by many that the reasons for Dutch mastery throughout the North Sea were down to several facts. First, they were connoisseurs of the herring and knew how to look after it. Herring, being an oily fish, goes off quickly once caught. Although Yarmouth fish merchant Peter Chivalier had introduced an improved method of salting herring (the Egyptians and Chinese were salting fish 4,000 years earlier, so it was not an unknown process) in the twelfth century, it was a Dutchman, Willem Van Beukels, who perfected the method of gutting and cleaning the fish and packing them into barrels with copious amounts of salt. To us it might seem obvious today that the gutting and cleaning was vital to preservation, but back then it obviously was not. Second, it was another Dutchman from Hoorn who remains nameless but who, about this time, invented the drift-net as we know it today with lead weights, floats and trains of nets tied together, and header ropes and strops to regulate the distance from the surface to the top of the net. What these two factors show was that the Dutch were busy catching herring at a time when the Baltic herring was supposedly in total command and that it wasn't a fact of the Dutch simply taking over from the Hanse at their downfall, but that they were already building up a substantial fishery.[5] Once the Baltic fishery collapsed, they achieved total command and fished the North Sea alone, often within sight of the British coast to the chagrin of the English Crown. Their method of using 'busses' – so called large bulky vessels that sent smaller open boats to fish, to return with herring that were cured aboard so that they could stay at sea for several weeks – produced copious amounts to satisfy the home market as well as the export to Eastern Europe.

The fact didn't go unnoticed for long and James I, after the Union of 1603, took steps to counter the Dutch, creating territorial waters. Although the Dutch, through previous agreements, were supposedly not to fish 'within sight of the shoar', they did.[6] By 1622 James had set up a Commission which later legislated to prevent the Dutch fishing anywhere near Shetland, Norway and Ireland. The Dutch responded by sending in naval escorts with success as the British seemed unable to act or control its own waters. On several occasions French and Dutch boats attacked each other in British ports while the locals simply looked on powerless. Britannia in no way ruled the waves in those days! On one particular instance a French privateer chased a herring buss right into Yarmouth harbour, killed several Dutch fishers, and robbed their boat before sailing off. The town bailiff fired off a couple of shots before politely asking the French to desist. This was met by various gestures that one can only imagine though the next day the privateer was trapped by two Dutch warships and their only escape was to beach the boat at Lowestoft. Wading ashore they were arrested and thrown into a Yarmouth prison though their ultimate fate is unknown.[7] When Cromwell overthrew the monarchy, he began to take action which ultimately saw the demise of the Dutch mastery in the North Sea in the eighteenth century, though long after his death.

Attempts were made to develop a fishing industry in the early eighteenth century. In 1704 Queen Anne allowed all harbours and shores to control the landing of fish, as well as introducing a bounty on Scottish exports of £10 4s per last (£24 for red herrings). Foreign fishermen were given the same rights and import duties were freed on imports for fishing boat building.[8] Then, in 1727, The Commissioners and Trustees for Improving Fisheries and Manufactures in Scotland offered small prize totalling no more than £100 to the first fishermen to spot the herring shoals upon their shores.[9] There are, in fact, many discourses written about ways of increasing the capability of the British fisheries, and especially the herring.

Views of a herring curing station on Loch Torridon, drawn by Thomas Newte in the 1780s.

The English and Scots decided the best course forward was to emulate the Dutch buss fishery, as put forward in some of these discourses, and a bounty was introduced on vessels. This bounty amounted to thirty shillings, paid annually for each decked vessel of twenty to eight tons built and based in home ports. In 1750, when the bounty was raised to fifty shillings, the Free British Fishery Society was founded and four years later they were operating forty busses, encouraged by the payment of bounties introduced by the government. By 1759 there were only four busses left in their fleet, such was the difficulty the Society was having financially.[10] Then, in 1787, the bounty system was altered to take into account the thousands of small boats fishing within sight of the shore around the Scottish coast and the North Sea coast of England. Instead of concentrating on paying out just on fleet tonnage, this was reduced to twenty shillings per vessel and a new bounty of two shillings and eight pence was paid on each barrel of white herring exported, one shilling and nine pence on full red herrings and just a shilling on spent red herring. 'Red' herring in this instance refers to ungutted herring while 'white' is gutted prior to salting.

It is probably true to say that the bounty system was the first time that fishermen had to deal with day-to-day paperwork for it created a massive amount of bureaucracy for both them and the fishery officers overseeing it. The same is said for the paperwork for exemptions to paying the Salt Tax and the procedure was said to be so complicated that few bothered because of this and the amount of money and time needed to apply.[11]

It was about this time that George II approved 'An Act for the Encouragement of the White Herring Fishery' which allowed coastal people to fish any part of the British Isles unhindered, use all the natural ports and harbours free of charge, and use all the beaches and uncultivated land for 100 yards above the high water mark for the purpose of drying nets and land and cure fish. For the first time fishermen could work as they please though the Act was largely irrelevant in the more far-flung corners of the country where they were fishing as they pleased anyway. It did have effects on fishers residing on the edge of any growing towns as suddenly they had the rights they had been attempting to enact.

Several writers travelled the Highlands and Islands looking at, among other things, the fishery. The list reads well: Thomas Pennant, James Anderson, Thomas Newte, Thomas Garnett and John Knox, all reporting back though it was Knox who was most influential and prolific. He, an Edinburgh bookseller, wrote and published *A View of the British Empire, More Especially Scotland, and Some Proposals for the Improvement of that Country, the Extension of the Fisheries and the Relief of the People* in 1784. Two years later he was off again and returned to produce *Observations on the Northern Fisheries with a*

Discourse on the Expediency of Establishing Fishing Stations, or Small Towns, in the Highlands of Scotland, and the Hebride Islands and the following year *A Tour through the Highlands of Scotland and the Hebride Isles* though this was more of a précis of the former. Nevertheless, Knox had clout and folk listened. At the same time the government commissioned no fewer than seven reports from the 'Committee appointed to enquire into the state of the British fisheries' between 1785 and 1786, so that the British Fisheries Society was set up in 1786 with the Duke of Argyll as president. Learning from the past errors of previous royal fishing companies and fishing societies, they planned to build fishing communities much as Knox suggested. The theory was that those 'cleared' (evicted) off the land where they had lived for generations, all in the name of sheep rearing, at least those not dead or emigrated, would supply the workforce if coastal villages were built in places with suitable shelter for boats to operate from. On the west coast three villages were built at Tobermory on Mull, Ullapool on Loch Broom and Stein at Lochbay, Skye. Knox had advocated forty. Another five reports emerged from the Committee in 1798–99. To the south of Wick, in Caithness, a fisher village and large harbour was built and named Pulteneytown (today it is regarded as part of Wick) and this was the only real success for the Society although Ullapool had limited fortunes. Tobermory and Stein never really took off as fishing villages. Around the coast, though, the herring fishery progressed without interference or investment and, with the repeal of the dreaded Salt Tax in 1825, a huge boost was given to the curing process and one really did begin to see the beginning of a thriving herring industry.

Around England, Wales and Ireland the story was one of little government help. Ireland was exporting herring to England while markets began to open up overseas to the whole of the British fishery. In the West Indies the sugar plantation workers – slaves until the 1830s – consumed thousands of barrels while the Mediterranean countries were also importing both the smoked and cured variety. In Wales the herring only came in autumn and was fished by a small number of beach-based fishers and the same could be said for the west coast of England. On the west coast of Scotland there were huge shoals in the lochs as well as out into the seas off the islands. Busses operated out of Campbeltown though they were prohibited in fishing close to the shore which meant the lochs were no-go areas. Loch Fyne's herring had been recognised for its excellence since Hector Boece noted in 1537 that there 'is mair plente of herring than is in any seas of Albion'.[12]

In the Isle of Man the herring fishery had been thriving since the days the Vikings colonised the island. Old Manx laws attempted to preserve the stocks of herring as they obviously understood the threat from overfishing. A law of 1610 declared a closed season for herring within 9 miles of the coast from the beginning of the year until July.[13] But by the 1820s the visiting Cornish and Scottish boats generally ignored this and before long the Manx boats were doing the same. No fishing was allowed from Saturday night until Monday morning as was the case in many parts of the country – parts of Scotland, especially among the islands, and in Cornwall and parts of Ireland.

It was always the North Sea that overshadowed any other parts of Britain in terms fish landed. The fleets of boats chased the shoals southward from the Shetland Isles in the early spring, along the Scottish and English east coasts progressively over the summer to arrive off East Anglia for the Great Autumnal Fishery there, as it became known, though locally it was the *hoom fishin*. Boats from all over – though most notably Scotland, Northumberland, Yorkshire and East Anglia, and Cornwall and the Isle of Man on the south and west sides of England. That was after about 1860 when bigger boats had been built, decked over as Washington had advised in his report, as discussed in the Introduction.

It would have been about this time that the difference between fishing as a longshoreman and that of a serious herring fisher became obvious. The long-shoreman always worked off his own shore, wherever that was, using the same boat for various forms of fishing, depending on the season. Seasoned herring fishermen, on the other hand, were chasing the shoals in their bigger boats that could remain at sea for longer periods and had a basic, if not comfortable, accommodation aboard for extended fishing away from home. For the first time fishing boats from Scotland could fish off southern Ireland and Cornish luggers were able to join in for the North Sea herring fishery.

A large part of this was due exactly to the fact that the boats were luggers, not burdened by squaresails or the sprit rig. On the east coast of Scotland they built fine northern 'scaffies' in a sort of expansion of the Scandinavian

Wick, in northeast Scotland, in 1865 when it was considered the herring capital of Europe. A thousand boats landed into the harbour during the herring season, the cured herring being exported to all points of the compass.

St Monans, on the Fife coast, with some of its fleet of fishing boats. These large boats are fifies, named after the region, and were rigged with two huge dipping lugsails that needed a large complement of crew to work them. St Monans was also home to J.N. Millers & Sons who became renowned boatbuilders over a 200-year span.

influence brought over centuries before, while in the south of the area it was the straight stemmed 'fifie' that was favoured by the fishermen, a design said to have been influenced by Dutch boatbuilders. In the 1880s a hybrid of the two became the popular vessel: the Zulu. At over 80ft in length, this was a huge vessel, powered by two huge dipping lugsails, having an upright stem and a heavily sloping sternpost at the after end which gave a long overhang. In Yorkshire they fished with their Yorkshire yawls and in Cornwall again they favoured the lug-rig upon their mackerel and pilchard drivers (drifters).

The Manx soon followed the Cornish, building similar luggers which they called 'nickeys' as we shall see in a later chapter. As the boats grew in length, so did the number of the drift-nets they set each night, hastened on by the changeover from hemp to cotton nets. Cotton was lighter hence nets could be longer for the same weight.

For centuries it was the drift-net that herring fishermen relied upon, but, on the shores of Loch Fyne, fishermen from Tarbert were busy changing that in the 1830s. Misuse of a drift-net as a seine-net from the shore, across the mouth of a bay, with the help of one small boat, was producing abundant catches of herring. The next stage was obvious: use of the same net with two boats hauling it around in a circle to trap a shoal of herring and within ten years this was being widely used. However, it was immediately regarded as trawling and the hundreds traditional drift-net fishermen that worked up the loch voiced opposition. They feared the new method was inferior in that it damaged the spawning grounds, and would lead to the situation whereby 'the Lochfyne fishing which has for centuries been famed for its herrings will be annihilated and its industrious fishermen ruined complete'.[14] The method became known as ring-netting.

The opposition had the advantage of the support of the fish curers and they went to work drawing up an anti-trawling petition and forming a delegation to lobby MPs and the Herring Fishery Board. For sure there were the altercations between the two groups of fishermen that sometimes became violent, and the most vocal made their point. Within time a ban on trawling was introduced and nets and boats were confiscated and impounded though it seems unclear whether this happened when the fishermen were caught red-handed while fishing or simply by coming across their inactive gear.

There was always the threat of jail too for flouting regulations. Angus Martin tells how his great-great-grandfather John Martin, along with his crews, were convicted of contravening the closed season for herring fishing in 1861. This ran between 1 January and 31 May. They were caught landing herring at night in March and all but John Martin was jailed for ten days. Later that year three Campbeltown fishermen were imprisoned for thirty days for breaking herring regulations.[15] Fishing ever since has been an occupation where the courts can inflict almost as much damage to the fishers as can the sea itself.

The ban never completely stopped ring-netting even after young fishermen Peter McDougall was shot by an officer and a marine from HMS *Jackal*, a gunboat sent to police the loch. That was in 1861 and within a couple of years those that were originally against the use of the ring-net were adopting it, realising the financial rewards it could bring. Six years later the same people were lobbying for the ban to be lifted and in July 1867 a bill was passed repealing all the legislation banning the method. By 21 August of that year

FISHING BOATS IN GIRVAN HARBOUR

Fishing boats in Girvan harbour. The eastern side of the Clyde had for many generations being actively involved in herring fishing and these boats – known as 'nabbies' and nicknamed 'slopemasts' – were prolific until the advent of the motor.

'two smacks, seventeen skiffs, eight trawl-nets, one sail, and sixteen fish-boxes had been returned to their owners'.[16] Ring-netting commenced in earnest, a method that was technically much improved over the next hundred years and yet one that eventually died out in the 1970s, probably partly through its own success, and partly because of the other, much more effective, methods that superseded it.

Although ring-netting spread to the Isle of Man, the west of Ireland, parts of eastern England, especially around Whitby and other areas of Scotland, there were the communities that remained steadfastly against its use, such as the Outer Hebrides. Stornoway was a harbour that never really accepted ring-netters though the motorised boats did occasionally berth there after the Second World War, always fearful of any reprisal from the drift-netters.[17] Before the war they preferred to take their catch over the Minch to Ullapool or Mallaig. The ring-net was in use throughout the Minch, around all the islands, and after the war some of the fishermen of the Outer Islands adopted the method themselves.[18] Some parts of the coast remained steadfastly opposed to it but generally the fortunes of ring-netting brought incredible wealth to many families, families that still exist and benefit from it. Furthermore, the ring-netters produced some of the prettiest work boats seen in British waters – the Lochfyne skiffs and the motorised ringers – and some of the most endearing written social histories.[19]

3

THE CROFTER-FISHERMEN OF SCOTLAND

Nowhere in the British Isles was fishing so vital to the economic well-being of the people than in Shetland.[1] The islands don't lend themselves to much land-based productivity but being close to rich fishing grounds it's hardly surprising that it was seaward that the inhabitants went in search of food. Shetland also remained the last bastion of the crofter–fisherman up to and just after the Second World War.

Before the eighteenth century when much of Shetland's fishery was controlled by German merchants, the fishermen would take themselves up to some 10 miles offshore in their four-oared boats (fourereens) and set long lines for cod and ling. This became known as the 'haaf fishery' – 'haaf' meaning deep sea in Old Norse. One of the earliest records of this was written by Captain James Smith who sailed there in 1633 and found the Hanseatic merchants from Lübeck, Hamburg and Bremen, as well as merchants from Scotland and England buying cod and ling. The Shetlanders were fishing in the yoles 'two or three leagues' off the coast, returning each day with sixty or seventy fish. Ling sold at threepence a pound and cod twopence. Smith loaded 11,655 ling and 834 gild cod which were salted aboard and then taken to London.[2]

By the eighteenth century it seems that many tenants were paying their rents in kind – fish, butter, fish-oil and woollen stockings – and thus the lairds became traders, filling in the gap left by the Germans, so that they could raise coinage to pay their taxes, etc. Before long the lairds had then taken to buying the fish directly from their tenants thus enabling them to pay rent in cash. However, it was often the case that the fishermen didn't know the price they would receive for their fish until well after the end of the season, and even then they had to wait at least to November for the cured fish to be sold and to receive any money.[3] The long and the short of this was that eventually the lairds demanded participation from the fishermen in the haaf fishery, as part of the tenure of their homes. 'No fishing, no home' and many were evicted. This in fact was a truck system in which the tenant was paid in vouchers or tokens that were only redeemable in the shops belonging to the laird so that they gained in every sense of the word 'capitalism'. If indeed the men had been paid in cash then they probably would have been able to purchase twice as much from local suppliers. The fishermen were, in reality, cheated by the employers, as happened in many other industries. Although Parliament passed an Act in 1831 making this system illegal, it did not apply to the Scottish haaf fishers. Nothing was to change in over half a century.

The haaf fishery began traditionally on Beltane Day (1 May) and continued up to Lammas Day (1 August) although the fishing seasons changed and some years they started 'from the month of March and gave it up on 12th June'.[4] Beach huts or lodgings were set up around the Shetland coast upon suitable shingle beaches where boats could be drawn up, with access to the ocean. These were mostly on the outlying areas of Shetland: around Sumburgh in the south and upon Unst to the north with several on the west side of the Mainland and the odd few on Bressay, Whalsay and Fetlar. In all forty-one such haaf stations, including one each on Fair Isle and Foula, have been identified.[5] Fishermen slept side by side with the curers, gutting folk, boys, old men and agents and remained at the station throughout the season. They would fish in their bigger six-oared boats – sixareens – sailing out some 30 miles offshore, to the edge of the continental shelf, to set their lines where the best ling were to be found. These lines could be 6 or 7 miles long and were left down overnight, which meant the fishermen had to sleep in the boat. Sometimes they stayed out three days, hauling and then reshooting the lines, meaning at least two days sleeping in the bottom of the boat, with only the sail for shelter, no mean feat in an open boat out of sight of the land. But these fellows were among the most experienced boatmen in the British Isles, being able to forecast the weather by simply watching the waves and cloud formations. They needed to be, to survive in these conditions. Piltocks were caught at the start of the trip which they used as bait.[6]

Once they had returned to the haaf station, the fish were unloaded, weighed and salted by the curers who would have been ready and waiting, though they often handed the gutting job to 'beach boys' and older men.[7] Often the fish were dried on the stones in the natural sunlight. The fishermen themselves didn't rest and they had to take their smaller boats out to catch bait – usually young saithe or herring.

The sixareen boats were indeed remnants from the Viking age. Norway was almost nearer than Scotland – certainly nearer than, say, Aberdeen and given that Shetland remained part of the Norse kingdom until 1469 when they were returned to Scottish control as part of the dowry of a Danish princess to her betrothed Scotsman, it is not surprising that Norseness influenced much of island life. Trees are rare on the islands and domestic timber was imported

Double-ended Shetland boats. These smaller boats were used for the inshore fishery whereas the larger sixareens, although similar in shape, sailed out into deep water away from the coast.

from Norway. However, contrary to this, boats were imported in kit form and assembled – a fifteenth-century version of IKEA maybe – and these, too, were of Scandinavian design. Furthermore, in true Viking fashion, the boats are all referred to by the number of oars in the Norwegian way.

In 1774, an average sixareen was 20ft in length and open. They set one mast with a squaresail for the journey out to the fishing grounds, though this was later replaced with a dipping lugsail around the beginning of the nineteenth century when they were being built on Shetland by home-based boatbuilders and were up to 35ft in length.[8] Nevertheless, the timber was still imported from Norway. The boats were clinker-built using wide green planks of Norwegian fir on sawn oak frames, or bands as they were called in Shetland, fastened with iron nails. In Viking tradition, the bands were not fixed to the keel, only the garboard planks, so that the keel could easily be renewed if worn through being dragged over rough beaches.

The fishermen usually undertook two voyages a week over the normal twelve-week season. Sunday remained a day of no labour though some ignored this. It was advocated that Parliament prescribe a rule for this: 'That all nets shall be hauled before one o'clock on Sunday morning; and that no nets shall be wet before one o'clock on Monday morning.'[9] Shetland was the main European source for ling and, just as Captain Smith sailed away with a much higher amount of ling than cod, so was the case up to the end of the haaf fishery in the 1880s as the herring fishery gained ascendancy. Cod was available from Norway, Iceland and Newfoundland whereas ling was not.

However, according to Coull, a cod smack fishery was based in Shetland in the nineteenth century and a hundred smacks were once based in Shetland with over 1,000 men engaged in it. These boats sailed up to the Faroe Islands, Iceland and Rockall. The fish were salted aboard the vessels and then dried on the beaches once landed back to the cod bases dotted around the Shetland coast or in inner Shetland.[10]

The crew of the sixareens tended to share their earnings equally though the skipper might have a bit extra. Boys would only receive a half share as was normal throughout fishing communities everywhere. But there were big differences of pay structure between island and island. Whereas the haaf fishermen only received tokens for their fish, Donald Moar of Gloup, North Yell, reported to the Royal Commission that he received half the fish he caught, the other half going to the boat owner in what was known as the *half-catch* system. After the cod and ling fishery he went to the herring fishery until September, a fishery which was booming at the time of the Commission in 1883, chaired by Lord Napier and set up to specifically inquire into the conditions of the crofters. During the winter he cared for his croft and repaired his fishing gear. The croft was considered something to fall back upon during the lean months and potatoes were the main crop though they did grow grain. Donald Moar had three cows and six ponies but no sheep and his family looked after the croft while he was away at the fishing. He paid his rent from the earnings of his fish.[11]

Gloup seriously suffered after the storm disaster of 20–21 July 1881 when fifty-eight fishermen, thirty-six from the village, were drowned and ten sixareens were lost, another example of the harsh conditions these men had to work in. Thirty-four widows and fifty-eight orphans were left behind. One century later a memorial was erected in Gloup with the names of the fishermen etched into stone. Sadly, the British coast, and especially that of Scotland, is littered with such commemorative structures. The *Shetland Times* ran the story of one survivor:

A fleet of about 30 boats was at sea the night of the disaster, 26 from the north half of Yell, most of them from Gloup, with others from places such as Gutcher and as far south as Whalfirth (near Mid Yell.) There were a few among the number out from Unst and Feideland. The night was very fine, and we went off from the land about 20 miles, though it is difficult to recollect the distance after so long an interval of time.

The storm struck us suddenly, and as soon as it struck we were in a fearful sea, and in darkness, in spite of it being the month of July. In our boat we held to our lines and did not leave our position till we had got all our lines on board. We then set sail and turned for home, sailing before the wind. In such a sea it was necessary to steer for each wave, veering away from side to side according to the precise direction from which the wave pursued us. Two men stood by the sail (a square sail) in order to handle it, both for the veering, and because, if a sea threatened to break over us, the skipper would make them lower the sail, thus easing the boat and allowing the wave to go past us before breaking.

At last as the day broke (about 4 p.m.) we saw that we were nearing the land – it was then pouring with rain as well as exceedingly tempestuous, with dark overladen sky. The first hint we got of any disaster was a number of oars floating in the water, for we had seen no other boat during the night. As we approached the haven at Gloup Voe we saw an empty boat driving ashore, overturned on its side, mast and sail keeping it in that position. Then as we entered the Voe itself, we saw a great concourse of people – wives, sisters, parents, and some children – gathered on the shore with a great lamentation, and a boat manned by twelve men rowing towards us to get hold of the upturned boat. The people had come from miles around to view what they dreaded and expected, for the storm had broken suddenly in the midst of a fine night, and they knew their men were at sea. When we landed they asked if we had seen any other boats, but of course we said we had not.[12]

It was the development of a serious herring fishery based on Shetland – the fishermen knew all about herring here having been forced to watch the Dutch master Shetland waters back beyond the 1700s – that resulted in the slackening of the grasp of the lairds over their tenants as they shunned the haaf fishery in favour of the summer herring. Boats were again imported (and many owned), this time from the east coast, though the local builder Hay & Co. produced several of the new breed of decked boats. For a short while herring was king, until the markets collapsed in the second decade of the twentieth century.

There's an old Hebridean proverb that says '*Dh'iarr am muir a thadhal*' – the sea wants to be visited. Over on the island of Lewis in the Outer Hebrides, the small harbour at the Port of Ness was once base to more than fifty fishing boats. Ness is actually a conglomeration of some sixteen villages including Lionel, Habost, Swainbost, Cross, North and South Dell, Cross Skigersta, Skigersta, Eorodale, Adabrock, Knockaird, Fivepenny and Eoropie. Before 1784 there was no shelter for vessels along the northeast coast of Lewis and around to Stornoway. In 1803 it was described as 'a terrible sea to fish on, and as terrible a shore to land upon'.[13] After Lord Seaforth, the owner of Lewis, arranged parcels of land for the fishermen to work from, it was decided a harbour was vital to the well-being of these fishers. The first pier was built by 1836 with a second phase being completed twenty years later. Even so, there was little shelter for boats. Then, on the night of 18 December 1862, while

Orkney yoles landing at Skippigeo, Bressay. These are two-masted boats, though the main has been lowered here for the run onto the beach. Boats were either lug-rigged or sprit-rigged, depending whether they were used in the north or south of the islands. Subtle hull shapes and boatbuilding techniques differed between the two areas, dependent on usage, the southern boats working in the notorious Pentland Firth and thus being heavier built. (*Courtesy of Orkney Library Archive*)

the boats were out at sea, a storm rose up and the entire crews of five Ness boats were lost, thirty-one men in total, in what has become known as *Am Bathadh Mor* – the 'Day of the Great Drowning'. This one disaster emphasised the urgency in the fishers having a proper harbour of refuge. No fish meant there was no money to pay rents which would only lead to eviction. Thus, by 1885 an inner harbour had been built though it was immediately a failure because of silting up. Within five years work started on moving the harbour entrance and building a new breakwater, as can be seen today. However, the harbour suffered from poor design, shoddy construction, erosion and more silting so that it was never a successful enterprise even if fifty boats were once based there.

Boats were able to use it though, even if it dried out. The *sgoth Niseach* (Ness skiffs) were large 32ft beach boats – in fact the largest beach boats in Britain, probably brought about by the fact that they were initially designed for use in a harbour that was not intended to dry out. Like all the Scandinavian-influenced fishing craft, they were double-enders, not dissimilar to the Shetland boats, also rigged with a dipping lug, replacing the earlier square-sail. Later boats adopted a long overhanging stern, similar to that of the east coast Zulus.

Macdonald gives a lovely description of how the boats were launched and beached on the open shores, how they pushed them down on pieces of wood called *lunnan*, ballasted with stones, the four oarsmen at the ready and the bowman, on his shout, pushing the boat out as the rowers dipped their oars. Coming back in was even more skilful, especially on a dark and stormy night. They hove-to close to the shore to ready the boat – sail and mast down and stowed, lines and nets placed out of the way, ballast dumped overboard and the skipper prepared for his perfect timing through the *fath*, the calm period between the waves, and onto the shore, the bowman ready to jump. The thrill of the event is almost tangible.[14]

These *sgoths* fished for ling and cod in the same way as the sixareens did, though they didn't sail out to the edge of the continental shelf which was many miles more distant from Lewis. They were the lucky ones for rich pickings of the fish could be had a mere 2 miles off the east coast of the island. Again it was the Lewis factor and his tacksmen (farm tenants) who instigated the cod and ling fishery early in the eighteenth century and compelled the tenants to fish, providing them with boats and fishing gear. Refusal meant eviction.

The Royal Commission provides a good insight to the building of these boats. Boatbuilder John MacLeod told them how he could build 'six or seven a year' for both fishermen and curers, the latter giving their crews the boats on three years' shares. The cost was £30 for a boat and if they managed to pay £10 a year for three years, then the boat was theirs. Total cost for boat,

A Ness *sgoth* in the harbour at the Port of Ness, Isle of Lewis. The shape again is reminiscent of the Scandinavian double-ended boats that so encouraged Shetlanders and the Lewis men to copy in many respects.

sail and fishing gear was '£42 or £43'. A good boat could catch 1,000 ling in a year though he remembered a time when 6,000 was the normal. MacLeod also suggested building a better harbour as many of the local fishermen had to travel to the east coast to work on the herring boats there as, with the harbour not suitable for larger vessels, they were unable to compete with the larger boats for the herring fishery. They, on average, returned with £5 to £20.[15] Today the harbour at Ness is quiet, bar for a few boats but it could have been a different story. It's a lovely harbour, all twisting and turning, longer than wide and still tidal. But maybe if the owners had listened more to the fishermen and those who knew, they wouldn't have ended up with a harbour pretty useless for its purpose.

Today Ness is more renowned for the *guga* (young gannets, considered a delicacy thereabouts) hunt on Sula Sgeir, an uninhabited island some 40 miles to the north of the Butt of Lewis. In 1549 it was reported by Dean Munro that the Ness men sail their small boats and 'fetche hame thair boatful of dry wild fowls with wild fowl fedderi' and they continue the tradition right up today, with a special licence granted by Scottish Natural Heritage.[16] It is probably true that the fishermen were practising this for generations before Munro, given their fanaticism for the young birds in the face of a monotonous diet of fish and potatoes, and it's good that these traditions have survived, even if there are groups opposed on the basis of cruelty.

Fishing was often about travel, with or without a boat. West Coast ringnetters went to the east coast, while east coast fifies and Zulus fished around the Outer Hebrides. The Manx ring-netters fished in the Minch while Cornish fishermen worked just off the Isle of Man coast. In the 1850s the fisherfolk from Buchan, on the east coast of Scotland, sailed 150 miles around via the Pentland Firth to fish the Minch. They set up bothies on Lewis or camped in local barns near Port nan Giuran and Pabail where they could moor their craft. By 1880 there were at least a dozen boats at Port nan Giuran, fishing for herring in summer and cod and ling with long lines (great lines), often staying away from base for weeks at an end. The fish was cured in salting houses along the shore, three of which were in Port nan Giuran.[17] But many of these fishers were still crofter men who lived off both land and sea. The sea might want to be visited, but any visitor wants to be sure there's a safe haven to return to.

When the Royal Commission visited Skye, Angus Stewart spoke for the crofters. Aged 40, he was one of seven living in his father's house at Peinchorran, on Loch Sligachan, where small crofts ran down to the shore. He began by saying that it was the poverty that they complained most about. 'It is great hardship that all of our earnings at the fishing we have to put into meal for the support of our families.' Part of the problem seemed to be the sub-dividing of the crofts:

In my grandfather's time, there were five tenants in Peinchorran and now there are twenty-six or twenty-seven. When the land is sub-divided, the new crofter has to build his own house … I cannot tell the exact acreage of my father's croft but I can say there is not one acre of it worth cultivating or worth putting to seed into. It is rocky, mossy ground.

On the west side of Skye it was Norman Robertson who spoke:

I am not a fisherman now. We seldom fish for cod and ling. Those who have nets go to the Loch Hourn herring fishing but there are not many in our township who have nets. They are not able to buy them. People would go to the fishing if they had more nets. The south county people are spoiling the fishing in Loch Hourn – fishing it in daylight and trawling, and so spoiling it for the poor people – trawling even on the Sabbath.[18]

He continued:

Herrings were 2s.6d. to 18s. per cran last year. 2s.6d. is a very small price. If the poor people could salt them they could wait and get a better price for them. If they money to buy barrels and salt, they themselves could sell the herring when they had cured them.

So, not only was it the grasping lairds taking all their earnings, it was the ring-net fishermen from the Clyde and Loch Fyne that were taking their herrings. This was 1883 remember, and trawling for herring with a ring-net had been legalised some sixteen years earlier.

Others cited the lack of harbours as one reason for the lack of commitment in fishing. From Reiff, north of the Summer Isles, Duncan Mackenzie pleaded on behalf of the forty young men who needed help to buy bigger fishing boats and gear, and a harbour where they could land their fish. The present harbour was exposed to the southwest and they had to draw their boats up the beach.

In Tarbert, Loch Fyne, there were few crofter-fishermen according to Hugh Carmichael:

Perhaps half a dozen. They work them partly themselves, and their families, but they do not remain at home from the fishing to work their crofts. With the Loch Fyne fishing as it is at the present they would do as well without crofts … There is more fish landed now in the village, owing to the trawling system … It is skiffs we use here. We have got them larger now; this year or two back some have been getting what they call decks and they can live on them now.[19]

Loch Fyne had two distinct advantages: the proximity to the Glasgow markets and the more predictable Loch Fyne herring and the Commission learned how fishing in Loch Fyne was a profitable alternative to crofting and this would point the way to a more equal social structure. One wonders!

Crofter-fishermen did not go away as the nineteenth century faded into history. Angus Duncan lived on the small island of Scarp, off the coast of Harris and regarded all the men as crofter-fishermen, which, he says, described them perfectly. He remembers how in his youth (he was born in 1888) 'all able-bodied men were absent during the East Coast herring season, leaving home when the planting was done and returning in time for the harvest'.[20] In winter the men turned their attention to the lobster fishery. Duncan also says that the long-line fishery was unknown in his day though when it was in vogue the men went off to sea for 'a day or two' with the dried fish being sent to Stornoway. Boats from the east coast came to set long lines, based on Fladday where they lodged in huts on the beach. His mother, she told him, recalled having tea with a woman in one of the huts so some of the men must have brought their family over with them for the duration.

On Eriskay it was the same. Before the herring fishery it was the haaf, fishing out on the 60-fathom line where the only visible land was the top of Bhen Mhor on South Uist.[21] With the arrival of the herring fishery, it was just left to the old men and the very young to fish with lines. The young men went herring fishing, especially when nearby Castle Bay had a thousand herring boats in the bay during the summer season. One dramatic story, or near disaster, Angus MacInnes recounts was in the early 1900s when the herring fleet of a thousand boats was sailing up the Sound of Sandray when a strong south-easterly wind rose up quite unexpectedly. Boats collided with each other and one after another crew had to be rescued while boats were sinking. A count was made in Castle Bay and, although thirty-seven boats had been sunk, there was, almost miraculously, no loss of life. Every one of the three hundred or so crew who lost their boats was saved. But by this time the crofter-fisherman on Eriskay was a thing of the past, as it was throughout the majority of Scotland.

Then, of course, the change to steam created similar circumstances. Despair came as the fish disappeared and the locals were unable to compete. In 1914, the Provost of Stornoway explained to the Scottish Departmental Committee in their report of the North Sea Fishing Industry:

> There were some men who had the boats, but they became disheartened with the boats and became hired men … The pith is knocked out of the fishermen with their sail boats, so that they cannot compete with the steam drifters nowadays.[22]

4

LONGSHOREMEN OF ENGLAND

According to the Oxford dictionary a 'longshoreman' is a North American word for a docker, but sometimes the dictionary is wrong as that is not all it is. A longshoreman is also a person who makes his living on or along the shore, or close to it, and this normally refers to a fisherman who works with a small beach boat which he lands and launches from the beach, who fishes not far from the coast, and who often has a shack at the top of the shore where he sells his fish. That is, indeed, the case in much of Europe, though throughout the rest of the world the first two descriptions might be accurate, but it will be unusual to see the fish being sold from a shack and is probably sold in a nearby spontaneous market – or taken home to feed the family.

Regardless of their geographical location, longshoremen are a vast part of the army of small-scale fishers of the world. Their contribution is immense: small-scale fishers account for some 95 per cent of all fishers. Using their simple fishing gear small-scale fishers capture somewhere in the region of half the world's seafood though they only use a tenth of the fossil fuel that large-scale fishers use with their diesel-guzzling industrial vessels plundering the oceans. Small-scale fishers also hold a huge amount of knowledge concerning the waters around them and the life living in them. They are at one with their surrounding environment and care for the future unlike those on the deep-sea boats who are learned at operating machinery and gazing at screens but have little care or thought for their surroundings. They have to service large loans to banks and are more beholden to bankers and financiers than to the oceans. Small-scale fishers, and their indigenous, often colourful, vessels are also well photographed as any visit to the postcard shop in any seaside town or a look through any travel magazine will tell you. Like the fishers from a gone age, they, in a world of waste and technology, are photogenic, have an encyclopae-dic intimacy and remain ecologically sound when many around them are not.

Contrary to crofter-fishermen, longshoremen earn all their living from the sea unless they find it financially vital to have a second employment to sub-

Adrian Sellick, known as the last mud-horse fisherman, working his nets set out across the mud in Bridgwater Bay, Somerset.

sidise the first. For instance, Adrian Sellick who operates stake nets on the muddy Sterk Flats, in Bridgwater Bay, Somerset, and who uses a wooden mud-horse to bring his catch ashore, works in a local factory to supplement his meagre income from fishing. He is a true longshoreman. But why then, you might ask, does he do it? Because it's in his blood and his father Brendan taught him, and his grandfather before him did it, much the same as was once widely heard throughout fishing communities everywhere.

In Brendan's own words:

> Well, I started when I was fourteen, when I was a kid. My dad was here all his life and I carried on from him. I've done it for sixty odd years, my dad did it the same, his father did it the same and the grandfather before him started it in 1820 or something. He was a stonemason, he picked up with a local fisher girl and she persuaded him there was no money in fishing and that's how we came here. Of course there were a lot of families doing it in those days. Any amount. When I started there were three or four families, a dozen blokes, nine brothers and that. Fifteen years ago there were two families. All had their own patch and a licence. That's only a few quid today but it gives us reassurance.[1]

He paused for a few seconds before continuing:

> Yes, non-stop for sixty odd years, I can't believe it. Adrian went out when he
> was six or so. Some blokes from Burnham did it using a boat to get out to
> their nets. I remember one father and son one Sunday whilst we were out.
> They disappeared whilst out trammelling in their punt. Went in they did and
> weren't found for three weeks. Probably one got caught in the net when it
> went over and the other went in to save him. Lost their knife they must have.
> Yes, many have lost their lives out here where all sorts of things can happen.

It's a danger well voiced in fishing circles and it isn't just the boats working in
the extremes of the North Atlantic who are vulnerable from the perils of the
sea. Respect for the sea doesn't protect anyone, life jackets don't prevent crew
members getting caught in nets as they are shot over the side and dragged
down to the seabed and lifeboats cannot always reach casualties. The sea is a
dangerous platform to work upon and just as fishers drown in the sea, even
mud-horse fishing has its dangers if the unwary fisher stays out too long and
gets caught by the incoming rush of tide.

The nets Brendan and Adrian have staked are a mile out into the bay and to
get there involves a drive in the 4x4 jeep, out as far as the beach allows, along
a well-worn track among jagged rocks, to the edge of these. Ahead is a sea
of glistening mud and the several hundred yards of this have to be traversed,
pushing the mud-horse out to the distant line of nets. There are twenty-eight
shrimp nets there, nets with a square mouth several feet across and which are
funnel-shaped to decrease the cod-end some 6ft downstream. Each is untied,
the contents emptied into a sieve before the net is carefully tied up again. The
catch is sorted – the small fish, weed and bits of rubbish are extracted – after
which it is added to the slowly filling basket. This catch consists of shrimps,
dabs, Dover sole, whiting, the odd mullet, dogfish and skate, the latter being
expertly sliced to separate the edible wings. You can certainly tell an experienced fisherman by the way he cuts a skate. Then Adrian clears the few
stake nets which held the odd fish before trudging another few hundred yards
through mud and water out to a further line of stake nets set out by the low
water mark. Here maybe are two more skate, mullet, dogfish and a Dover sole.
All the time he's watching the tide.

Adrian goes out most days but sometimes hangs the nets up if there's nothing in them to save the tide ripping them. A good wind also brings a lot of
weed down off the beaches, and hanging them up saves time as he has a limited amount of time out before the tide catches him out. Only then can he
load his baskets and push his contraption straight across the mud back to the
jeep. By leaning upon the framework, he can push it forward without his feet

sinking too far into the mud. It does look hard work, though, he says, not as half as hard as carrying the fish in a basket. Being a longshoreman is hard work and dangerous, he adds.

Longshoremen work all around the coast of England and Wales – and Scotland too but we've discussed the fishing there in the last chapter. However, several regions of the country jump out as being more resilient than others in that the practice has survived up to today even if that very survival is now under threat. In these following pages we shall consider various parts of the English coast in sections.

The Northeast Coast

There's little evidence of fishermen operating a dual economy in Yorkshire and that fishermen were farmers during the quiet season. It's true to say that a few did work in the iron mines in winter during the nineteenth century but these were more the exception than the rule.[2] Generally fishermen worked from one of the many coastal settlements that existed from Berwick upon Tweed down to the River Humber, working their locality although some did join the autumnal herring fishery off East Anglia in the nineteenth century. Lines, trawling, potting and drifting for herring were the main fisheries.

From an inshore fishery point of view, both Northumberland and Yorkshire were well served by square-sterned cobles, those quintessentially British boats that are a mixture of Scandinavian and English techniques with a catalyst emanating from what is still today an unknown influence. They are unique among British fishing boats which, in a way, must make the fishermen themselves different from the rest. It's 'ceubles' in the north and 'cobbles' in the south and the point of merging is said to be around Redcar. The etymology of the word is unclear: some say it has Celtic connotations as Celts used *ceubal* for 'boat' while *couple* is said to have originated from the Lindisfarne Gospels of the year AD 950. The boat itself has obvious Scandinavian influence and has been developed over the years for working directly off a beach. It is a complex shape with a pronounced forward sheer, slightly curved stem, deep forefoot and lean entry into the water giving an almost Viking appearance. The after end of the body was shallow with flat floors, hard bilges and a high sheer. The keel only extended over the forward part of the boat and a ram plank, a flat plank onto which the floors were fitted, continued to the sloping transom. The hull had a degree of tumblehome which was unusual for British working craft and was built in true clinker fashion with wide planks called strakes. A deep rudder descended a long way beneath the boat. The design suited the coastal conditions where heavy breaking surf was often encountered both on launch and recovery. Boats were normally beached stern first and horses were often used to haul the boats up the beach on trolleys with huge wheels, such as at Filey, though a steam-powered winch was used at the North Landing at Flamborough.[3]

There are 170 miles between the Tweed and the Humber and until the rivers were dredged out for shipping in the nineteenth century, harbours were few and far between though rivers may have afforded some protection. South Shields was an early settlement for fishers – 'Shields' coming from the Norse word *scheles* taken to mean 'simple fishermen's summer huts along the shore' – though is today nothing by comparison. One example of a small coastal settlement that has survived as such is Low Newton-by-the-Sea, a cluster of fishermen's cottages built on three sides of a square, the open side facing the sea. Today though the fishermen have gone, to be replaced by holiday homeowners, who play on the grass where the net poles, once vital to the upkeep of the nets, once stood.

Cobles also came in various sizes, depending on the time of the year and the fishery it was working. Winter and spring were the times for trunking, potting and line-fishing in 30ft cobles, crewed by three men, said to be older men by some. Trunking was an old method of catching lobsters and crabs which survived longer in Yorkshire and Norfolk than anywhere else in Britain.[4] A trunk was a net attached to an iron hoop with two bands across in which the bait was held. The trunk was set on the seabed, marked with a buoy, and while other trunks were being set, it was hoped a lobster or crab would find the bait and begin eating. Then, when a short time had elapsed, the trunk would be carefully hauled, hoping the crustacean had fallen into the net. The next trunk would then be hauled and so on. In a night's fishing (which was preferred) the whole fleet of trunks could be shot and hauled up to fifteen times. A similar method were used on the east coast of America, in New England, where the net was dropped and the fisherman stayed above, watching for the lobster or crab to climb onto the net before hauling it in.

In June they got their larger cobles out when the weather was more reliable. These were the herring cobles that they called ploshers and they followed the herring into the autumn. These cobles could be as much as 42ft in length and powered by a dipping lug sail, the same as the smaller boats. As motorisation affected all the fleets in the first and second decades of the twentieth century, the hull shape was altered to incorporate a tunnel in the after part of the boat so that boats could still work off beaches. A few ploshers were double-ended though most retained the transom, and some were half-decked.

In about 1875 a double-ended 'mule' was introduced into Yorkshire, a keel boat which has been described as a cross between a coble and a whaling boat. These were half-decked and tended to work out of the small rivers, such as at Staithes or Whitby.[5] The small river out-flowing at Staithes gives a sheltered refuge for boats and it can be difficult to envisage that this was the largest

Fishing for salmon with a seine-net from a salmon coble on the River Tweed. This type of fishing mirrors that depicted on the Naxos vase. These cobles were different to those to the south, being smaller and less pronounced in shape.

harbour along this coast in 1817 when there were seventy cobles based there, a figure that increased to a hundred later that century.[6] Today it is home to a mere handful of cobles and keelboats.

The fishers were independent folk as elsewhere but it is said that in Filey they kept completely to themselves. They lived in the old town, apart from both the other inhabitants who opened lodging houses and other fishermen from along the coast.[7] Sunday fishing was frowned upon. Filey fishermen, other than having their cobles worked off the beach there, owned Yorkshire yawls, larger two-masted boats of about 50ft in length that were kept at nearby Scarborough harbour.

Today's cobles are numerous and remain the chosen working platform of the modern fisher though most are motorised and are based in the rivers and harbours that today dot the coast. At Filey, sheltered mostly by Filey Brig, however, things haven't changed at all and the boats still sit on the Landing on metal trolleys with big wheels, the only sop to modernisation being tractors instead of horses. Another spot along this coast that hasn't changed much and is worthy of mention is Robin Hood's Bay, an almost cliff-hanging village, the haunt of smugglers and fishers (often the same thing), where boats are hauled over the scaur (rocky platforms) onto the track leading down the hill. It's hard to believe today that some thirty-five cobles operated out of here during the fishing heydays of the mid-eighteenth century.[8] Here too the village had its own Robin Hood's Bay Mutual Shipping Insurance Company, formed in 1806, which insured vessels worth £94,300 in 1867. It is said that the fishers went with the Whitby whaling fleet and came back with money enough to put into trading vessels. At that time there were 174 ships owned by Bay men and registered at Whitby. 'The trade in fish had given way to the trade in coal' lamented one visitor in 1858.

A comparison of prices is useful. In the Whitby district, in 1730, the annual rent of a small fisherman's cottage was forty shillings to five pounds whereas herrings were ten to twenty a penny and haddock ten to twenty pence a score (twenty). Beef and mutton were two pence a pound, small chickens two pence, butter at twice that a pound. Local farm workers earned eight pence a day in winter and one shilling and sixpence in summer, both including board.[9]

Nearby quaint Runswick Bay has a similar atmosphere of intrigue and secrecy and was once centre of a large fishery, while in between Whitby retains the charm of a fishing station and a bustling river and is said to be one of the most atmospheric towns in the whole of Britain. Further north, the Northumberland coast is regarded as the unspoilt coast of Britain and has gems of villages along it such as Beadnell and Craster and here the cobles are notorious for the canvas cover they set over the forward part of the boat. Many survive and are in use daily in an area where longshore fishing is alive and well. Boatbuilder Fred Crowell of South Shields is kept busy today in his small yard off the River Tyne, repairing and rebuilding cobles, among the other fishing boats he works upon.

East Anglia

There are two types of longshore boat of interest in this part of the east coast of England – the north Norfolk crab boat and the Suffolk beach boat. A third, the Yarmouth shrimper, was based in the river and there is no evidence that it ever worked directly off the beach.

Along the thirty-mile stretch of coast between Wells and Sea Palling, fishing has been characteristically small scale, mainly done from beach-launched boats.[10] This was centred on the neighbouring towns of Sheringham and Cromer, both of which had attempts at building some form of shelter for boats at the end of the medieval period. None seemed successful except for a harbour at Shipden Ness, just east of Sheringham, though this was engulfed by the sea in 1430. The coastline here has been for centuries one of erosion and changing and shifting sands, made worse by the fact that this part of England is slowly sinking. Fishermen have had to work directly off the beach and they continue to do so today.

By 1724 Daniel Defoe noted that the market town of Cromer was famous for its lobsters which were sold in Norwich or taken to London. He described it as a dangerous coast.[11] In 1771 an agreement was made between 123 fishermen of Cromer and the London markets for the supply. As the century concluded, Edmund Bartell in his *Guide about Cromer* (1798) wrote that 'Lobsters, crabs, whiting, cod-fish and herring are all caught here in the finest perfection.' He continues that:

> the lower class of people are chiefly supported by fishing. The herrings which are caught are cured in the town, a house, within a few years, having been erected for that purpose, which, I believe, answers well, both to the proprietor and the fishermen, who now find an immediate market for any quantity they may bring in.[12]

When William Daniell passed through in the early nineteenth century, a new jetty had been built, the older one having been swept away in March of that year, 1813. Sea bathing and fishing appear to attract a similar interest to Daniell though not for the first time do we see the growth of a resort simultaneous to the development of the fishery, where the fishermen are partly responsible for both through the colourfulness of their way of life and the use of their craft to take day-trippers out during the summer season. This always allowed a small extra earning for them. In 1875 Frank Buckland, in preparation of a Parliament report, found fifty crab boats in Cromer, a hundred in Sheringham and perhaps another fifty from other north Norfolk beaches. Each boat carried some twenty pots and that they had only come into use some twelve or fourteen years before. Before this they used hoop nets – the same as trunk nets. The lobster and crab fishery preoccupied the majority, if not all, the fishermen.[13]

The boats of the crab fishermen are unique in British craft and have been described as a cross between a coble and a keel boat. Again they work directly off the beach into the surf and are recognisable from the oar holes they have in the top strake, known locally as 'orrack' holes, used to slide oars through so that the boat can be carried up the beach. Boats were built locally and were some 16ft in length while a slightly larger boat at 19ft, known as a 'hoveller' or 'hubbler', was used for whelk fishing, drifting for herring and mackerel, and long-lining for cod when the lobster fishing was slack.

When the creel-type pots were introduced in about 1860, possibly from Yorkshire, they were made by the fishermen and called 'flotums' at Cromer and 'swummers' at Sheringham. They were made from hazel bent into hoops and fitted into an oak floor, the whole thing covered in hemp netting, with the entrance spout ('crinny') at the side.[14]

With the development of motorisation, use of the traditional wooden double-ender continued though tractors and trailers became the normal mode of hauling the boats from the water. The shape, although similar, fattened up to take the extra weight involved, and the dipping lugsail was done away with. Their usage continued throughout the twentieth century and, in 1996, the last vestiges of the wooden boats were still working though the newer lighter one-man boat called the skiff was being introduced. These still work the beach and most fishermen have, since the 1970s, had their own tractor and trailer. Beaching still attracts holidaymakers in the season as, although boats tend to set off in the very early morning, they return any time after nine o'clock. Unknown to most of the onlookers, this is the most dangerous time for the fishermen, especially when there's a heavy swell running, for there is the ever present danger of a boat overturning and trapping a crew member underneath. To add to their woes, each beach was different.

The transgression from wooden double-ender to fibreglass skiff might save the payment of wages to a second hand but doubtless has led to an increase of the risk of accident. However, with the decline in fishing fortunes leading to many choosing to turn away from the sea, the increase in the cost of living and wages, it has been necessary for many fishermen to survive to work alone. Not only on this coast, but all around where longshoremen continue to serve the inshore fishing sector, it's the same story. With shrinking quotas, fierce competition from the large-scale fishers taking the catch before it reaches the coast, and general legislation, longshore fishing is increasingly under threat and at the same time we see many of the traditions stretching back generations, being discarded. That the Cromer and Sheringham lobster fishermen continue in the same vein as their ancestors, albeit as a part-time occupation in many cases, is surely something to celebrate when so many other walks of life are changing, and not always for the best. Like the survival of the coble in modern-day fishing, the beach boats of north Norfolk have perhaps faced their toughest challenge and are now secure in their survival for the next century, especially after the very recent construction of a wooden crab boat.

Further down the coast, into Suffolk, and the story isn't quite the same. From just south of Lowestoft, at the small village of Pakefield, right down to Bawdsey, close to the mouth of the River Deben, a series of small (and larger) villages were once served well by the sea. These communities favoured a transom-sterned punt to work off the beaches and some continue to do so today. The largest fleet lies at Aldeburgh and a 1588 map clearly shows boats and crab capstans on the beach, so this beach fishery appears to have been long established then.[15] The beaches are shingle here, and shelve more deeply than the sandy beaches of north Norfolk, and the Suffolk punts evolved to cope with this.

The herring and sprat fishery was the lucrative fishery of the autumn. Boats were known to have been overloaded with sprats and Robert Simper tells of one fisherman, Billy Burrell, who recalls how, in 1938, after engines had just been fitted to Aldeburgh boats, these were removed for the sprat fishing so that more fish could be loaded aboard. In summer they chased the salmon and took trippers out.

Simper also mentions the small hamlet of Shingle Street where the people lived with little outside contact. They fished, and at the same time were wild-fowlers, poachers and beachcombers, all contributing to a meagre living. They even devised a huge underwater spoon which they used from a boat to dredge up coal from sunken ships off Orfordness.

Many of the fishermen of these east-facing Norfolk and Suffolk beaches were often life-savers. The sea offshore the coast is wild and in the nineteenth century hundreds of vessels sailed past in these waters, often coming to grief. The fishermen set up beach companies to act as rescue and salvage operators, working with what have become the renowned East Anglian beach yawls. Each beach company had its own headquarters and open double-ended yawl (or *yol* from the Norse *jolle*, meaning open boat). Some beach land-ings had more than one beach company and competition could be fierce. Although primarily acting as rescue boats, they were also used as supply boats for the passing ships, taking out whatever was needed. They maintained a twenty-four-hour lookout and if a vessel was spotted in distress, the yawl was launched with speed and raced to the scene. From Happisburgh in the north, right down to Shingle Street, beach companies were based in almost all the places were boats could be launched and landed. This was often a much more lucrative business than fishing, which then took second place.

But the sailing the yawls was often more risky than fishing, given the urgency with which they were sailed. First to the casualty got the job. Some boats were three-masted, setting big dipping lugsails. Simper tells of several that were lost: two from Sea Palling in 1842 and twelve men lost in the space of five weeks which would have been a great loss to a small community. The three-masted *Increase* from Great Yarmouth, which had the largest number of beach compa-nies, capsized in 1853 and only one of the eight men aboard was rescued.

The Southeast Coast

Today Hastings is probably the best known beach-based fishing community in Britain. It is a place where boats that fish out into the English Channel are landed and launched from the shingle beach and is said to be the larg-est beach-launched fishing fleet in Europe today. Although declined from its heyday, it is still a magnet for folk – holiday-makers and residents alike – who come to lap up the atmosphere when the boats come in to the water's edge, to be dragged up the beach using wooden sleepers under the keel and tractors to do the hauling work.

A century ago things weren't that different except that the boats were sail-ing craft, full and round, mostly clinker-built and rigged with two lugsails.

There were big craft – the luggers – and smaller vessels – the punts. The luggers exhibited lute or elliptical sterns while the punts were transom-sterned. All were built on the beach and, being rounded in the hull, sat upon the beach pretty well upright.

However, although Hastings is today the only real survivor in terms of the longshore fishing, this whole coast was one of small fishing communities in the nineteenth century. From Selsey Bill to North Foreland, beach fishers worked from Selsey, Bognor Regis, Worthing, Brighton, Newhaven, Eastbourne, Bexhill, Hastings, Dungeness, Hythe, St Margaret's Bay and Deal. Newhaven, Folkestone, Dover and Ramsgate, although having fishing fleets, had harbours to accommodate these fishers so were not beach based.

Tourism overtook some of these towns in the eighteenth century with the popularising of sea-bathing for health reasons. Then, with the growth of the railways in the nineteenth century, day-trippers flocked to the south coast from London and the days of commercial tourism had arrived, filling the pockets of the local traders and town councils alike. Fishing became the work of undesirables and they, in their insular communities, were pushed to one end of the town. This is obvious today in Hastings where the Stade is their base today on the east side of town: the well off were housed to the west. The

'Lugger on the beach' by E.W. Cooke from the early nineteenth century. Although this lugger was probably from near Brighton where Cooke produced many etchings, the boat would be similar to those in nearby Hastings.

irony is that, with its renowned tall net sheds and vibrant beach, it is today more popular than the west side of town.

Brighton might be the gem in the crown but was once merely the small fishing community of Brighthelmstone that is said to have sent boats into the North Sea to fish for 'linge, codd and herrings' at the beginning of the seventeenth century.[16] The Brighton 'hog-boat' was the favoured vessel and, like many of the craft of the Sussex coast, mirrors those of the French–Belgium border area across the Channel. These were all flat-bottomed craft, squarish in plan and sluggish to sail. Many were featured in drawings by such artists as Edward Cooke.[17] Like the Hastings fishers, those of Brighton (as it became known) were also pushed to the edge of the town. Unlike Hastings, the fishing didn't survive in the same way, partly due to the construction of a marina and partly from the growth of the town in other ways.

Trammel-netting is the mainstay of the Hastings fleet.[18] It's an old method of fishing and is pretty ingenious. The net is in fact three layers of net – a central net or lint with a small mesh of between 4 and 5 inches either side of which hang larger mesh nets with head and foot ropes attached. These outer nets are known as the 'armouring' or 'walling' and hang looser when set on the seabed. Fish swim in through the large mesh, force their way through the inner mesh so that fish and inner mesh pass through the other large mesh netting to form a bag from which there is no escape.[19] According to Holdsworth, the name of the net is said to come from the Latin *tres maculae* (three meshes) and was introduced to English fishermen from those of France, which seems fairly likely given its proximity.[20] The trammel is used extensively along this coast for plaice and sole in the spring and is also used in the Channel Islands and Cornwall. Hastings men trawl from May onwards, and occasionally set gill-nets. In the summer they also hand-line for mackerel, and drift-net for herring in early winter.[21]

Today the Hastings fleet survives, though not with the help of the policy makers in Brussels. Sheer determination is what keeps the beach alive. The boats have changed somewhat and now catamarans and mono-hulls made from fibreglass, steel or aluminium are more likely than wooden elliptical-sterned craft. But the traditions handed down through generations show through just as brightly allowing the fishers to continue to make their livelihood. For sure, crews amount to just one which adds a further danger to the job but these men are built for the sea and take this in their stride just as they do up and down the coast. Longshoremen have so much to offer society by way of their local knowledge, their crewing lifeboats, their watching the coast for unusual phenomena, as well as the obvious supply of freshly caught fish into the food chain using methods of fishing that are, mostly, as ecological as is possible. Long may they continue.

5

WEST COUNTRY PILCHARD FISHING

On 22 November 1872 fleets of both mackerel and pilchard drivers – so-called as they were regarded as driving the fish into the drift-nets – from the Cornish village of St Ives were fishing some miles offshore when a gale-force wind rose up unexpectedly. The smaller pilchard luggers were nearer to home so they hauled in their gear and safely reached shelter, but the bigger mackerel drivers had a harder beat home. By the early hours of the next morning eight boats were still unaccounted for and though some made it to safety, two making Newquay, one to St Agnes and one to Ilfracombe. However, two boats – *Mystery* and *Captain Peter* – never did and ten fishermen were lost, leaving six widows. But of course this wasn't the only instance on this weather-battered coast where just the loss of one single boat was a tragedy. In 1880 the Mousehole lugger *Jane* was smashed to pieces on the rocks just outside the harbour entrance and all the crew killed as those on the shore watched, being completely unable to do anything to help. That night boats sank at nearby Newlyn while eleven sank at their moorings in Mousehole harbour.[1] Just as the small coast-hugging fishing communities of most other parts of the British coast suffered their own tragedies, the fishermen of Cornwall certainly had their own, their working grounds facing, as they do, the onslaught from the Western Approaches. Whether pilchard fishing, potting for shellfish or trawling for white fish, there are always stories to tell. Here, though, for the moment, we are only interested in fishing the pilchards.

Fishing for pilchards was done in one of two ways: driving and seining. Both had advantages and, seemingly forever, there were disputes and verbal arguments between the two branches of the fishery. It seems that seining had the upper hand, largely due to Acts of Parliament from the seventeenth and eighteenth centuries, and it was often said that the drift-net fishermen were the poorest while the seines were run by well-off businessmen. Given the fact that drift-netting involved a far greater investment in terms of lugger and nets in contrast to the small boats of the seines, then this is perhaps understandable. The

Acts, it was said, were to protect the interests of the majority in that they virtually prohibited the use of the inshore drift-net during the pilchard season.[2]

Perhaps the most severe was enacted in the time of Charles II when harsh penalties were placed on the drift-net boats so that:

> … from and after 25th day of May, 1662, no person or persons shall in any year, from the first day of June, till the first day of November, presume to take fish, in the high sea, or in any bay, port, creek or coast, of or belonging to Cornwall or Devon, with any drift net, trammel stream net or nets, or any other nets of that sort or kind, unless it be at the distance of one league and a half at least from the respective shores, upon the penalty of forfeiture of the said nets so employed, or the full value thereof, and one month's imprisonment, without bail or main prize.

Pilchard seining, by its very nature, was an age-old profession dating back from at least the Middle Ages. It has been described as a 'colourful and extraordinary sight unique to certain parts of Cornwall and south-west Devon'.[3] Some of the legislation protecting its use dates back to the late sixteenth century, the time of Elizabeth I. In 1602 there was much discussion about the seines and drivers:

> But the least fish in bigness, greatest for gain, and the most in number, is the pilchard. They come to take their kind of the fresh (as the rest) between harvest and Allhallowtide, and were wont to pursue the brit, upon which they feed, into the havens, but are now forestalled on the coast by the drovers [*sic*] and seiners. The drovers hang certain square nets athwart the tide, through which the shoals of pilchards passing, leave many behind entangled in the meshes. When the nets are so filled the drovers take them up, cleanse them, and let them fall again.
>
> The seiners complain with open mouth that these drovers work much prejudice to the commonwealth of fishermen, and reap thereby small gain to themselves; for (say they) the taking of some few breaketh and scattereth the whole shoal and frayeth them from approaching the shore; neither are those thus taken merchantable, by reason of their bruising in the mesh. Let the crafts-masters decide the controversy.[4]

The pilchard is one of the commonest fish around the western part of Britain and is, in fact, a mature sardine, as those seen off the western coasts of Portugal, Spain and France, and into the Mediterranean. It also has been caught off southern Ireland and off parts of west Wales, such as at Fishguard where Richard Fenton introduced 'the business of preparing these fish [pilchards], their fry or sprats, in the same way as the Spaniards did and export[ed] them to Italy'.[5] That was in the eighteenth century when, it seems, a sprat was regarded as being the fry of anything that looked in any way similar! Fenton built a tall, four-storied warehouse with cellars and racks for curing both herrings and pilchards, the building existing still.[6] Two hundred years or so before, in 1603, it was said that the pilchard was not so rife as it had been in earlier years and that pilchards and mackerel took second place and were nothing in comparison to the herring.[7]

From a Cornish perspective, there were few parts of both the north and south coasts that didn't participate in the annual pilchard fishing before the end of the nineteenth century. They didn't swim much beyond, say, Trevose Head although Port Isaac, Port Gaverne, Port Quin and even Harlyn Bay just north of the Head, were bases to seines. Furthermore, rarely is a pilchard seen further up-channel than Start Point, though, in 1722, a considerable amount was caught at Totnes Bridge, right up the River Dart, after a shoal was chased in by porpoises. When landed by the locals with their boats, Daniel Defoe says they fed the locals for several days.[8]

Not only is there a distinct difference in the way pilchards are caught using drift-nets and seines (and we will have more of the latter soon), but the way shoals are spotted is somewhat distinctive in British fisheries. I say 'somewhat' for the task of spotting pilchards from cliff tops has been copied in other fisheries but was first practised in the process of pilchard seining.

> The job of spotting is that of the 'huer', sometimes called a 'balker', a man who: standeth on the cliff side and from thence best discerneth the quantity and course of the pilchard, according whereunto he cundeth [instructs] (as they call it) the master of each boat (who hath his eye still fixed on him) by crying with a loud voice, whistling through his fingers, and wheezing certain diversified and significant signs with a bush which he holdeth in his hand.[9]

In later times this was traditionally shouted as '*heeva, heeva, heeva*' through a trumpet-like speaking horn when he had spotted a shoal. However, a huer was only useful when fishing close to the shore where the cliffs were high enough to be of use. Offshore, the man in charge was the Master Seiner who directed the operation. As to the word 'heeva', it has been interpreted as meaning various things and Noall suggest it probably means something like 'Here they are'.

So how do they spot them from atop the cliff? Like the herring fishermen watching for the 'natural appearances', the huer would spot the shoals when they were close by. The huge shoals appeared as stains of red, purple and silver in the water and this would be chased by screaming gulls and diving gannets overhead. They swam in from the west and split on meeting Lands End so that both the north coast and south coast profited from the fishing.

Two or three boats are employed in one Seine Company, as a group of fishermen operating a particular seine are called. Each seine was licensed to work a particular area and often a company owned several seines, such as T. Bolitho & Sons of St Ives who owned thirty-three seines in 1869.

The main boat was the seiner, a low open boat of 35–40ft in length, usually double-ended and carvel-built as these were regarded as the fastest and able to carry the largest net as the seine-net was. They carried no sail and were propelled solely by six oarsmen. The second boat was named variously as the 'folyer', 'volyer' or 'stop-seine boat' and it carried the stop-seine, sometimes called the thwart-seine, aboard and was a few feet smaller than the first boat. The third boat was called the 'lurker', much smaller at sixteen to eighteen feet in length, and was used to direct operations with the Master Seiner aboard. When they were working close inshore the lurker was dispensed with, all directions coming straight from the huer's mouth, so to speak, atop the cliff.[10] Often there were two huers, the assistant being responsible for the stop-seine.

The main boat would shoot the seine by understanding and anticipating the instructions from the cliff top or Master Seiner who was in charge. These were in the form of semaphore signals which would direct the boat this way or that, so that the net would be eventually shot around the shoal. The folyer would help and if the catch was huge, the second net, the stop-net, would be employed to close off the mouth of the net. The seine-net could be up to a quarter of a mile long and 60ft deep. Once surrounded and sealed, the seine would be towed by both boats to shallow water where the fish would be extracted. Sometimes the process of taking the fish ashore had to be delayed, for example if the curing process could not keep up, so that the fish would be held in the net for days, with a guard left twenty-four hours to make sure no one else helped themselves. The largest catch was said to have taken place in St Ives in the autumn of 1851 when it was estimated that 17,908,800 pilchards were caught. This catch took a week to land and the overall profit was £7,500 which is over half a million pounds in today's sums.

The net itself needs a mention. It has been described as a:

… cumbersome affair … about 160 fathoms in length (320 yards) and could be as deep as 8 fathoms (48 feet). A net of this size would weigh three tons. This included the lead 'sinkers' which were placed on the foot rope causing the net to drop like a curtain into the sea and prevent the fish from escaping underneath the net close to the sea bed.[11]

Hauling it from the sea would take several men; hauling it ashore would take far more manpower.

Daniel Defoe, when being rowed to view the river's entrance and castle at Dartmouth, experienced the excitement of the sighting of a pilchard shoal. In his words:

> … I observ'd some small Fish to skip, and play upon the Surface of the Water, upon which I ask'd my Friend what Fish they were; immediately one of the Rowers or Seamen starts up in the Boat, and throwing his Arms abroad, as if he had been betwitch'd, cryes out as loud as he could Baul, *a Scool, a Scool*. The Word was taken to the Shore as hastily as it would have been on *Land* if he had cry'd Fire; and by that time we reach'd the Keys, the Town was all in a kind of an Uproar.
>
> The matter was, that a great *Shoal*, or as they call it a *Scool of Pilchards* came swimming with the Tide of Flood directly, out of the Sea into the Harbour. My Friend whose Boat we were in, told me this was a Surprize which he would have benn very glad of, if he could have had a Days or two's Warning, for he might have taken 200 Tun of them, and the like was the Café of other Merchants in Town; for in short, no body was ready for them, except for a small Fishing Boat, or two; one of which went out into the Middle of the Harbour, and at two or three Hawls, took about forty Thousand of them.[12]

Local bye-laws restricted the fishing ability further. For fishermen there must have been a confusing amount of legislation, perhaps comparable to that which fishermen have to cope with under today's EU Common Fisheries Policy, which we will attempt to clarify in a later chapter. These bye-laws included prohibiting fishing on a Sunday night. But it wasn't just the seiners that attracted the attention of the lawmakers, as we've seen, so that the drift-net boats were not to be shot during neap tides, nor before half-tide in spring tides. In 1631 an order was made that no herring fishing boats were to shoot nets before the feast of All Saints 'but if they Drive with nettes before they may according to the auntient custome'.[13]

Some of the photographs of seining tell the same story: large groups of people involved in the process of emptying the nets, called the 'tucking' of the pilchards. The seine boat was pulled into the seine so that the pilchards could be removed with the tuck-net which was lowered into the seine and brought out, bringing up with it some pilchards which were then transferred to the seine boat using dip-nets or baskets called dippers. Once full, the seine boat then carried the pilchards to the shore where it was beached and then unloaded once the tide had dropped, using horse and carts. Some writers refer to a tuck-net boat which presumably was a boat for carrying the pilchards to the shore in the same way as the seine boat was used, while others call the boat for carrying the pilchards to the shore a dipper. Nevertheless, the tucking was another spectacle not to be missed and was described thus:

> Tucking is a sight which the stranger should not, on any account, neglect to witness, especially when it is performed on a calm, clear night; it is then impossible to imagine a more exquisite scene: the boats moving to and fro, their oars scattering brilliants at every stroke, and the quiet, yet busy action of the fishermen, as they plunge the basket into the water, and at each dip, raise, as it were, a stream of liquid silver, produce an effect at once unique and beautiful.[14]

The scene is easy to imagine. The fish splashing and writhing in the seine, the splosh of the baskets as they are plunged into the oily water, the shouting of the men as the work progresses and the general hubbub of the spectators, for it wasn't only at night that a stranger could witness the performance as seining itself was a daytime occupation. Night-time tucking happened when, in winter, the daylight hours were short. For the men it was back-breaking, cold, monotonous and dangerous work for little pay.

All along the south Cornish coast there were few beaches or coves that did not have a seine company. For the rockier north coast, the places seines operated were more drawn out. Wherever a seine worked, nearby there would be a pilchard cellar, the place where the pilchards were cured. Take Portwrinkle, for instance, a small village close by Rame Head. It has a small drying harbour and above this are today the remains of the seventeenth-century pilchard cellars. In 1813 there were simply fishermen's huts along the shore and a curing house.[15] At that time the whole population of the hamlet would be involved in the pilchard fishery, especially the tucking and curing. A decade earlier some 200 hogsheads – a hogshead was a barrel containing about 3,000 fish – were captured. In 1834 an advertisement announced the sale by public auction of the equipment and cellars of 'The Portwrickle [*sic*] Fishery Company', consisting of three seines, boats, tackle and all shore equipment, and ninety tons of new and thirty tons of old salt.[16]

At the other end of the scale – and the county – St Ives, the principal Cornish seining station, had the largest number of seining companies. The numbers recorded in the St Ives Seine Registrars' Book show fluctuations: in 1867 there were sixty-one seines, the following year 266, 286 in 1869, 285 in 1870 and seventy-two in 1871. Numbers declined thereafter and were down to thirty-six by 1882. 1870 is said to have been the peak year and afterwards catches fell due to several factors – a dearth of fish, the pilchard drivers and loss of the traditional markets.[17]

Other places with a tradition of pilchard seining were Newquay, Mousehole, Newlyn, Mevagissey, Fowey, Polperro, Looe and Cawsand. Other smaller villages renowned for seining were the tiny village of Portloe on the Roseland Peninsula, Cadgwith Cove, better known these days for its crabs, Portreath on the north coast and the nearby expanse of beach at Perranporth. Here a huer patrolled the cliff top and sounded his trumpet at the sighting of a shoal. Several seines were based here and there were some one hundred fishermen, between whom there was considerable rivalry.[18] Porthleven, traditionally a fishing harbour, was closely connected with the drift-net fishery though there was a little seining there.[19]

Men were normally paid a wage – in about 1670 this was 3s 8d a month plus a further £1 14s 6d at the end of the pilchard season – though a part-share system was adopted in the nineteenth century as an incentive bonus. Fishermen were also paid extra for specific jobs such as barking a net or hauling the seine-net to a boat while huers and Master Seiners received a lot more than the average fisherman. They were in a top class while shooters were second class and the seiners (average fishermen) third. *Blowsers* were men ashore and they received a minimum wage too. The season was rarely longer than eight or ten weeks though very occasionally went to four months.

Work on the drift-netting luggers, on the other hand, was not seasonal and offered a more stable employment and earnings. Pilchard driving occurred from June to late autumn and it was not unusual for the fishermen to hand-line for hake while drifting to their nets. Catches of two hundred hake were not unusual, adding to the income. Out of the pilchard season many drivers went to the hook and line fishery, and to the mackerel drift-net fishery, so that many of the crew aboard the luggers were employed throughout the year. During the off season in late winter, the boats would be overhauled, scraped and re-painted with pitch. Sails and the boat's rig had to be maintained, and it didn't matter whether you were a seine fishermen or crew aboard a driver – the old hemp nets, later replaced by cotton, had to be constantly repaired and barked in a tannin solution of oak bark (and later cutch) to stop the seawater rotting the fibres.

Once ashore, the pilchards had to be cured in a speedy manner as, like all oily fish, they go off quickly. Salt has for centuries been used for this purpose, both dry salting and brining, though smoking has long been another fine way of preserving fish. Before the onerous Salt Laws were abolished in the nineteenth century, it was an expensive commodity. However, just across the channel, French salt was untaxed and this led to boats bringing in cargoes for use locally, regarded as free trade though others termed it smuggling!

That there was a considerable amount of money made from operating seines is obvious by the amount of investment needed. A seine company needed a pilchard cellar, boats, nets and tackle. Businessmen do not invest if the envisaged returns are not high, and they were. For instance, the most profitable fishing ever seen in Cornwall was at St Ives in 1862 when 3,500 hogshead were taken. These fetched seventy-five shillings per hogshead (total £14,112 10s including sale of oil and other), and the overall profit was calculated as £10,153 18s 5d after wages and expenses were paid. Salt was the highest expense. However, it was not a meagre sum for a day's fishing![20]

The pilchards were carried ashore from the dippers in *gurries*, open wooden boxes with carrying handles at either end which could hold some 1,200 fish. These had to be 30 inches long, 21 inches across and 19 inches deep and were marked by the Registrar as being compliant. The Registrar was empowered to enter any cellar or boat to measure nets, ropes, gurries or casks to ensure they were of the correct size. Any new seine net had to be inspected prior to use.

The floor of the pilchard cellar consisted of smooth pebbles set in cement, sloping so as to drain away. The pilchards were then 'bulked' – built up into solid rectangular blocks between layers of salt some 5ft high, this work being mostly done by women and girls. The fish remained in this for four or five

Processing the pilchards in a pilchard cellar. The presses are counter-balanced by the heavy beam running overhead and pressed down onto the barrels with their packed fish. Although this scene doesn't compare to that described by Collins, nevertheless the actual pressing task didn't alter much in generations.

weeks with the oil, blood and brine seeping out and draining into a sump called a train-pit. The oil was sold off for manufacturing and the 'drugs' (dregs – blood, brine, etc.) sold as manure (hence 'other' above). The pilchards were then washed and laid into casks known as hogsheads, these being more straight-sided than the traditional barrel. On top of the pilchards was laid a circular wooden cover, called a buckler, which was weighted to press down on the fish. Heavy boulders of a hundredweight or so were used to create the pressure necessary to bear down on the bucklers and these bore down for a week, with more oil being forced out between the timbers of the cask. In that week more pilchards were added as the level shrank. The hogsheads were then sealed and branded with the curer's name. They were then ready for shipment as some 95 per cent of the cured pilchards were exported, a large amount going to Italy.

In the region of up to 40,000 hogshead were needed in a good year, which in itself created a vast industry, just as the Scottish herring fishery had a need for huge numbers of barrels. One can again imagine the bustle of activity at a pilchard cellar with the arrival of the gurries, coopers making the hogsheads and the women preparing to bulk. The smell itself must have been overwhelming but Victorian novelist Wilkie Collins in his *Rambles Beyond Railways* (1851) was one to overcome this and describe the vivid scene he saw in St Ives:

Here we must prepare ourselves to be bewildered by the incessant confusion and noise; for here are assembled all the women and girls of the district, piling up the pilchards on layers of salt, at three-pence an hour; to which remuneration, a glass of brandy and a piece of bread and cheese are hospitably added at every sixth hour, by way of refreshment. It is a service of some little hazard to enter this place at all. There are men rushing out with empty barrows, and men rushing in with full barrows, in almost perpetual succession … then we advance further, get out of the way of everybody behind a pillar; and see a whole congregation of the fair sex screaming, talking, and – to their honour be it spoken – working at the same time, round a compact mass of pilchards which their nimble hands have already built up to a height of three feet, a breadth of more than four feet, and a length of twenty. Here we have every variety of the 'female type' displayed before us, ranged round an odoriferous heap of salted fish. Here, we see cronies of sixty and girls of sixteen; the ugly and the lean, the comely and the plump; the sour-tempered and the sweet – all squabbling, singing, jesting, lamenting, and shrieking at the very top of their very shrill voices for 'more fish', and 'more salt'; both of which are brought from the stores, in small buckets, by a long train of children running backwards and forwards with unceasing activity and in the hands move as fast as the tongues; there may be no silence and no discipline, but there is also no idleness and no delay. Never was three-pence an hour more joyously or more fairly earned then it is here!

Collins also writes of *cabing*, the snatching of pilchards from the gurries by children. Boys, armed with sticks, were employed to accompany the gurries on their way to prevent such attacks. The children received a smart blow across their hand if caught in the act.[21]

The use of the seine-net declined sharply after about 1870 as seen above, and hardly figured in the twentieth century: the last seine was shot in 1922 though nothing worth talking about was hauled in. The fortunes of the drivers continued somewhat longer, thanks to the development of canning, though the disappearance of the pilchard did later bring about their abrupt end and it wasn't until the late twentieth century that any pretence of a pilchard fishery surfaced. Most of the cellars were idle and the market was little if not sparse. However, Newlyn, with its single Pilchard Factory, did survive and went a little bit further by developing a growing market.

Today's fishery for pilchards is a very different fishery however. Health regulations simply do not allow fish to be processed in such unhygienic sur-roundings. No longer are drift-nets used, while a seine is, but, alas, a very different seine-net, something half way between a purse-seine net and a ring-net. It's shot from one boat – two fishermen usually working at night when the pilchards feed off the surface of the sea – and is some 600 yards long, shot around a shoal found, not by the huer or the natural appearances, but by sonar. Pilchard fishing, like all fishing, has adopted the technology of computerised fishing. The sonar shows the fish as dark red squares looking like blocks of high-rise flats on the screen. Sometimes, when the shot is made, the dark red squares dive and swim out before the net is closed. Once the shot is made and the end of the net is picked up, then the bag is closed by tightening the purse rope which is threaded through rings attached to the bottom of the net, to create a bag out of which there is no escape. The fish can then be brailed aboard, to be later landed and taken to market.

Today's Cornish sardines in their little jars and pretty cans are, in reality, simply Cornish pilchards relabelled as, for many, the word 'pilchard' has the ring of poverty and obnoxious times. However, just as likely, the same consumer will have on the shelf a can of pilchards from South America, given the state of today's fishing market. At the same time sardines come from the Mediterranean, Portugal and the West African coast and are welcomed on the shelves. Gone are all the traditions of the pilchard industry and, sadly, few remember it. The Cornish used to refer to pilchards as 'meat, money and light' – food, a living and oil for their lanterns. Today few eat it, a very few get an income from it and no one lights their lamp with its oil. It's gone, largely, as has a whole way of life.

6

FISHING THE IRISH SEA

From a fishing point of view the Irish Sea is of prominence as it encompasses part of each region of the United Kingdom: England, Scotland, Wales and Northern Ireland, and also includes a chunk of the Irish coast. Bang in the middle is the Isle of Man whose growth has been accredited with the development of a fishing industry (and centre of a smuggling trade) several centuries ago. The Irish Sea thus gave all the coastal settlements along the coastline that have survived from the fisheries a common bond.

It's a fish-rich sea with a biodiversity almost matching that of the North Sea. Channels either end – the North Channel between Scotland and Ulster, and the St Georges Channel between southwest Wales and Ireland – link it to the Atlantic Ocean (north) and the Celtic Sea (south). With a proximity to the Bristol Channel with its second highest tidal range in the world, the Irish Sea is washed twice a day by the tide, helping it to maintain a diverse amount of sea-life.

Fish traps were once prolific along this coast as attested in an earlier chapter. Although shellfish have also long been caught in the tidal waters and other fish caught with lines, it was the herring that was the first fishery of any significance and the Manx were the first to prosecute this fishery to any serious degree. But even so, before it became an organised fishery in the nineteenth century, the herring had been landed into the island from the earliest times. Certainly there is documented evidence of herring being landed during the first half of the fourteenth century, and some of this was by strangers from outside the island, according to the *Chronicles of the Kings of Man and the Isles*, in which it is stated that Thomas, Bishop of Sodor (*c.* 1330–48) was the first to exact from the rulers of Man one tenth of all the taxes paid to them 'by all the strangers in the herring fishery'.[1]

By 1610 various regulations were laid down in the *Manx Statute Book* including a law enforcing a close time for the herring from 1 January to 5 July, within 9 miles of the shore, and prohibiting the shooting of nets before sunset.[2] It would appear that the fishing was highly controlled and operated in an organised and disciplined manner by a Water Bailiff ashore and Admirals of the Herring Fleet at sea. The latter reported misdemeanours while at sea to the Water Bailiff who held a court every Saturday during the herring season and was able to summon skippers held to break the rules. These included shooting nets too soon, crossing another boat's nets, cutting buoys or corks from other nets and taking their fish. Fines were also imposed for minor offences such as bad language.[3]

Blundell tells us that, in the middle of the seventeenth century, the fishermen had to hand over a good percentage of their catch. The Lords of the Isle took 20 per cent and the Church the same while the Water Bailiff only demanded a modest share of 5 per cent, leaving something in the region of 55 to 60 per cent remaining.[4] Blundell also noted that 'the sea feedeth more Manksmen than the soil' and that they are eaten as they are and never smoked. Among the other fish they caught are salmon, cod, haddock, mackerel, rays, plaice and thornback.

At about the same time (1603) it was reported that such was the abundance of herrings around the coast of Pembrokeshire it was as if it 'were enclosed in with a hedge of herrings'.[5] All sorts of fish were available according to the same source:

> … turbot, halibut, burt, sole, plaice, fluke, flounder, ling, millwell otherwise called cod, hake, mullet, bass, which breeds twice a year as says Rondelet, conger, gurnet, grey and red, whiting, haddock, shad, the friar, bowman, sea smelt, sea bream, the cow, swordfish, sprat or sandeel, the earl or needle whose fins grow forward contrary to the nature of all fish, rough hounds, smooth hounds, thornback ray, shark, with many other kind of sea fish …

A further list gave the various shellfish present at that time. Of the herring, it was said that fish:

> … collect in large numbers and so large are the shoals of herrings that they cannot be caught, but after the autumn equinox they divide themselves into columns. They change their places and wander through the oceans in shoals, as a result of which it happens that many are caught at the same time.[6]

Tenby, on the south Pembrokeshire coast, was the centre of a huge herring fishery about this time. In fact, its Welsh name *Dinbych-y-pysgod* literally translates to 'the Little Fort of the Fishes', a fact reflecting its fishing position from the fourteenth century when its harbour was built, and probably earlier.

In North Wales documented evidence comes from much earlier with regard to the herring fishery. In 1294 at Llanfaes, a custom of one penny on

every mease of herring landed was charged, a mease being about 500 herrings. Furthermore, every herring boat entering or leaving port owed the
king one mease, worth about two shillings. Llanfaes at the time was home to a
thriving trade in fish even though it was a tiny hamlet on the Isle of Anglesey
(Ynys Mon), at the eastern end of the Menai Strait. Probably the money thus
raised went to pay for the castle at nearby Beaumaris which was finished the
following year.[7]

The Welsh Port Books show the extent of the export of herrings from
the island and the amount suggests that a further development of the fishery
occurred in the sixteenth century. Salt was brought in from the Cheshire
salt mines by ship via Chester, with salt herring being sent back to the port,
or sometimes to Liverpool. By the sixteenth century herring was becoming
a well-traded commodity. In 1564 a Scottish boat was said to have landed
'6 lasts, 4 hogshead of shotten herrings, 30 copules of ling, 20 copules of
codfish' into Milford and in 1566 the Pembrokeshire fishers were working in Irish waters as well as up the River Severn and into North Wales. In
1571 a French boat landed sixteen lasts, eight barrels of white herring into
Carmarthen and four years later a Tenby boat brought sixteen barrels of herring from La Rochelle to Milford. Strangely, though, little mention is made of
exported herring during this time which suggests a lull in the shoals.[8]

Herring certainly must have been an important part of the local economy
in Beaumaris by the following century, as in 1722 and 1723 the town elected
two men – Lewis Davies and Richard Morris – as the official packers of
fish there.[9] In 1797 huge shoals 'sometimes visit the Anglesea coast, which are
taken, dried, and exported; being considered by the knowing ones in delica-
cies, as particularly excellent'.[10]

To the south of the Irish Sea, across the Bristol Channel, lies the delightful
village of Clovelly, on the north coast of Devon, with its tiny harbour at the
foot of the cliff. In 1630 Thomas Westcote noted that herring was being caught
there and up the coast at Lynmouth, the latter being known 'for the marvellous
plenty of herrings there taken'.[11] The Rev. John Robbins, vicar of Clovelly
from 1730 to 1777, reporting the ups and downs of the herring, wrote that:

> In this year 1740, God was pleased to send his blessings of a great Fishery
> among us after a failure of many years. This thro' His mercy continued in
> 1741. In this year 1742 the fish was small and poor and in less quantity. In
> this year 1743 but an indifferent fishing. In this year 1744 worse than in the
> preceeding. In this year 1745 still worse. In the year 1746 much worse.[12]

One wonders whether it could have got any worse! However, this is
the very nature of the herring: a fickle fish that can change its migratory

Gordon Perham in his Clovelly picarooner shaking herring from his nets before they are basketed ashore. Stephen Perham has continued fishing in the same way although the prospect of a total ban on drift-netting in the European Union threatens one part of his livelihood.

pattern at the drop of a hand. Nearby Minehead had a vibrant fishery in the seventeenth and eighteenth centuries when the small quay was crowded with smokehouses. 'Herring and bread, go the bells of Minehead' so the saying went. In late autumn some 4,000 barrels of herring were being exported. By the twentieth century the fishery had all but disappeared. Clovelly, however, bucked the trend. At the beginning of that century Charles Harper reported that 'Clovelly fishermen are famed for their endurance and Clovelly herring for their flavour.'[13] Nothing can be truer today when each autumn Stephen Perham goes out fishing in his small open picarooner (the small single-masted lugger of the village), sculling or sailing depending on the wind, to lay drift-nets not much more than half a mile from the harbour, and catch several thousand of the small sweet-tasting fish. His is a niche market – and two others fish though using engined boats – and over the last few years the quality of the herring has improved year on year. To celebrate the fact, the village holds an annual Clovelly Herring Festival each November, the only annual herring festival remaining in Britain.

In the first half of the nineteenth century the Irish herring fishery was thriving along the coasts of Counties Down, Louth, Dublin and Wicklow. Here small boats reminiscent of Scandinavian design worked inshore while larger boats worked offshore, many being second-hand Manx vessels. Ardglass became a major fishing station where, in 1835, there were some 300 boats based there for the summer season, a third coming from Penzance, the rest equally between Irish and Manx boats. Scottish fish dealers came to Ardglass to buy the catch and cure it there, and it was later sent to Liverpool or Dublin by lugger or wherry.[14]

But in the nineteenth and twentieth centuries it was the northern part of the Irish Sea that benefited from a thriving herring fishery. By the time the English Crown took possession of the Isle of Man in 1765 after the passing of the Revestment Act, bounties had been introduced in the buss fishery. Duty on the import of herrings into Great Britain was abolished and, in some cases, the Manx fishers prospered from the bounties. Towards the very end of the eighteenth century the numbers of boats increased dramatically after the bounty was introduced for small boats. After the Douglas Bay disaster of 1787 the Manx had adopted the smack as a fishing vessel and numbers belonging to the Island amounted to some 343, according to the Custom House in Douglas, of twelve tons, and each carried a crew of seven or eight men, although larger vessels were being introduced at that time. Some fifty larger smacks were buying the herring and salting them aboard before being barrelled ashore. These were then sent to ports such as Liverpool or Dublin. The fishers were paid on a share basis and were not full-time but only worked the four-month season. Outside of this they were employed as farmer labourers or mechanics.

There was a steady expansion of the herring fishery in the first decade of the nineteenth century when there were as many as 600 local boats at times working the herring. By 1823 numbers of local boats had fallen to 400 and three years later had further declined to 250. However, Cornish and Scottish fishermen had by that time started following the herring around the island. Both fished in large luggers which had stemmed from Cornwall, where two-masted dipping luggers had been drift-netting for mackerel as described in the last chapter. The Manx fishers liked the rig, finding it more powerful than their smacks, and especially effective when lying to the nets with the mizzen lug set. During a decline in the fishery in 1835, they shortened the boom of their gaff sail and added another mast with a small dipping lugsail, creating a dandy rig. At the same time they stepped the mast in a tabernacle on the deck instead of it passing through the deck to the mast step resting on the keelson. In this way they could lower the mast when lying to the nets just as the Cornish and Scots did.

Then, in 1860, the obvious happened and they copied the design of the Cornish boats, building their own two-masted luggers. These became known as 'nickeys', the name said to have come about through the high number of

Cornishmen called Nicholas, although another suggestion was that the first boat from Cornwall was in fact the *Nicholas*. The first boat of this design was *Alpha*, built by William Qualtrough of Port St Mary in 1869. Thus, not for the first time, fishermen broke the local tradition of using the same boat of their forefathers and adopted that from another area because of the effectiveness of that vessel. In Britain, for the herring fishery in the days of sail, two boats from opposite ends of the country were found the optimum – the West Cornish lugger and the Scottish fifie, and both shared so many similar characteristics that it is hard for some to realise that they evolved independently of each other. They were designed by fishers for fishers and, until the Scottish Zulu came about in the last days of sail, were the very best in vessel technology for the intended use of drift-netting.[15]

The nickeys were larger than their Cornish counterparts and were renowned for their speed, increased possibly by the use of mizzen topsails and mizzen staysails. They could accommodate seven fishermen and a boy in a space in the aft end some 15ft in length. This included a stove for cooking. Forward of this was the fish hold, then a net room with a bosun's locker up front. These boats sailed south to join in with the lucrative mackerel fishing off Kinsale, on the southern coast of Ireland where French, Cornish, Scottish and other English boats mingled with the Irish boats during March and April. Then it was back home for the summer herring and some nickeys sailed to the east coast of Scotland to follow the shoals southward into East Anglia. It was almost possible to fish continuously all year, with a little time off in the winter to overhaul the boat.

In 1879 it is said that a thousand boats were fishing in the waters between the Island and the Irish coast including native Manx boats and those from Scotland, Ireland and Cornwall. In 1881 there were 334 Manx boats recorded as taking part in the herring fishery, most being registered at Peel or Port St Mary. Such was the trade in these boats that renowned Cornish boatbuilder William Paynter from St Ives began a boatbuilding business in Kilkeel to satisfy the local demand. Sadly, this enterprise did not thrive and, after a fire burnt down his yard, he retreated back to Cornwall. However, he left a great legacy of the boats he built atop the beach at St Ives.[16]

It was around this time that the Manx fishers began to follow the Clyde fishermen in their use of the ring-net. Locally, this initially raised anger because of the supposed destruction to the habitat and to the quality of the herring. Trawling was also being blamed for the disappearance of the herring spawning grounds off Douglas and Laxey, although this has never been proved one way or the other. From the available evidence it seems that the herring was already in decline in the Irish Sea, a point that soon became apparent and thus cannot necessarily be blamed upon the antics of the ring-net fishermen.

What did happen, though, was that for the second time the Manx fishers turned to other areas to copy the type of boat in use, this time northwards to the boats of the ring-net – the nabbies and Lochfyne skiffs.

Although outside the geographical area of the Irish Sea, it would seem pertinent that what occurs in the Clyde affects the whole of the Irish Sea. Ring-netting, as it became known for it is the setting of a net around a shoal and thus creating a bag as in seine-netting, the difference being that the net is trawled between two boats in the process. A very brief summary is needed.

The introduction of ring-netting at Tarbert in the 1830s gave rise to serious arguments among the fishermen, with those from the upper reaches of Loch Fyne particularly in favour of retaining the traditional drift-netting and believing that the huge hauls of the ring-netters would all but empty the loch of herring within a few years. This was discussed in Chapter 2.

Once trawling had recommenced in earnest and some of the original objectors had joined in, as had one fish-curer who had realised the advantages of the method. In that same year, 1867, under great pressure from all sides, the government repealed all the Acts and amendments, making the use of a trawl-net legal once more: within a year all trace of an era of law enforcement had disappeared.[17]

Initially the Lochfyne fishers had used wherries to fish, a common type of boat around the northern part of the Irish Sea and favoured by the smuggling trade. They then adopted the half-decked smack in the 1820s and then introduced the lugsail sometime in the 1840s. In turn they developed the double-ended lug-rigged drift-net and line-fishing boat similar to the boats of the northwest coast. The lug rig was introduced from Ayrshire where double-ended nabbies were small open line boats. Ring-netting necessitated a larger boat as a crew of four or five was needed, and so the Lochfyne skiff was introduced into the ring-net fleet in the early 1880s, a similar size increase taking place with the nabbies of the east side of the Clyde. Accommodation was available aboard the vessel for the first time so that they no longer needed to sleep ashore in temporary shelters or take a large lugger for use as sleeping quarters. For by this time the fishermen were spending longer periods from home in the quest for herring.[18]

Two years after the Lochfyne skiff was born, the first of the new types arrived in Peel and soon became known as the Manx nobby, though bearing no relation to the Morecambe Bay prawners across the sea, also referred to as Lancashire nobbies. The nickey owners at first adopted the nobby rig of a much smaller mizzen but then they were quickly phased out in favour of the new type which was smaller and required a smaller crew. Like their predecessors, they followed both herring and mackerel where the Irish, so impressed with the vessels, built their own versions which worked both on the east and west coasts.

The next development in the fishery was motorisation, which began to take effect on this area in the first decade of the twentieth century. Steam had impacted in the previous century and steam trawlers were working out of Fleetwood, a deep-sea fishery port that had grown out of a tiny hamlet at the mouth of the River Wyre. Sailing trawlers, and then steam, worked the rich grounds off Iceland and further north, bringing back vast amounts of cod and other fish (this will be the subject of another chapter). Milford Haven briefly became a major herring port in the 1920s when steam drifters landed there but the business was short-lived even if several smokehouses survived into the 1960s.

From the point of view of the herring industry, it was the development of the motorised ring-net boat that started in 1922 at Campbeltown when the first of two canoe sterned boats arrived to work. In time this led to what became the motorised 'ringer', a beautifully shaped, varnished hull with a substantial sheer line, low on the waterline to enable the net to be worked over the side, pretty wheelhouses and a small sail until the engines became reliable enough to dispose of any rig except a boom used for lifting the baskets of herring ashore. These were built mostly in Scotland, with Alexander Noble & Sons Ltd of Girvan producing some of the best craft, although others came from east coast yards and several from the Isle of Man.[19] In time the Scottish type of fishing boat became the ubiquitous boat seen all over Britain and many worked the Irish Sea ports such as Maryport, Workington, Whitehaven, Liverpool, Holyhead, Aberystwyth, Swansea and Cardiff, as well as the smaller Cardigan Bay ports. Liverpool was said to be the base of a thousand herring boats in the mid-nineteenth century though these, according to Robinson, were fast cutters and sloops that sailed from the Mersey to buy the catch all over the west coast.[20] They sailed home and cured the catch, ensuring it was barrelled within the requisite three weeks demanded by regulation.[21] Holyhead enjoyed a brief flurry of herring activity in the 1950s but this was short-lived. Moelfre, on the east side of Anglesey, was base to a small beach-based herring fleet which survived until the 1960s, with a daily train from the local station that took the fish to Liverpool market. It was said that the Welsh sea captains who sailed the seven oceans in their trading ships, came home for the brief herring season in the autumn, making more money in those six or eight weeks than they did all year. The same was said for all the small Welsh ports and creeks.

The herring fishing survived up to the 1970s when the last ring-net was shot. With a decline in stocks, the European Union placed a ban on herring fishing after Norwegian and Scottish boats clobbered the stocks with their huge purse-seine nets. After the ban was removed, fishing in the Irish Sea was never the same again. Herring were scarce except for sub-species types as

A fine view of Morecambe Bay nobbies gathered at the Mersey River race in about 2002. These boats that fished for prawns and white fish, sometimes even drifting for herring, have survived well and an active fleet still sails and gathers for annual races around ports of the northwest. Note the beam trawl on the nearest boat. (*Courtesy of David Wilson*)

caught today at Clovelly. Irish Sea fishermen relied upon trawling for white fish and prawns, potting for shellfish, and mussel, cockle, oyster and scallop fishing to survive.

The one fish we have not mentioned so far, and one that was once caught in abundance, was the salmon. Generally in these parts, the salmon was fished in the rivers – though in some parts it was fished in drift-nets off those estuaries of the rivers where salmon were known to swim into to spawn – and these rivers saw some varied and ingenious ways of catching what was once a widely eaten fish until stock declines brought about the opposite: the food of the privileged few. There were days when the servant population of the middle and upper classes threatened strike action when they deemed they were being fed salmon too many times a week. Ah, if only we could now made such claims. Instead we see salmon upon salmon lining the supermarket fish counters – insipid farmed salmon containing inferior chemical-fed colourings and antibiotics and other additives on which it is fed to counter the disease from parasites such as sea lice, and bacteria from its faeces. For the home market most is farmed in Scotland and northwestern Ireland by companies today largely Norwegian-owned. Norway, with its fjords of cold fresh unpolluted water, appears to be the market leader in what is a thriving business. Other species such as bream, turbot, tilapia, sea bass, carp and trout are also farmed with success while other fish such as cod are not having the same results.

In the Irish Sea rivers the following methods of salmon fishing are practised: the drift-net in various Irish estuaries, the haff-net in the Morecambe Bay rivers, whammel-netting in the River Lune, draft-netting on the River Dee, coracle fishing in many Welsh rivers, the compass-net of the River Cleddau, and seine-netting in various rivers. In the rivers that feed into the Bristol Channel other methods include the lave-net, stop-net and long-net of the Rivers Severn and Wye, the pitch-net in the River Parrett, the putchers and putts, withy constructed baskets to trap fish, in all these rivers, and the draft-nets of the Rivers Taw and Torridge in north Devon. In Bridgwater Bay the stake-nets occasionally catch salmon. On the Irish side, salmon were caught with draft-nets in the River Boyne where coracles were once used too, and in the southeast, in the Rivers Suir, Slaney and Nore, both snap-nets and draft-nets were used. Draft-nets were basically seine-nets set across the river as were long-nets. For each of these fisheries, a particular boat evolved through usage and thus we have the Lune whammel boats, the Dee salmon boats, the compass-net boats of the Cleddau, the stop-net boats and the long-net punts of the Severn and the Taw salmon boats. Across in southeast Ireland, various different cots worked snap-nets and draft-nets, while coracles and prams worked the River Boyne. Coracles from the Welsh rivers and the Severn and Wye came in various sizes and shapes.

Often a forgotten mode of fishing, trawling for shrimps and prawns in Morecambe used to be practised using horses and carts to tow trawls. Perfect for shallow water trawling, the horses were superseded by tractors in the twentieth century. (*Courtesy of Jennifer Snell*)

The stop-net, like the compass-net which was the almost same thing on a smaller scale, was unique and both were probably the most interesting and ingenious of all the salmon fishing methods. The stop-net was a bag-net suspended on two 24ft-long pieces of stout Norwegian spruce called 'rames'. These were held in a 'V' by a spreader while weights at the apex of the frames completed the frame. Once the stop-net boat was moored fore and aft to its 'chain', one of the many wire warps lying perpendicular to the stream attached to a stake ashore and anchored in deep water, broadside on to the river, the frame was lowered into the tide so that the bag opened up below the boat. Hence the shallow draft of the vessel and lack of much of a skeg which would both entangle the net and create more drag as the boat sits across the current. Five feeling strings were attached to different parts of the net and to a 'tuning fork' – a wooden stick – which was held by the fisherman. A wooden prop supported the weighted apex. Once a fish was detected through vibrations in one of the feeling wires which resonated in the stick, the fisherman kicked the prop out – called knocking out – and helped by his weight the net came up out of the water with, hopefully, the fish still in. If so, this was extracted through the 'cunning hole' which, when untied, was a concealed entrance to the cod end where the fish ended up. A quick thump with the 'knobbling pin' consigned the fish to the thereafter and the net was again tied up and dropped back into the water, propped up to await another unfortunate fish. When the fishing was good several salmon could be landed during the three hours of fishing though when the tide was strong or the water calm they might get nothing.

Coracle fishing was undertaken in pairs, two coracles floating down stream with the current with a net suspended between both vessels. Again feeling strings told the fisherman of the presence of a fish and the net would be hauled up to trap the fish. Haff- and lave-nets were similar in that the fisherman stood in the river, facing the direction from which they assumed the salmon would come, and when a salmon struck the net it was flipped up to trap the fish. The art was in the positioning of oneself in the path of an oncoming salmon. Pitch nets were similar and used in the muddy waters of the River Parrett where the swimming salmon had to come to the surface to clear, and the fisherman then judged by experience where he would surface the next time to net him. All these methods pitted man against fish and those who understood the patterns of the fish tended to gain most and, this in many quarters, was regarded as an art. But, like so many other traditional skills, much of this fishing has disappeared as technology takes over at the expense of skill and overfishing has seen stocks plummet. Added to the problem for these river fishermen is the angling brigade who are supported by riparian owners who can earn a huge income from them. Licensing authorities, often in the hands of these owners, have reduced both licences and the fishing season while raising the fees for the licences so that those determined to see the traditions kept alive do so at a financial loss. But, other than a bit of trawling, prawning, lobster and crab potting, and mussel, cockle and scallop fishing, that's about all that's left in the Irish Sea for the fishermen to take a living from.

7

TRAWLING THE SILVER PITS

The 'Silver Pits' have, strangely, no connection to the silver darlings, and the only silver to come out of them comes in the form of silver coins. Maybe they should have been named the golden pits, for that was what they became, a source of untold wealth for fishermen – in the short term.

Many charts name this phenomenon the 'Silver Pit', as that is exactly what it is: one undersea valley stretching some 25 miles in a north–south direction, the northern end being 28 miles out from Spurn Head at the mouth of the River Humber. This valley, 300ft at the deepest point, lies close to the southern edge of the sandbank known as the Dogger Bank which occupies an area of 6,800 square miles of the southern North Sea, half way between England and Denmark. In contrast to the Silver Pits, Dogger Bank is in effect a large sandbank with depths ranging from 48 to 120ft. The name comes from the *dogger*, the Dutch fishing boat that resembled something like a herring buss but one that is said to have trawled over the banks in the seventeenth century.

The first documented evidence of trawling as such in Britain comes from 1376 when a device called a *wondyrychoun* was being petitioned by the Thames ports to Edward III against its continued usage. This was likened to an oyster dredge with a closed-net mesh. A year later what was described as a 'machine' which consisted of a 10ft beam with a frame at either end shaped like a 'cole rake' and the whole thing was 3 fathoms long. A sketch from 1635 shows a beam trawl affair although there is no sense of size.[1] It has been suggested that it was a device imported from the Zuider Zee, another instance of the Dutch teaching the English and Scots how to fish.[2]

Its use attracted plenty of criticism, and like the ring-net in Loch Fyne in the 1830–1860s, there were plenty of strict regulations enforced and fishermen were fined for using small-meshed nets and 'unlawful engines'. However, up to the eighteenth century, trawling was confined to inshore waters and sometimes dragged along beaches as happened in Filey. Horse trawling for prawns continues right up to today, as we shall see in a subsequent chapter, though nowadays it is tractors not horses that pull the net along.

The beam trawl was described thus in the early 1900s:

The beam trawl was an apparatus consisting of nine distinct parts. These were the beam, the trawl heads, the ground rope, the bosom, the cod or purse, the draw rope, the running pieces, the pockets, and the bridle. The beam was proportionate to the size of the net. The wood usually employed to make it was elm, experience proving that this was the best material. For the smaller beams, which had a length of about 36 feet, it was not difficult to find single pieces of wood which could be used with little or no trimming. If, however, the trawl beam was very large, two or three pieces of elm had to be scarfed together and secured by iron bands. This was the form most commonly seen on the Dogger when the trawling had reached its height. To each end of the beam an iron trawl head was fixed into a socket. A pair of trawl heads stood in relation to the beam as the runners do to a sledge. The lower part was quite flat, the front part being curved and the back and top practically straight. The object of the trawl heads was to keep the beam about three feet above the ground and so afford an uninterrupted entrance to the net itself. The upper part of the net was known as the back, the bottom portion was known as the 'belly'. The front edge of the back, technically called the 'square', was fastened to the beam; but the 'belly' part was extensively cut away so as to form a sort of semi-circle on the ground. The middle of this curve or sweep, the 'bosom', was thus at a considerable distance behind the beam and in front of the net, the distance, as a rule, being about equal to the length of the beam itself. The ground rope protected what might be called the lower lip of the net. Generally, the ground rope was an old hawser 'rounded' or covered with small rope, which served two purposes – to make it heavier and to prevent chafing. But there was a greater object than that to be served, and this was to stir up the ground and so rouse the fish which, as a rule, would immediately make their way into the net, and having once done that, there was little chance of escape. It was essential that the material forming the ground rope should be old, so that in case as obstruction was met – and this frequently happened on rough ground – the rope would be destroyed and the net itself saved.

The net would sometimes have a length of 100 feet, the meshes being of four different sizes, varying from 4 inches square near the mouth to 1.5 inches at the cod end. The net with a length of 100 feet would have a width of 50 feet at the mouth, so that there was an immense triangular bag towing at the bottom of the sea, which, if it came across a shoal of fish, would scoop a tremendous haul. It was a not uncommon for 3 tons of fish to be caught at a time, and on the Dogger I have seen one of the old beam trawls so crammed full with haddock that it could not be hauled; as a matter of fact, the net burst and the dead haddock were as thick on the surface of the water as an icefloe.

The most interesting part of the beam trawl net was in the old days, as it is now, the cod end, for here the fish are found when the net is hoisted inboard and the moment comes for the big bag knot to be unlashed and the catch released. The cod end is a narrow jail for the fish, and once in it and in the pockets there is about as little chance for the creatures to escape as there is for a convict to get out of prison. It must be remembered that the fish are swimming against the tide and that the net is being towed with it, so that, the more they try to escape, the smaller is their chance of freedom. If, however, fish turn about and try to get away from the enveloping meshes, they seek to do so by keeping to the two edges or sides of the net. In this case they are doomed, because then they swim into the pockets. These pockets, two in number, are placed near the cod end and are made by lacing the upper and lower parts of the net for about 16 feet. Each pocket is practically a reversal of the cod end, and is literally a trap, for the entrance consists of a valve or curtain of netting, called a flapper. This flapper is so constructed that, although it allows free admission to the fish, still, it prevents them from returning. If they turn at all, they must go into the pockets, which are practically inverted cod ends, so that there is no chance whatever for them to escape, especially as fish are constantly entering the net and often enough forming a solid mass.

To the trawl heads, by means of shackles, the bridle was attached, and to this in turn was fastened that important part of the trawl's equipment – the warp. The warp had a length of 150 fathoms, consisting of two sections of 6 inch rope spliced together.

In the old smacks the trawl was invariably kept on the port side, and when the beam was not in use it formed, with its trawl heads, net and gear, a very prominent feature of the vessel. The great beam usually projected beyond the stern.[3]

In the same century eating fish became fashionable and, as we all know, when something becomes fashionable on the tables of those able to pay for it, the price rises. And when the price of a commodity shoots up, then the supply has to keep pace and thus those responsible for that supply have to work harder to prosper. Prices thus soar. Out in the North Sea the fishermen had to stay fishing longer hours and developed the well-smack, modelled on Dutch boats that were able to keep the catch fresher longer by keeping it in wells in the belly of their vessel. Long-line boats from Harwich and Barking were foremost at this so that they could stay at sea until the well was full. Harwich was at the time the premier port of this coast, though Barking was later to eclipse it.[4] The well itself consisted of bulkheads across the boat to create a watertight box amidships and, with holes drilled in the planking of the boat, the well being flooded by the sea.[5]

Daniel Defoe noted these craft in the early part of the eighteenth century:

> One thing I cannot omit to mention of these Barking fisher-smacks, viz.
> That one of those Fishermen, a very substantial and experienced Man, con-
> vinced me, that all the Pretences to bringing Fish alive to London Market
> from the North Seas, and other remote Places on the Coast of Great Britain,
> by the New-built Sloops called Fish-Pools, have not been able to do any
> thing, but what their Fishing-Smacks are able on the same Occasion to
> perform. These Fishing-Smacks are very useful Vessels to the Publick upon
> many Occasions; as particularly, in the time of War they are used as Pres-
> Smacks, running to all Northern and Western Coasts to pick up Seaman
> to Mann the Navy, when any Expedition is at hand that requires a sudden
> equipment: At other Times, being excellent Sailors, they are Tenders to
> particular Men of War; and on an Expedition they have been made use
> of a Machines, for blowing up Fortified Ports and Havens; as at Calais,
> St. Maloes, and other Places.[6]

The men of Barking, a hamlet aside a tiny creek off the Thames, had been catching herring since at least AD 670 and the hamlet was well placed to supply the London markets. Well-smacks were introduced here in 1798 and thirty-five years on there were 120 such craft based there. Twenty years later trawling was well underway as there were 134 smacks trawling and another forty-six long-lining off the Norfolk coast.

Long-lining is, of course, an ancient way of fishing and has been practised all around the coast for centuries. They consist of lines with thinner strops called *snoods* spaced out along their length with hooks attached to the snoods. The length of line and number of hooks differs greatly and varied from twenty to 6,000. They may be worked from boats, set on the seabed, near the surface or simply by placing them on the sands at low water and checking them on the next ebb. Great lines were common in northeast Scotland and down the east coast of England and were traditionally baited ashore by the women, old men or boys. Baits varied but it was once the norm for the fishermen to gather mussels to use as bait though in other areas sometimes the hooks were baited with herring as they were shot. Long-lining was prolific until the advent of, especially, steam trawling. A typical cod smack carried sixteen dozen lines, each 30 fathoms long. Each had a snood at some 7ft intervals which was

Two Lowestoft
trawlers sailing out
of the harbour. These
were hugely powerful
craft capable of towing
heavy trawls.

30 inches long. A train of these lines of about 6 miles in total length carried about 5,000 hooks with an anchor at either end and buoys at every mile.[7] The amount of boats needed to supply these lines was immense and some forty vessels were busy exclusively collecting bait from the Wash for them.

As the power of sail increased, so did the ability to tow trawls across the bed of the North Sea and English Channel. It is said in many circles that the small Devon village of Beer had much to do with the growth of trawling. 'Beer made Brixham, Brixham made the North Sea', the saying goes. For, even before the Barking folk were trawling the North Sea, the Brixham boats were annually joining in with the Yarmouth Herring Fair back in at least 1200. Devon boats were travelling far and wide in their search for fish and were the protagonists in sailing across to Newfoundland for the cod fishery in the sixteenth century where they went to search for fortunes. By 1785, there were seventy-six sailing trawlers working from Brixham although it is said that the first men working trawling out of Brixham were Beer men in their small three-masted luggers.[8] Some say that it was the Dutch again who taught the Brixham men to trawl.[9] These trawlers were working the North Sea, some basing themselves for the season in Scarborough and by the end of that century were up to almost 80ft in length. Indeed, many Brixham skippers took their wives and families to Scarborough where they resided at temporary homes during the fishing season while their husbands supplied the town with fish for the growing tourist trade. At the same time the smaller smacks were working over the Dogger Bank.[10]

The story goes that it was the Brixham boats that discovered the Silver Pits in 1837. John Dyson tells us how William Sudds, a Brixham fisherman who settled in Ramsgate, was master of one of several boats dispersed in a winter storm in the early winter that year. When he limped home his boat was said to have been staggering under the weight of fish – 2,000 pairs of soles for which the Silver Pits became renowned.[11] Robb Robinson puts Sudds aboard a Margate-built smack *Betsy* which he first registered at Hull and then re-registered in Ramsgate in 1838.[12] A further suggestion was made that the Silver Pits were in fact discovered in 1838 and then 'rediscovered' in 1844.[13] Perhaps Sudds kept quiet about his discovery, took it back to Margate and then returned to the area as he was master of the 18-ton smack *Ranger* in 1844, a boat owned by J. Todd, a Hull fishmonger.

Life in the smacks in the North Sea was not fun. In a smack there were normally five crew. Bottom of the rung aboard was the boy, that doer of everything no one else wanted to do. He was, of course, learning the ropes, later to climb up the crew, and later still to literally climb up into the wheelhouse to take command. He was cook, cabin cleaner, washer upper, tea maker, water drawer, clearer of the decks of fish scales and all, and getter rid of the 'brash' or rubbish in the net. He learnt to box the compass, steer, mend and brail nets, coil the ropes and generally keep everything in its rightful place.

Next came the fourth deckhand who wasn't much further up the ladder than the poor boy. He was expected to be able to do everything the boy did which isn't surprising as it is quite likely that he *had been* the boy prior to the arrival of the new boy after, probably, a higher member of crew had left. Most of the crew had worked their way up from the boy's position, learning everything there was to know about sailing a smack and towing a big trawl in all sorts of North Sea weather, just as their fathers and grandfathers and great-grandfathers had before them. He was also meant to be able to handle the vessel, to set the sails and watch how they react to the wind. He'd watch the trawl too, for a snagging could have dire consequences. He'd be able to

The boy had all the unpleasant and tedious jobs to do, here seen peeling spuds. Redding the tarred headrope down into the hold was one of the most unpleasant of all!

splice and whip ropes, mend sails, braid a cod end and repair nets and take the soundings. And when he wasn't doing any of that he'd be attending the fishing and gutting the catch.

It used to be said that it wasn't uncommon for a crew member to drop off the stern of a smack, tripping up or missing his foothold while working. On dark nights, with the wind whipping across the faces and hands of the crew, to secure the trawl and then turn the smack around quickly was impossible and that crew member unlucky enough to fall in wouldn't have a chance anyway. The vast majority of fishermen couldn't swim. If they could the cold would have had them before the smack was able to have even the slightest chance of finding him. It was easier to succumb to the water as quickly as possible. Most times they didn't even bother to attempt a turnaround as they were acutely aware of the situation and it was merely an acceptance within the job. There's no truer statement than 'it's not fish, it's men's lives'.

The job of the third deckhand was slightly more taxing as he'd stand watch for eight hours at a time, manage to prepare the vessel to shoot or haul in the net and splice the warps. He would have to be skilled at net mending, checking the rigging and chafes, as well as fishing and the subsequent gutting and icing down.

The mate had to be able to run the vessel, to navigate, to watch for signs of fish, to attend to everything on the ship that needed attention. He was under the master but understood the master's job for if the master was absent, then he was in charge. He had to know the fishing grounds, when and where to shoot the net, the finer points of trawling.

The master was, of course, that. His word was final and he was responsible for the good running of the vessel, and its fishing efficiency. A poor catch meant there was no money to share out among the crew. With the share system, the boat took a portion of the money from the sale of the fish while the crew shared the rest out. The master had a double share, the mate one and a half, the third and fourth one share and the boy half a share. Sometimes the proportions were slightly different but the idea was the same. Once the smacks became larger in the second half of the nineteenth century, there was often another hand aboard as cook who was employed to look after the crew and take part in the fishing at times. The boy was the deckhand, still the person to do all the menial jobs and learn the ropes. Some of these vessels preferred to pay wages and, in 1887, the average was a penny an hour, asleep or working, which amounted to fourteen shillings a week. He would also get a shilling for each pound of the smack's earnings which could bump his earnings up considerably. The mate got eighteen shillings a week in total, the third deckhand sixteen shillings, the fourth fourteen shillings, the cook ten shillings and the deckhand twelve.

Conditions aboard the smacks were pretty grim. Some boats were squalid, 'with verminous cabins, uncouth men and sordid life'.[14] However, that wasn't the case of all craft and, although conditions were by no means homely, there was a certain pride among the crew in keeping the vessel clean. Generally they ate well aboard as any skipper worth his mettle knows that a well fed crew works well: roast beef, dumplings, lots of potatoes, suet puddings, and fish for breakfast, the prime of the catch.

The large sailing trawlers were some boats, for sure. Built mainly in Brixham, Galmpton, Rye, Lowestoft, Hull and Grimsby, they were immensely strong vessels capable of towing a 55ft beam trawl. Some older smacks were lengthened to cope with the increase in the size of the gear. Scarborough was said to have several being worked upon on the open beach there. As boats became larger, so their cost increased. A first-class trawler by the 1880s was a big investment at £1,500 but with steam trawlers beginning to make inroads on the fisheries, some second-hand vessels came up on the market for those skippers who could not afford a new vessel.[15] The 1870s proved to be the peak of their trade. Fleets sailed from Hull, Grimsby, Yarmouth, Lowestoft, Ramsgate and Brixham and they worked throughout most of the year. In winter fishing was mostly confined to the Dogger Bank and the banks to the southward and in summer they would venture further out towards the Danish and German coasts, and off Helgoland (Heligoland) which was British territory between 1807 and 1890. Brixham boats continued to sail far and wide though in winter they worked their local grounds until moving away in March, some to Penzance, the French coast and southern Ireland while others moved to the North Sea, landing into Yarmouth or Lowestoft.[16]

One of the most important developments in the trawl fishery was the introduction of the otter trawl in 1895. Instead of a beam trawl that dragged the net over the seabed on the iron shoes, two boards were so fixed to the tow ropes that the pressure of water on them forced them apart, thus keeping the mouth of the net open. Although it was able to run along the seabed, for the first time the trawl could be operated above the seabed. Wood's description is still relevant:

Experience proved that the beam was unwieldy and unnecessary, and there came into being the ingenious contrivance which is known as the otter gear. It was not until 1894 that the new method superseded the old plan of fishing. Like all other improvements, the Otter was at first ridiculed and condemned; but the opposition died very quickly, for even the most conservative smacksman saw in it a welcome change from needless labour, a vast improvement in fishing, and a means of greater profit. In place of the beam, two boards, about 4.5 feet square, were attached to the mouth of the net, where the trawl heads had been, and so arranged that on being dragged through the water they kept the mouth open in the same manner as the rigid beam and irons. An enormous advantage, too, was the lightness of the contrivance compared with the weight of the old apparatus, and the possibility of shooting and hauling in weather which would make the employment of the beam impossible. With a lessening of weight and the further use of steam, the labour of handling the net has been very much reduced. Powerful steam winches have succeeded the hand and donkey capstans; yet even today the final work of getting the net on board is hard enough to satisfy even the most robust of toilers.

At the outset a modified form of the Otter apparatus was used, and I remember photographing one of the earliest types of 'gallows' – a square invention which was unpleasantly suggestive of the real thing which is stealthily concealed in unassuming sheds in gaols. Today the 'gallows' consist of arched girders fitted to the trawler's side, and they form a prominent feature of her equipment.

At the outset many patents were secured for the Otter apparatus, and it was necessary to pay a fee of £25 yearly before it could be used; but, as improvements were put on the market and the demand for the modern appliance grew, the charge was abolished, and today the principle is employed, free, in all modern steamboats engaged in trawling.[17]

Two other factors contributed to the growth in the fisheries. First, there was the increased availability of ice to keep the fish fresh while at sea, which enabled the boats to venture further from home. Ice had been imported from Norway and kept in ice houses for many centuries and, indeed, the remains of various ice houses can still be seen today especially in parts of Scotland, where it was widely used to pack with salmon brought down from the east coast to London. The one in Barking was said to have had a capacity of 10,000 tons and in winter 3,000 men cut ice during the winter, the ice lasting the fleet until November. 1874 was the first appearance of artificially made ice though it wasn't until the end of the century that this became the chief source.[18]

Second, the railways were a major source of this growth as fish was suddenly able to move about the country to markets that were previously unreachable. With a growing population, especially in the developing cities where industry was making a mark in the mid-eighteenth century, fish was becoming available at prices that could be afforded by many working people. Boats could land anywhere within reason and get their fish to any market around the country if they so wished. The pace of fishing simply grew and grew, without much thought to the nature of the stocks. With the introduction of the steam trawler, conditions might have improved slightly for the crew, though not for the fish. The old smacks slowly disappeared and motorisation took its toll on the oceans.

The Silver Pits have become synonymous with North Sea fishing but in fact were only a huge source of sole, not white fish in general. Today they are still there, abandoned through a dearth of fish, like much of the North Sea where stocks are at an all-time low, if some are to be believed. Others, fishermen among them, say they have turned the corner and are rebuilding. Indeed, the evidence points more and more towards the words of these experienced fishermen.

Nevertheless, the North Sea remains full of names that conjure up images of the past, some in today's Shipping Forecast: Smith's Knoll, the Sole Pit, the Coal Pit, the Skate Hole, the Great Fisher Bank, the Outer Silver Pit, the Cockle Lightship, the Haisboro' Light, even the German Bight. Find a chart of the southern part of this sea and the names are all there, seemingly, however you look at it, a silent monument to the great days of North Sea fishing.

8

FISHING BEYOND THE
CONTINENTAL SHELF

In 1997 the replica ship *Matthew*, with modern-day technology and intrepid crew, set out from Bristol to Ireland and thence on to North America, mirroring the journey of John Cabot 500 years before. When they arrived to a fanfare of celebration, the once-great cod fishery off Newfoundland was quiet, fishing all but banned after Europeans and locals had hammered it so much, the fish were gone. However, when Cabot had returned from his exploration the following year, he told stories of the sea swarming with cod as big as a man and 'so many that this kingdom would have no further need of Iceland'. This then was the firing gun for the beginning of an Atlantic rush from England to fish these bountiful waters though, surprisingly, the boats were not a commercial success at first. Cabot's comments do back up the theory that boats were already sailing to Iceland to fish the waters around that coast and that England was being supplied by a flourishing Icelandic cod fishery as well as its own inshore fisheries.[1]

Whether the sudden rush to the New World fishery did affect the Icelandic fishery is open for debate. According to Evan Jones, the Newfoundland cod fishery was developing in what he describes as a time of expansion in the Icelandic cod fishery. It had been earlier in the fifteenth century that vessels from Bristol, Hull and Lynn had visited Iceland after acquiring special licences, and half a dozen ships sailed there each year until a decline in fortunes towards the middle of the sixteenth century, although vessels from East Anglia continued. Prior to 1490, half the problem had been that there were heavy restrictions on Englishmen visiting Iceland though these were eased by the Anglo-Danish treaty of that year. The licences lasted seven years and they had to pay a heavy fee to leave the country.[2] What Jones maintains is that, even if the Icelandic fishery declined somewhat after 1530, some English ships still continued to follow the fishery. He notes eighty-five in 1533 and only forty-three by the 1550s. Nevertheless, although much of the blame for the decrease in number he places upon the Danes for increasing the duties payable by the visiting vessels, and to the English Parliament for passing a law that restricted the selling of the fish, vessels did continue to fish there. It was not a matter of stock level of fish. Added to the decline was the rise of Protestantism in England, at the expense of Catholicism, which meant less emphasis on the eating of fish on Fridays and other fish days, which had vastly inflated the amount of fish consumed. When Elizabeth I attempted to bring back these compulsory 'fish days' for 152 days a year – Fridays, Saturdays, ember days and throughout Lent, and later on Wednesdays – the law proved unpalatable to the people because it reminded them of papism, and it was found unenforceable and soon lapsed.[3]

By the beginning of the seventeenth century fishing was once again flourishing off Iceland. Generally this fishery was prosecuted by large boats capable of sailing the 500 miles of ocean between northern Scotland and Iceland, and of remaining at sea for maybe six months at a time as spring and summer was the time for this fishery. Many were built in Harwich and have since been termed 'cod smacks'. By the early eighteenth century these were fitted with fish wells to keep the catch fresh. The number of crew depended on size and the largest boats, up to 100 tons, had some forty men aboard. The whole journey from East Anglia could take a week if the wind was right, and a month if conditions were against them.

Fishing was using lines and Jones quotes John Collins in *Salt and Fishery*, published in 1625, in which hand-lines of 90 fathoms are described. The line is divided with a 'cross-stick' to two lines with two baited hooks, an early form of paternoster I assume. Long-lines were also employed.

On the other hand, the Newfoundland fishery was followed by vessels from West Country ports such as Weymouth, Poole, Southampton, Exeter, Bideford, Barnstaple and Plymouth. A few were said to have come from the east coast, most notably London. Theirs was an earlier start than the Icelandic fishery and they set sail in the New Year to face just over 2,000 miles of the winter Atlantic. First they chose the best landing places as harbours were few and far between. Sheltered beaches were sought where huts could be erected, drying structures and landing stages built and where timber was available. Sometimes those from a previous year might be reused, or sometimes destroyed to prevent someone else using them.

Hand-lines were used extensively and long-lines sometimes set, using small boats away from the mother ship. It was said that you could almost lean over and touch the back of a fish, they were so numerous. Fish were landed, split, dried and salted, the oil being collected from the swollen livers. When the French boats came, they were seen away by the English and they sailed south to discover the Grand Banks where the cod were just as prolific. They tended to process the fish aboard, returning home when the boat was full, and returning so that they made two journeys each year.[4]

The fishery progressed throughout the eighteenth century with some of the fishers deciding to settle in the New World. Each year the boats sailed over, filled up with fish over the summer and sailed back to Europe to sell the dried fish. Portugal, Spain and the Mediterranean countries bought the catch which was sometimes traded for other commodities such as spices, wine, velvets and other items that could be taken by the England to be sold for hard money. However, in the 1790s, there was a decline in the migratory fishery and the fishermen of the West Country refrained from visiting again, the fishery being left to the Newfoundlanders who then controlled it for the next 150 years, before the Europeans came once again and contributed to the total collapse in this fishery in the late 1980s and the subsequent ban on fishing in 1992.

The Icelandic fishery, on the other hand, was already a distant memory. The seventeenth century started well but by 1660 it was obvious to the East Anglian fleet that the cod fishery was in decline. In 1668 there were thirty-nine ships working Icelandic waters, and a decade later twenty-nine. By 1680 it was said to be a quarter of what it had been and, at the turn of the eighteenth century, only 10 per cent of those previously employed in it were still fishing. No ships were sent by Yarmouth, one of the main cod fishery ports. Fishing became focused on the North Sea which was being opened up by sailing smacks from Barking and Brixham.

It was Charles I, desperate to raise revenue, who started the rot by increasing duties in 1630, the time of the heyday of the fishery. At the same time there was a refusal to allow the reclaiming of salt duty from salt imported from Biscay that was used in the fisheries. Increases in salt tax meant, in the end, that the English were forced out of the Icelandic fishery because they were unable to compete and much of the cod that was then imported into the country came from the Dutch who were, at the time, also commanding the herring fishery in the North Sea.[5]

We saw in the last chapter how the North Sea was opened up in the eighteenth and nineteenth centuries. The late part of the nineteenth century saw the peak of the era of the sailing smacks working the North Sea and Shetland waters, but it wasn't until the development of steam vessels that opened up the Icelandic waters to trawling and steam lining. Liners from Hull and Grimsby also worked around the Faroe Islands and the discovery of the halibut lining grounds known as the Faroe Banks in about 1880 saw interest from steam liners.[6] However, before we discuss the effect of steam on the Icelandic fishing, we'll have a brief look at the growth of ports that eventually commanded the northern fisheries in the late nineteenth and twentieth centuries.

In the main these were Aberdeen, Hull, Grimsby and Fleetwood. The latter grew from what was little more than an uninhabited area around the estuary of the River Wyre in the beginning of the nineteenth century into a major fishery station in half a century. Built by the Hesketh family of Rossall Hall

A postcard view of a Fleetwood trawler leaving port. These boats sailed right up to Iceland and beyond in their constant quest for fish. (*Courtesy of Sankeys*)

who owned most of the land between Rossall and North Meols, the name 'Fleetwood' came from a marriage of Roger Hesketh to Margaret Fleetwood whose family had originally owned Rossall Hall before they wed in 1733. By 1860 there were thirty-two small vessels working from Fleetwood harbour and this number doubled over the next fifteen years. When the Wyre Dock was opened in 1877, the arrival of the first steam trawler heralded a phase in the town's fortunes that were unsurpassed.[7]

In terms of the fishery, Aberdeen, at the mouth of the River Dee, was a late starter. In the 1880s there was hardly any fishing activity even if a thriving herring fishery was being prosecuted almost within sight of its harbour entrance and fish had been brought into the market from the surrounding area, something bemoaned by John Knox in 1784:

> ... there is not a single decked vessel fitted out from Aberdeen for the herring or the white fisheries: here is an excellent harbour, an active people conversant in trade, and possessed of capital; seated two days' sailing of the Shetland Isles, whose sole fishery is confined to a few open boats; the captures are insufficient for the supply of the inhabitants. If the merchants should also export cargoes of fifty or sixty vessels constantly employed in the herring and white fisheries, the port of Aberdeen would, in a few years, become the most celebrated mart of fish now existing.[8]

In 1882 a syndicate of local businessmen acquired a steam tug for trawl fishing and, even though the initial feeling was one of opposition, it didn't take long for the success of the trawl to be seen and within a few years 'fishing families from scores of villages all round the East Coast of Scotland were moving to Aberdeen to seek their fortunes and, backed by southern money, the fleet of steam trawlers grew and grew'. By 1900 there were 205, providing a living for some 25,000 people, both ashore and afloat.[9]

Hull, on the other hand, had sent ships to Iceland centuries earlier. In 1800 it was a major whaling port with something like 40 per cent of the country's whalers based there, though by the middle of that century this was in decline due to overfishing. About the same time interest in fishing surfaced with the discovery of the Silver Pits and the Humber saw an influx of Devon fishers. Grimsby mirrors the same growth in the fisheries in the mid-1800s, with the trawl fisheries seeing both expansion in the steam fleets and the development of fishing methods leading to both ports, like Fleetwood and Aberdeen, starting to look north for an ever-growing demand for white fish. Grimsby has the added notoriety of having the first purpose-made steam trawler launched based there in December 1881. The *Zodiac* was owned and operated by the Grimsby Steam Trawling Company. A second vessel followed immediately and was based in Hull.[10]

So, it was the steam trawler that started the return to fishing off Iceland by exploiting its surrounding waters which were rich in white fish. Large catches meant an increase in the number of boats working there. The first Hull steam trawler sailed for Iceland in 1891 and made fantastic catches. The following year boats from other ports repeated the exercise and it was almost as if a bonanza had been released. However, at the time Iceland was governed from Denmark (as were the Faroe Islands) and, not keen on the sudden influx of trawlers, in 1893 a 50-mile fishing limit was declared around its coast. However, this was not recognised by British trawler owners and generally ignored and the 1890s were regarded as an 'El Dorado'.[11] Danish gunboats patrolled the area and arrested several boats which were escorted into port and fined, with the catch confiscated. In 1896 an agreement was signed whereby British boats were able to shelter in Icelandic ports as long as they stowed their gear and nets and didn't fish to the east of the country. Some arrests for so-called 'illegal fishing' still continued although the outbreak of war in 1914 curtailed the fishing and no further agreements on the issue of Icelandic fishing were made.

It is worth noting that steam trawlers made inroads into fishing in other parts: around the coast of Ireland, out into the Atlantic to lonely Rockall, down into the Bay of Biscay and even further south to the Moroccan coast. To the north, trawlers sailed to the rich fishing grounds off Murmansk in 1904 and thence to Jan Mayen Island, Bear Island, Spitsbergen and even Greenland and Labrador. Sometimes the boats fished illegally and were caught and arrested but the boats persevered. Just before the outbreak of the First World War there were 25,000 fish and chip shops in Britain and the demand was insatiable.

The impact of steam was colossal in that the boats could go further, stay at sea longer and shoot longer trawls. The development of netting, from hemp and cotton nets to manmade fibres resulted in larger and larger nets being used.

Ironically, the quality of the fish coming down from the north, having been encased in ice for maybe two weeks, was not as it should have been even if half the cod being consumed came from that direction. It was said that the smacksmen of old would have condemned such fish as substandard and consigned it overboard. Quantity, at the expense of quality, was the nature of the day and steam trawling – or some trawling in any form – always resulted in poorer supplies of fish. However, fishmongers demanded a supply and it was this that was the driving force behind steam trawling.[12]

The typical steam trawler of the time was about 120ft in length and had a triple expansion reciprocating engine of about 60 horsepower. The engines were big and took up a lot of the space, with the weight well aft. Accommodation was in the forward end and in rough seas the bow could rise and fall a vertical distance of some 20ft which made being there unbearable at times. As the great bow pitched downwards, everything not fixed down tended to remain in the air. Then, as the bow lifted again, the objects which were left in midair and which had only just begun their own freefall descent met the rising boat with a loud, bone-crunching thump. To supplement life in this living hell, water poured in nearly continuously from every part of the riveted hull. Yet by 1909 there were 1,336 steam trawlers in England and Wales, 514 of which were based in Grimsby alone and 449 at Hull. Scotland had another 278, although in many parts of that country they tended to be more sceptical about trawling, and retained the belief that it destroyed more than it benefited.[13] They were pretty ramshackle boats and it's a wonder they survived for so long. John Dyson quoted one fisherman who remarked, 'These paddle-jumpers are held together by cement, iron-rust and God's mercy!'[14] He also describes how they developed, with wheelhouses, winches, improved trawls and other small improvements to make life slightly easier. Often it took five days to reach the fishing grounds and the boats would be overloaded with coal for such a long trip, some being taken aboard as deck cargo until supplies decreased below so that this could be stowed in the bunkers before fishing started. When fishing did start in earnest, it wasn't abnormal to work thirty hours at one go and then sleep for four hours before being summoned on deck again. Shooting and hauling, with gutting in between times, occurred almost constantly, and sleep was at a minimum. Dyson tells of crew falling asleep in their food and even one poor lad fell asleep while on the lavatory and the crew filled his trousers with cod livers. Urinating on someone's hands was the only way for that fellow to tie a knot. Gloves were frowned upon. The one blessing for the trawlermen was that each boat had a full-time cook who would serve up ample amounts of food.

Navigational aids were non-existent and skippers relied upon dead reckoning. Skippers didn't need to hold tickets until 1894, reinforced in 1904 when the Merchant Shipping Acts brought in requirements for skippers and mates on vessels larger than twenty-five tons to hold official competency certificates. The tests were mostly oral and were very basic. Nevertheless boats had collisions, strandings and total losses. In 1904 twenty-one British trawlers were lost at sea.[15] In the seas off the Icelandic latitudes the perils were much worse – ice, storms, icebergs, long hours of darkness and a low-lying coast devoid of habitation. Storms took their toll as described by a skipper and published in the *Toilers of the Deep* in 1893:

The storm began with a blinding downpour and a gentle puff of wind at intervals, each one stronger than the last, until at last it rose and increased in fury to a hurricane; and then, in a moment, it dropped to a dead calm without any warning. The wind had been from the southwest in the squalls and our aneroid was rushing up at an alarming rate. This, coupled with the sudden dropping of the wind, was a very bad sign so we hove up our fishing nets and prepared for a 'blow hard' ... . Nearer and yet nearer on they came [clouds], and in about two minutes the gale in all its fury was upon us, screeching, roaring and howling, bearing our vessel over almost at once on her broadside; whilst the wind was so strong the sea was comparatively smooth. What we had to fear now was the wind dropping. This happened towards tea-time then up rose the 'sea lions', roaring, frothing and leaping in savage fury at our devoted ship. The first huge mountains of water broke on board whilst we were at tea, washing the man at the wheel off the bridge, entangling his legs in the wheel chain and seriously injuring him ... dark grew the night, higher rose the seas – rushing and leaping in mad fury, threatening at every moment to engulf our vessel as she lay, a mere toy, upon that wild waste of waters. Sleep was out of the question and we remained fully dressed, dreading the worst, yet trying to persuade each other that we were hoping for the best. About 11 p.m. the second great mountain of water broke on board. We heard the watch on deck shouting 'Water!' and springing up the companion hatchway I heard the words, 'Lord Save Us!' and 'Oh my poor wife and children!' We were all on deck by this and saw that awful sea rushing at us … We could hear the crashing grinding noise as it rushed at us and not one man aboard but thought his last moment had come.

We felt our poor vessel tremble with the vibration of that thundering sea, towering as it seemed to us some twenty feet above us. Our ship seemed to be drawn broadside-on right underneath it, heeling over towards it, and then it fell. In a moment we were buried fathoms deep. How can I describe the next few moments? Screams of mercy, cries for help, ejaculatory prayers, soul-stirring indescribable sounds, the artillery-like cracking of the torn sails, howling wind and roaring sea. It was God's mercy that we ever came to the surface again. But what a change! Masts, funnel, ventilators, lifeboat, trawl beams, nets, bridge, compass, companion hatchway – all had gone; but worse than this, our cabin was full of water and there was four feet of water in the engine room. Our pumps were choked with small-coal and would not work. We were half drowned, bruised and bleeding, and totally unfit to cope with this danger, knowing, too, that with one more sea like the last all would be over. And this was likely to happen at any moment.

However, life is sweet and the fear of death, coupled with hope – truly the sailor's sheet anchor – gave us courage to fight the raging elements above and below us, and taking off our seaboots and oilskin caps we began our battle for life. It was bale, bale for eight hours without one moment's rest, but the strain mentally and physically was telling, and with two feet of water yet in the cabin we could do no more. Thoroughly exhausted we sat on the lockers and more than half dead we watched our clothes and bedding floating around us. All that day our vessel lay in the trough of the sea, at the mercy of the wind and waves. Four times that night we were hove down on our beam ends and each time we did not expect she would right again. Higher and higher rose the water in the cabin, darker grew the night, louder roared the sea, without food or fire, bitterly cold, up to the armpits in water we sat, worn with toil, anxiety and fear, expecting every moment the dread summons to appear 'across the river' …

I think it would be about four or five o'clock next morning I was startled out of a stupor into which we had all fallen by the extra heavy rolling of our vessel and the water rushing about the cabin. I felt sure this was a good sign, and ventured to peep on deck. Oh how glorious! The sky was perfectly clear and fairly studded with beautiful stars ... After our smoke we set to work to clear the wreck but it was not until fourteen more hours' hard work that we were able to get steam up and steam slowly home.[16]

Icing up was something else: a build-up of ice above deck, on the rigging, anywhere where ice could build up layers and thus increased the height of gravity of the vessel; and the more it crept above the centre of buoyancy, the greater the chance the boat would capsize. And they did, going down without any trace of them, the dreaded news to relatives back home arriving days later with the simple implied message – such and such a boat is missing, presumed lost with all hands. It was a cold, dangerous place to work on top of the long hours, and it has been said that tiredness in some cases resulted in skippers making the wrong decision such as when to seek shelter when the clouds warned of storm conditions on their way.

In the year up to June 1909 some 222 men who crewed aboard fishing vessels were killed and out of these over half were the fishermen (121) themselves as against the other members of the crew such as skippers (twenty-six), second hands (twenty-one), apprentices (five), boys (three), engineers (fifteen), firemen and trimmers (fifteen), and cooks, stewards, etc. (thirteen). The official figures give individual numbers for sailing and steam vessels and is further subdivided between those registered under Part 1 of the Merchant Shipping Act of 1894 and those that aren't – i.e. first class or not. With regard to first-class steamers, the figures still show a total of 110 deaths, almost half of which (fifty) were fishermen. Read further and the cause of death is surprising. For these first-class vessels there were no men lost through founderings that year though twenty-one died in strandings and six in collisions. Ten died working fishing gear, seven were carried overboard or killed on deck and six when throwing ashes over the side. Ten died through 'miscellaneous accidents' and one when ferrying fish. Six were drowned returning to their vessel, presumably under the influence when in harbour and one was '"found drowned" in rivers, docks, harbours etc'. Three committed suicide, including one skipper and another died of a 'supposed suicide'. Two were listed as missing at sea and seven died of disease. In all six skippers of steam vessels died, two in strandings, one working fishing gear, one when returning back to the vessel, one in suicide and one from disease. Read what you like into these figures but Walter Howell, at the beginning of his report, states that the total death rate among fishermen was one in 475 while for those registered under Part 1 of the Merchant Shipping Act quotes one in 229.[17] Fishing beyond the continental shelf was indeed the most dangerous fishing of all. Compare with the rates in 2010: a total of 12,703 fishermen in the UK and there were five fatalities, giving a death rate of one in 2,541.[18]

9

COCKLES, MUSSELS, OYSTERS AND SCALLOPS

All too often fishing is regarded as being at sea, away from the land, shooting nets or lines and so on down into the sea and landing thrashing-around, bumper quantities of fresh fish, whether it's by a longshoreman or someone deep-sea. But, away from the excitement (or humdrum for those doing the work), fishing close to and even on the foreshore, still remains an important sector of the job.

Cockles, mussels and oysters can either be picked fresh from the foreshore or dredged from vessels. Scallops generally are only dredged as they tend to live in deeper water. In Britain 98 per cent of scallops are caught using dredges and the rest by divers.

Cockles

There is much archaeological evidence from middens of prehistoric humans eating cockles among other shellfish, as did the Romans. In Australia, such middens have found the Sydney cockle (*Anadara trapezia*) to have been part of the diet of early Aboriginal humans. In more recent times, the accounts from medieval religious houses prove that cockles were widely eaten. Later on, the consumption of shellfish was regarded as the food of the poor people. Angus Martin mentions that between 100 and 200 horse-loads of cockles were removed from the Barra sands at low water every day of the spring tides over two summers in the late eighteenth century. These were either boiled and eaten out of their shells or stewed in milk and eaten as a soup.[1]

According to another source, cockles 'live in sandy areas … they are collected for sale as food for the public from Barra in the Outer Hebrides to the south coast of England, as well as Ireland'.[2] There are four notable areas in which cockle gathering is a distinct commercial fishery: Morecambe Bay, the Burry Inlet in South Wales, the Rivers Thames and Swale, and the Wash. Other areas of somewhat lesser importance, although not insignificant, are the Solway Firth, the Ribble and Dee estuaries, the Lafan Sands and parts of the Menai Strait and Anglesey, parts of Cardigan Bay, the River Towy, parts of Cornwall and Devon and many more sandy estuaries and small creeks.

Morecambe Bay

Morecambe Bay is an area about 10 miles across and 18 long, and consists of huge sand-flats at low tide. There's approximately a 30ft tidal range and the tide can flood in at an enormous rate – once said to be quicker than a trotting horse. It is also an estuary of five rivers – the Wyre, Lune, Keer, Kent and Leven.

In 1868–69 records show that £2,000 worth of mussels and cockles passed through Morecambe station. The occupation was primarily a family affair, and usually was the job of the women and children. Children were often reported absent from school during the season that was then mostly in winter and spring. Some say the women used to work barefoot throughout the year.

A tool used for bringing cockles to the surface is the jumbo, which consists of a metal framework of two uprights and a crossbar, attached to a wooden base, about 4ft by 18 inches. Some called them 'tamps'. All-wood versions have been used for possibly centuries to expose the cockles that lie about half an inch below the sand. They are rocked forwards and backwards to suck the cockles upwards. Both Jenkins and Davis mention them as being used.[3] According to Kennerley though, use of jumbos was illegal through most of the year in the nineteenth century for it was believed they damaged the cockles.[4] For a period in the twentieth century they were banned altogether.

Although some used jumbos at times, others looked for the telltale air bubbles in the sand that denote their presence. According to Jenkins, keen observers could spot 'the siphons of the cockle, the tubes through which the respiratory and food-containing currents of water are inhaled'. Another trick was to tread the sands with the feet, thus bringing the cockles to the surface. It has been said that, at times when the use of jumbos was banned, that children had planks of wood tied to their shoes to stamp around, unseen, to bring the cockles up. A craam, a five-pronged rake, is used to gather the cockles.

The jumbo purportedly came about after the working mothers brought their babies out onto the sands in their cradles, the rockers of which were seen to bring the cockles to the surface as they rocked vigorously. According to Wakefield, a woman with a two-week-old baby was heard to say she wouldn't feel well again until she 'could get to t' cockles again'.[5]

In those days the only mode of transport available to move the shellfish off the beach was by pony and cart, the pony, according to Wakefield again, looking 'as if it had been dried in the sand and salt water for centuries'. Horses were also used to drag a shank-net over the sands behind a horse to catch shrimps. It wasn't until the early 1960s that tractors gradually replaced horsepower.

In the *Report of the Commission on Sea Fisheries 1879*, it was estimated that £5,000 worth of cockles were taken from the south side of Morecambe Bay and that it followed that some £20,000 worth were taken from the whole Bay. Furthermore, they were unable to trace any decrease in the yield of the fishery. Thus it must have been a substantial fishery. In 1890, according to Wakefield, 3,162 tons were fished at Flookburgh, at an average price of £2 8s a ton. This was the best year ever known. Three years later it had shrunk to 1,335 tons. In 1895, after a devastating frost that killed much of the harvest coupled with poor demand, the take fell to 822 tons. But the next year it was down to a meagre 50 tons after a minimum size was introduced, although improvement followed, the take increasing to 195 tons the following year. Such is the capricious nature of fishing! However, by 1911, 65,500 cwts (3,275 tons) were taken, indicating a substantial revival.[6]

The cockle fishers of Morecambe Bay have received more than their fair share of publicity when, on one cold night in February 2004, twenty-three Chinese cockle gatherers were drowned on the notoriously treacherous sands of the Bay after failing to return from gathering, the blame being attached to unscrupulous gangmasters who sent them out without a thought of the conditions. Only one survived.

A few years ago I spoke to one of the pickers working on the same sands as the Chinese about the nature of the job:

> We get about five hours out on the sands. Us locals, the British so to speak, go out four hours before low water but some of the others chance it and go earlier. But it can be pretty dangerous out there. We've lost three tractors before and that's £120,000 each. I took one up to the Solway a few weeks ago, but that's closed now.

I asked how much someone can earn:

> Price depends on time of year and quality but it's about £450 a ton right now. Most are going to South Wales just now. Sometimes it's as high as £1,400. Each bloke picks by the bucket, two buckets to a bag and six bags is the average right now. Sometimes he can get a ton but the pickings aren't very good at the moment here. But they should recover in May and then the Spanish buyer comes and the price goes up. They should really close this area now.

The East Coast of England

In the Wash they used to have an ingenious method of 'blowing out' for cockles. For this they needed a boat with a large engine power and a heavy stern anchor. Once anchored firmly on the cockle beds, the backwash from the three-bladed propeller was used to pile up the cockles around the anchor so that they could then be sieved and shovelled aboard the boat once the tide had ebbed. But the Wash fishery, like that of the Thames and the Burry Inlet, is a regulated fishery, not a public one as Morecambe Bay, and therefore is closely monitored by the Eastern Sea Fisheries Committee (ESFC) and 'blowing out' was banned in the mid-1980s, largely because it caused a high mortality rate to cockles, and other species caught in the backwash.

The fishery is today controlled through an entitlement system where there are sixty-four entitlements owned by fishermen which cannot be passed on or sold, but which revert to the Committee when given up. This entitlement enables the fisherman to fish for any shellfish such as mussels, cockles, whelks, clams and oysters. Each fisherman must buy either an annual or monthly licence at least once every two years to keep his entitlement to fish.

The majority of the cockles taken are dredged, in vessels that must be less than 14m long (unless fishing in a larger boat under the same ownership prior to mid-1991 can be proved) although some is handpicked. The fishery occurs in July and August and is confined to 8 tons per boat per day and fishing continues until the Total Allowable Catch (TAC) is achieved. In 2004 this was 1,500 tons and the fishing lasted for about four weeks. According to Rob Blyth-Skyrme of the ESFC, the fishery for 2005 was much lower. When the fishery falls below a level of 70 per cent of a takeable size, it is closed. This takeable or minimum size is 14mm, much smaller than the west coast fishing, and prices are accordingly lower, on average between £350 and £800 a ton. Most is processed in factories in King's Lynn and Boston, and much is then exported.

On the Thames, the cockle fishery is centred at Leigh-on-Sea where the fishery has been in existence for at least 200 years. Naval punts, surplus to requirements were used, which were taken out to the cockle grounds and grounded, and then the men raked up the catch before loading up and returning. These were later replaced by sailing cocklers, flat-bottomed boats that were capable of being run ashore where they waited for the tide to ebb before filling the hold. Sometimes they worked a double tide if the cockles were sparse. The 34ft Leigh cockler *Mary Amelia*, built in 1914 at Southend and now belonging to Jonathan Simper, often used to carry over 4 tons of cockles aboard, with only the top plank showing above the waterline. Just after the Second World War these were replaced by motor cocklers until, in 1967, handpicking was outdated by dredging.

South Wales

The South Wales cockle fishery is perhaps the best documented in all Britain, largely thanks to the recent work of J. Geraint Evans who was, until 1991, the curator at the Welsh Folk Museum at St Fagins, outside Cardiff.[7] The fishery also has the distinction of having some of the finest shellfish in Britain and supplies almost a quarter of that gathered in Britain. Today the Burry Inlet cockle has the Marine Stewardship Council (MSC) certification as a sustainable and healthy fishery, the only one for this species, achieved in April 2001. The MSC, a global, non-profit, independent organisation, is 'dedicated to reversing the decline in fish stocks worldwide and to encouraging a more sustainable fisheries management through the promotion of its seafood certi-fication and eco-labelling programme', according to Rupert Howes, the chief executive. Once given accreditation, the product is labelled with the MSC logo, ensuring traceability right back to its fishing. To date, twelve fisheries have been certified, with nineteen more under the assessment process, which together account for some 4 per cent of the world's total wild fish supply.[8]

George Owen mentions cockles, among other shellfish, as being collected in Pembrokeshire in the late sixteenth century.[9] When they were first har-vested in the Burry Inlet will probably never be known, for it must have been centuries ago. The first documented evidence seems to come from D.C. Davies who gave a paper to the Liverpool National Eisteddfod in 1884 and who noted that 'some five hundred families find employment; and the cockles and mussels taken are valued at over £15,000 a year. One little village, it is said, passes £2000 a year through the Post-office.'[10] Much of the catch was taken to the market at Swansea where the cockle sellers, women in flow-ing Welsh costume, were well known. Others went selling house to house, carrying baskets on their heads. Local lore has it that they walked in bare feet until reaching a particular bridge on the outskirts of Swansea, at which point they put on their best, and only, pair of boots.

In 1910 there were 250 pickers and these were almost exclusively women from the surrounding villages of Penclawdd, Croffty, Llanmorlais, Gowerton and Loughor – probably even the same women who sold the catch. Again they used a small rake or *cramm*, different from its Morecambe counterpart in that it had seven prongs, a small knife and a sieve. Whether the difference in spelling between 'craam' and 'cramm' is regional or erroneous is unclear. Net-bags were used at one time but banned in 1996 in favour of rigid sieves. Today little has changed and only hand-raking is allowed.

There are in fact two cockle fisheries under the jurisdiction of the South Wales Sea Fisheries Committee (SWSFC) after it was given the powers in 1965. The first, the Burry Inlet fishery, is carefully regulated with fifty-two licences being sold each year to, first, those fishing the previous year, and then any remaining to those on a waiting list that, currently, has 180 people on it, proving the popularity of the fishery even if a licence costs £684. The fishery, which covers the area of the inlet between Loughor Bridge and Pembrey Harbour, is open all year round, except for Sundays and at night. Each person has a daily quota of 250–350kg, depending on the level of stocks and other factors determined by the authority.

The other area is called the 'Three Rivers', these rivers being the Towy, Taf and Gwendraeth, and is the area north of line between Tywyn Point in the east and Ginst Point. Again there is a history of fishing in this area with, in 1910, 150 people active at Ferryside, fifty at Laugharne, fifty at St Ishmaels and twelve at Llansteffan. Matheson gives a landing figure of 9,949 hundredweight at Laugharne, worth £1,741 in 1925 and 25,905 cwt at Ferryside worth £4,532.[11]

Today, however, unlike the Burry Inlet fishery, this is a public fishery so that all that is needed is a no-cost permit from the SWSFC on demand, similar to the system at Morecambe. As Phil Coates, the chief executive of the SWSFC, says, they have no powers to charge even an administration fee for these permits. From the table below it will be seen how, up to 1998, important the Three Rivers cockle fishery was. The minimum size for both these fisheries is that cockles must be unable to pass through a sieve of 19mm by 19mm mesh. Interestingly, according to Phil Coates, jumbos were at one time used at Ferryside, although the Committee prefer to see hand-raking as the only means of gathering the fish. The practice didn't seem to last that long, although he did state that, technically, their use is not illegal. Because of the different nature of the sand, and the fact that the tidal range is lower, the only assumption is that they are not as effective here as they are in Morecambe Bay. J. Geraint Jenkins shows a hand-pulled cockle dredge in use on the west side of Carmarthen Bay in the 1950s with some success, and another unsuccessful attempt was made to reintroduce this form of dredging into the Llanelli beds in the mid-1960s.

Mussels

Prehistoric humans, along with their Roman successors, realised the benefits of gathering mussels – they are full of protein and easy to harvest. Coastal dwellers everywhere have followed this basic proviso that easily got, nutritious food is best reserved for the community.

Conwy, in North Wales, had an estuary full of the seafood. However, although originally gathered for food, it seems that in the nineteenth century they were sought after more for their pearls than any nutritional benefit. Sacks and basketfuls were collected by hand, and placed in an iron pot in a sort of pit, and stamped upon like grapes at wine-making time. Once reduced to a pulp and with water added, the animal matter comes to the surface, which is then collected. This is duck food, while on the bottom of the pan lie the pearls, mixed in with all the sediment and sand. Washing with clean water soon exposed these pearls. Pearl fishing in this way was by no means confined to the River Conwy, as many of the main Welsh rivers were worked. Conwy simply produced more than anywhere else.

J.O. Halliwell, travelling in North Wales before 1860, wrote:

> The mussels are found in considerable abundance at low water all along the shore at the entrance to the river, and are dredged by boatmen along the course of the river, as well as collected on the mussel banks. I tried my fortune with a dozen of them, a number which yielded nearly a dozen pearls, two of these the size of a pin's head; the others were exceedingly minute.

Up to 160 ounces were said to have been collected per week in the late nineteenth century and these fetched 2s 6d per ounce.[12]

By the 1880s mussels were being collected for human consumption. Before the age of mechanism these had to be dredged by hand. Two methods were adopted – either using a hand rake from a small rowboat, or simply by harvesting them by hand. In the latter instance, the pickers, usually women in old times, made their way to their chosen stop by boat and gathered by hand, using a small knife called a *twca* to cut clumps of mussels away from the rocks. These were then bagged and put aboard the boat for carriage back to the quay. On the other hand, those dredging afloat used a rake with eight or so prongs – nominally not bigger than 3ft across the mouth – attached to a long pole up to 30ft in length. The mussels were forced into the prongs of the rake by pulling the rake along the seabed and, when the handle was vertical, the rake was flipped over so that the molluscs fall into the bag-net attached to its back. They were then hauled aboard and dumped into the boat. Once it was full, the fisherman returned to the quay. This method had the added benefit of preventing destruction to the mussel beds.

Both catches were then sorted and washed before being purified by immersion in sterilised sea water containing chloride of lime to flush out their stomachs. Regulations stated that this process should take two days before they could be bagged, carried to the railway station by horse and cart and sent to markets in the Midlands. The first purification plant was opened in 1916 after national health scares.

Each family in Conwy had their traditional point of embarkation and there were two fishermen in each boat. In 1929, the year of the earliest records, there were fifty-five mussel fishermen and by 1939 this had increased to seventy-five, including eight full-time women. During the war years when the men went to fight women ran the entire fishery.

In the mussel purification plant at Conwy, alongside the now redundant fishing quay, fifty baskets of the shellfish are placed in each of four tanks, each tank holding three-quarters of a ton. These are left for forty-two hours, ultra-violet light being used to kill bacteria, before the baskets are removed, and the mussels fed into a conveyor system. They are then cleaned, riddled, scrubbed, brushed and finally bagged. Overall, three tons of mussels are processed every two days and fed into the British market.

It's important to clarify at this stage that Wales wasn't the only home of the mussel fisheries. In the Wash, on the east coast, the small Lynn yolls sailed out to collect mussels from the extensive grounds. In Morecambe Bay, and around the River Lune, small specifically built flat-bottomed mussel boats collected from the banks. Further north, there were beds at Duddon at one time, where huge amounts of them were taken off by farmers for use as manure. As mussels were in extensive use by the long-line fishermen all around the coasts, especially so on the Scottish east coast, the fishermen even suggested that they should be banned from being eaten by humans to protect the beds. In reality it was probably the farmers that exhausted the supplies there, and, needless to say, human consumption was never forbidden, just rigorously controlled. Part of the legislation first issued in the beginning decades of the last century ensured proper purification at government-regulated plants, like the Conwy premises, and effective sealing of the bags of refined mussels to verify this at market.

Mussels were often brought up in oyster dredges, but actual dredging for the bivalves never seems to have happened to any extent in Britain until the twentieth century. On the River Medway it is said that this was tested, but it obviously appeared ineffectual in comparison to hand-raking and picking. Whether the trawl was deemed inefficient, or purely a lack of sail power, is unclear, but it wasn't until our modern age of mechanisation that dredging began in earnest.

Today, however, the situation is very different. The largest supplier is in Bangor, North Wales, and the company dredges mussel spat and relays it upon the bed of the Menai Strait until it is ready for the market, at which time it is re-dredged and passed through the purification plant, then on to ready markets here and abroad.

Oysters

The Romans, it is said, had a special weakness for the oyster, collected around bays such as at Naples. The bloodthirsty Caligula was a fan, as was Horace, the leading Roman lyric poet, who once wrote:

When I but see the oyster's shell,
I look and recognise the river, marsh, or mud
Where it was raised.

Britain, as for cockles and mussels, was once home to a thriving oyster culti-vation business, although, it must be said, not on the same scale as that of the French, even then. In France, and especially Brittany, oysters are everywhere.

Essex is purported to have produced the finest British oyster, although such areas as around Chichester might perhaps disagree. However, oysters from the latter area – Emsworth, in fact – were fed to those at two corporation ban-quets in Winchester in 1902, resulting in the death of, among several people, the Dean of Winchester. The sale of oysters from the area was instantly banned, but the event served to awaken the authorities to the problem of sewerage outfalls and pollution in other areas. Generally public confidence in oysters collapsed. The compulsory purification of oysters wasn't enforced until the 1960s, and by then overall consumption was minute in comparison to what it had been. The price rose accordingly and it became known as the food of the rich!

Much of the British oysters were dredged up from various parts of the inshore waters and set down on specific patches on the open shoreline. In parts, at some times of the year when the sea temperature was high enough, oysters would spawn and the spat could be dredged clinging to shells and stones on the seabed. This was altogether a haphazard and chancy business. Spat, however, did have one natural ground to emerge in Britain, and that was in Loch Ryan on Scotland's west coast where the benefits from the Gulf Stream created conditions, especially in sea temperature, suited to spawning.

Wales had a flourishing oyster trade that was centred on the small sea-side village of Mumbles, to the west of industrial Swansea. Its other name of Oystermouth reflects the importance it once attached to the shellfish. Although seriously affected by the oyster's decline at the beginning of the twentieth century, the fishery in Mumbles had been in existence for several centuries, and was indeed in full flow in the seventeenth century, when it was said to be the best in Britain.[13] Here open boats were used to collect the undeveloped oysters which were then laid on beds on the beach in front of the village. These were split into perches so that each man or fishery had his own demarcated patch upon which his oysters were laid. These open boats became decked about the middle of the nineteenth century, at which time they were equipped with masts. A dipping lugsail was carried to begin with, but it seems that many adopted a two-masted shallop rig, as did the pilot boats from nearby Swansea. This type of boat remained in service until the greedy east-coasters arrived in the late 1800s with their big smacks to denude these oyster grounds, taking thousands of the prized spat off to their home grounds. This overfishing most certainly contributed to the decline in Mumbles fortunes around the beginning of the twentieth century. However, prior to that, realising that to compete they had to sail further afield, the South Wales men had already adopted the east-coaster's boat, bringing a whole host of these smacks in from outside. Most, it seems, were built in Devon and Cornwall, although the first to appear came from the River Colne in Essex. Their earlier craft consequently fell into disrepair.

The village of Port Eynon lies just around the coast on the south coast of the Gower peninsular. Here, too, was a thriving oyster trade much the same as at Mumbles. Small skiffs sailed out and collected oysters to be laid on their beach to grow to maturity. Like their Mumbles counterparts, they too changed over to the smack, abandoning their early open boats. Some have suggested the salt house on the beach at Port Eynon, still clearly visible after recent works, was built to supply the local fisheries with salt. Whether this was for the oyster trade, or a possible herring fishery, seems unclear. Oysters, it is clear, have no demand for huge amounts of salt.

To the west of Carmarthen Bay, oyster beds also lay to the north of Caldey Island and off Stackpole Head. These were dredged by small local Tenby luggers, solidly built craft that were used for all manner of fishing including drifting for herring, line fishing and oyster dredging.

The east coast boats sailed as far north as the Isle of Whithorn. In the other direction the big first-class smacks fished off the Dutch coast. They supplied London with a seemingly never-ending catch of fresh oysters to satisfy the demanding people of the city. However, it must be said, that some writers seem to over-dramatise these Essex smacksmen by describing them as the hardest working of all fishermen. They certainly appear to have been an egotistical and avid lot in the nineteenth century and before, almost circumnavigating Britain in their plundering of other's oyster beds, although they did receive some physical opposition in Scotland. Most fishermen have always managed to respect other's fishing grounds and it is generally thought that this lot did not.

Any mention of oysters must surely include the oyster fishermen of Falmouth. The fishermen here remain the only commercial boat people in Britain who still work under sail. On average there are some twelve Falmouth working boats that work the fishery, and under a local by-law, they must all dredge under sail. They might motor from port to fishing ground and home, but once the dredges are lowered, they must have their sails set. Two dredges are used, each being hauled by hand and the oysters hand-picked. Undersized oysters must be returned to the seabed if they cannot sit on a brass ring that is 67mm in diameter. They make a fine sight, these folk sailing back and forth around the bay, knowing that they, perhaps unwittingly, are keeping alive old traditions which, in turn, help to regulate the fishery.

The fishing process appears simple to the untrained eye but this is not the case. I know this from the experience of one trip out. The boat, sails set to produce the tiniest of forward movement, has the dredges set so that the boat drifts with the current, almost beam on if the wind is in the favourable direction. The dredges, which are simple steel affairs with net-bags, are light enough to be handled over the side, and are hauled alternately, remaining down for ten minutes or so, which is the time it takes to haul in the other, empty the dredge, shoot it again and sort through the catch. Fishing is restricted to the months of October to March and daily from 9 a.m. to 3 p.m., except Saturday which is 9 a.m. to 1 p.m. and no fishing on Sunday. The timings are strict and all trawls should be up out of these hours. A bailiff is employed to check, as he does, and also that no undersized oysters are landed. The fishery, as well as that for the mussels, is regulated by Carrick District Council under the Port of Truro (Variation) Order 1975, although this is set to change in 2015 when regulatory control passes to DEFRA and its agents. Some say this will harm the fishery as faceless bureaucrats take control over those that know it well. Others say the fishermen are going to be more involved in the running and that overall, the change will have no adverse effect on the fishery. They say the fishery regulates itself by only allowing dredging under sail which itself is governed by the weather in general and the wind direction. It is labour intensive and has been estimated to produce some 50 tons of oysters a year. Currently the price is around £3 a kilo so it is worth £150,000 jointly to all the fishermen. Licences cost £165 annually per dredge.

There are at least twelve who work under sail and about another ten who work from the so-called 'haul-tow' punts. These small punts anchor over the beds in shallow water and drift back with the tide. They then shoot their single dredge and, using a specially designed hand-powered double capstan, winch the boat back towards their anchor on one drum while the other drum winches the dredge. Once back to the anchor, the dredge is hauled in and emptied. Again each dredge costs the owner £165 in licence fees but they only have the one so this keeps the overheads down. Doing the mathematics, it is easy to see how, over seven months, the income isn't outstanding. Each dredge, on average, nets one and a half tons, worth £4,500, and that's in a good year. We were out for six hours and landed 18kg, perhaps worth a little over £50. Happily mooring fees at Mylor are free but over the winter it can be very cold out there, and lifting the dredges over the side hard work. And it's hard on the back, even in ideal conditions. When the dredges are full, mostly of anything but oysters, they are really heavy and the difficult moment is when the framework is almost aboard but the bag itself still hangs over-

Richard Clapham hauling in a dredge aboard the Falmouth oyster dredger *Holly Ann* in 2014. This fishery is operated entirely under sail.

board. There is a pivot point but it's the last few inches I found most awkward. But persevere they do although most of the fishermen do have another job of out necessity and often carry on simply to continue traditions. You'd never make a proper living out of solely dredging under sail. Nevertheless, young blood is welcomed and, after a year's fishing, the old-timers might just nod at the new boy.

Scallops

In 2010, the UK fleet landed 43,000 tonnes of scallops (family *Pectinidae*), worth an estimated £54 million into UK ports, and scallops are now the third most valuable part of the UK fleet catch. Approximately 60 per cent of these scallops were exported to European countries, France in particular.

The standard scallop dredge is effectively a large rake consisting of a 2.5ft wide metal frame fitted with a row of spaced teeth on the leading edge, which are fitted to a spring mounted bar. The spring means that if the dredge encounters any hard objects or obstructions on the seabed it allows the teeth to hinge backwards preventing the dredge from becoming stuck and preventing damage to gear and seabed. A number of dredges are attached to two poles which are towed behind the vessel. The number of dredges towed is, as is the physical dimensions of the dredge, strictly regulated and can vary from area to area depending on local by-laws.

Scallop dredges hanging over the side of the scalloper *Coral Strand II*, CN267, entering the Crinan Canal in about 1996. Built for trawling in 1969, the boat was later re-rigged for dredging.

The dredge is typically used on soft sand or shingle sediments and rakes scallops off the seabed or just below the surface which are then gathered by a collecting bag made of chain mail or netting. The fishing areas where scallop dredges can be used are strictly controlled with fragile seabed species and habitats being protected by Special Areas of Conservation (SAC) under the European Natura 2000 and proposed Marine Conservation Zones (MCZ) under the UK Marine Act. The majority of scallops are fished within the English Channel and the Irish Sea.

Although scallops had been fished by a few boats since the beginning of the twentieth century, most of the catch was being used as bait. Most of what was fished came from the English Channel and parts of the coast off eastern England. It wasn't until the 1950s that a substantial fishery developed, especially in the waters of the southwest, with boats working from Brixham. After 1975 this became a major fishery as the value of the scallop increased. Two specific grounds existed in the Channel: that between the Lizard and Portland Bill and the other between Selsey and Rye.[14] Smaller areas were discovered in Cardigan Bay and off Wolf Rock.

The Isle of Man is famous for the queen scallop (*Aequipecten opercularis*), a smaller scallop, generally known locally as the Manx Queenie. Whereas the scallop is found to the west, south and east of the island and to the south of the Chicken Rock, the queenies lie in a huge area lying to the east of the island and stretching from Burrow Head to almost Anglesey.

In the Isle of Man fishing started in October 1937 although it wasn't until 1969 that the queenies began to be fished. Since 1972 the scallop boats have worked further afield. Scallops tend to lie in hollows in the seabed, with the flat shell uppermost. On the other hand, queenies do not recess themselves into the seabed and can live on a harder seabed. Sometimes they lie on the same grounds and, before 1969, queenies were being thrown back into the sea as a by-catch, though now both are landed. The scallop fishery is today the main fishery in the Isle of Man, and superseded the herring fishery after the Second World War.[15]

10

LOBSTERS AND CRABS

Commercial lobster fishing in Scotland only developed relatively recently, around the mid-eighteenth century. In England, Daniel Defoe noted a lobster fishery at Cromer in 1724.[1] In Wales the earliest mention is by the Rev. William Bingley who noted a lobster fishery around Bardsey Island in 1800.[2] Prior to these times lobster fishing was primarily for local consumption. The growth in the trade only grew once companies were set up with well-smacks that collected the lobsters from the inaccessible parts of the country where they abounded.

Ireland, too, had a considerable lobster fishery in the nineteenth century and it was reported that 10,000 lobsters were sent to London each week. The same source states that 'immense quantities are also procured on the west coast of Scotland'. He declared that 30,000 lobsters were seen at Greenock coming from the Outer Hebrides. In 1887 in Scotland 681,100 lobsters and 2,215,700 crabs were landed, this being assumed to be an average year.[3]

Grimsay, a tiny island squeezed between Benbecula and North Uist, has been renowned for its lobsters which were largely taken off the Monach Isles and sent to the market in London, obviously via Greenock.[4] Since the 1840s the same family – the Stewarts – have been building small gaff-rigged double-enders specifically for this fishery. Today it survives, still with wooden fishing boats, some of which originate from Tom's Yard in Polruan, Cornwall.

In the same way each lobster community has developed its own unique boat. The Yorkshire men use their cobles while at Cromer the double-ended crab boats were once tractored into the water off the beach, as we saw in Chapter 4. Crab fishing there dates back to at least the thirteenth century and probably much earlier.[5] Up north, the Orkney fishermen use their small whills, similar to the larger yoles so favoured by the line fishermen. In Aberdaron, at the tip of the Lleyn peninsula, close to Bardsey Island where Bingley noted his lobsters, small double-ended herring boats evolved into transom-sterned, gunter-rigged boats especially developed to haul pots over the stern.

Nigel Legge of Cadgwith aboard his boat hauling in pots. This shape of pot, framed in steel bar, is cheaper and much less work to produce. (*Courtesy of Nigel Legge*)

Cornwall, too, has had a thriving lobster and crab fishery since the eighteenth century. Cadgwith, close to the Lizard, still survives upon this fishery. Their transom-sterned boats are still hauled up and down the beach as they always were. Fresh crabs can be bought from the tiny shack alongside the beach. Penberth is tiny cove to the west of Penzance where a few open lobster boats are still drawn up. Further east, Portloe seems like time has stood still with several potters on the hard while the small crabbers of Gorran Haven sit on the sand in the harbour as they've done for generations. Across the Channel, the islands of Jersey and Guernsey still retain their crab fleets. All very quaint and picturesque for the tourist, but just how long these remnants will survive is anyone's guess.

Just as the craft used for potting differ around the country, so do the pots themselves. Many of the Cornish used inkwell withy pots, as did some of the fishers from South Wales and small communities such as Clovelly, though the men of St Ives preferred inkwell pots made of wire. Hoop pots, also known as creeves, were favoured in Scotland and on the east coast of England. Today these are made from a steel frame, rectangular in plan with a curved top – the so-called cottage shape – although sometimes alkathene pipe is used to make the curved shape. All usually have three compartments and openings or eyes for the shellfish to enter and access by the fisherman is through a door that can be secured shut quickly and safely. Summer pots can be smaller with only two compartments and two eyes. Other local traditions have again created a number of variations of pots. Steel has the added advantage that it doesn't need weighting down with bricks.

Crail in Fife, on the east coast of Scotland, is generally regarded by many as the pre-eminent lobster harbour on this coast. However, back in the eighteenth century it was a 'great resort for herring fishermen from Aberdeen, Angus and the Mearns'.[6] By the mid-twentieth century much of this herring was gone and lobsters and crabs were the mainstay of the fishing industry.

The boat that was adapted for the hauling and setting of the lobster creels became known as the partan yawl, a 'partan' being a crab (*Cancer paguras*) in Old Scots. This was basically a smaller version of the bauldie, which in itself was a smaller version of the fifie. The partan yawls were double-ended and only about 20ft in length. Depending on who built them and for whom, the sternpost was either very upright or slightly raked. Today, many examples of these beautifully shaped boats can be found all along the Scottish coast from Fife to the Moray Firth, and sometimes further afield. In Fraserburgh, a variant was a Fraserburgh yole (the words 'yole' and 'yawl' both come from the Norse *yol* or *jol* literally meaning 'small boat').

Partan yawls, like their larger brothers, were undecked in their early days: they were generally indiscernible from these in their early days. The only difference was that they sought crabs and lobsters and only set one dipping lug.

Inkwell crab pots being made by Albert Braund and unknown in Clovelly. As well as herring which was an autumnal fishery, potting for crabs and lobsters was a successful fishery for Clovelly fishers. (*Courtesy of Stephen Perham*)

But, as decked fifies appeared in the latter quarter of the nineteenth century, so did the creel men copy this tendency. Then, as motor power arrived in the twilight of the twentieth century, these had small units added. As was the pattern elsewhere, the craft became fuller in time, especially around the after end, to compensate for this. However, transom sterns were never adopted, so that the creel boat of the first half of that century was a boat about 20ft long with a foredeck and side decks and a central hatch that was sometimes covered over. The engine sat beneath a box towards the stern and often a hauler aided the pulling in of the creels. These continued to be built until the 1960s, and many examples can still be found.

Some years ago I experienced a couple of trips upon Fife lobster boats. The first time, on a cold January morning, was out of nearby Pittenweem with brothers Graeme and Raymond Reilly. Creeling was their mainstay fishing, yet the boat, a 1980-built Cygnus 32 called *Comely III*, was rigged for trawling prawns when the lobsters were scarce. The winch sat on the wide aft deck behind the wheelhouse so that the deck had plenty of room to haul the creels aboard. We motored out, along the coast and past Crail, one of the most picturesque harbours along the coast, where the brothers both live and work out of in summer. Although it's well protected, there's a surge in the small harbour and not much room for their large boat. Their cooking shed lies upon the quay, from where fresh sales can be made in the summer season, but otherwise it's more convenient to drive the few miles from home to Pittenweem and work out of there.

It wasn't long before Raymond had brought the boat round into the wind and Graeme was using the boathook to catch hold of two plastic cans serving as markers. Creeling is, like most fishing, a tedious routine of hauling and re-setting. The line is bent round the Spencer-Carter hauler and brought up. Pots are set in trains, twenty pots to a train in their case, and each pot is hauled aboard in turn, emptied of its contents, re-baited and stacked aft. Lobsters are of course the prize, but in the first train we had more than a boxful of partan crabs, pinkish crustaceans that legally had to be over 5.5in across the shell, although the buyer insisted on 6in. These at the time fetched eighty pence per kilo whereas a lobster, the legal size being 87cm along the carpus, would fetch £13.50 a kilo. The lobsters were poor though, and, with over a thousand seal pups born that year on the island, the brothers weren't slow to attach blame to these mammals. Seals are the bane of the fisherman, and a seal pushing its nose into a creel can destroy the netting around it with ease. The proof was obvious. And replacement is a costly business.

Once all twenty pots were aboard and re-baited they were streamed out once more and left a couple of days being hauled again (weather permitting). The bait they were using was fish heads, bought from the filleting sheds of

Pittenweem for £2 a box. There's a certain irony here in that all these harbours along this coast were once a bustle of activity and now only Pittenweem has its landings of mostly prawns. Yet the filleting sheds are still active. Vans arrived each day with fish from far afield, mostly from Aberdeen, to be processed and then more vans picked it up each morning and drove all over Scotland, hawking the catch as 'fresh Pittenweem fish'. That's the nature of the business, which has been transformed from a local fishery to an international industry.

We motored over to the Carr Brigs off Fife Ness. Here the calmer waters seethed with buoys from dozens of trains of creels. Crabs caught in shallower water have less water content to counteract the water pressure, I was once told, and hence have more meat in them. But this produces another problem for fishers here, the proliferation of pots set by part-time fishermen. The East Neuk had some eight or nine full-time creel boats working and probably twice that in part-timers. The consequence is that the grounds are hammered. And it was winter, so imagine what it's like in summer when there's twice the number of creels down. Twice we had fouled trains when others had laid their creels over ours. 'There's one particularly thick fucker who's always doing that,' Graeme told me in exasperation after the two of them had spent fifteen minutes unravelling their train from his. Paradoxically this guy was the only part-timer they trusted not to lift their pots and empty them. 'You can never prove anything though, but sometimes you just know someone has been here before you,' he continued.

The next ten trains relinquished poor catches of both crabs and lobsters. Velvet crabs were plentiful, as were soft-backs. A market for the velvets had recently opened up and they were being processed into crab sticks but the soft-backs were thrown back in. Most of the lobsters were undersize – Graeme carefully measured each one before putting them back in. I didn't see him take one that was even a millimetre undersize. Here was one fisherman who understood sustainability and that adhering to the regulations would only benefit them in the long run.

Then the gas ran out. No more tea. That was worse than the poor catch. I began to feel like a Jonah. Then, out of the blue, we hauled a train further inshore that brought with it ten good lobsters – a prize indeed. Graeme had just been telling me that, at this time of year, three or four per train was average. Ten was amazing. But then the next train only had one. We moved towards Kingsbarns, just off the old harbour, where I was astonished later to read that a substantial fleet had once been based. It's little more than a few stones protecting an exposed beach, but then this was the norm back in the eighteenth and nineteenth centuries.

Eventually all the creels in this area had been hauled and put back in. Most of the bait had gone. The box of lobsters was nearly full – twenty-five kilos according to Graeme, not bad. Two boxes of crabs and another of the velvets. And a dozen codling that had found their way into the creels. We headed back to harbour, the boat punching into the force 5 at a steady eight knots, spray cascading over the boat. But she never slammed once and I was impressed with her performance. The brothers were thinking about getting a bigger boat with better accommodation for when they're at the prawns, but this one has certainly served them well.

It's not a glossy business, this fishing. Tedious, hard work and dangerous sums it up. So why do they do it? 'Ah,' they say in unison, 'there's no finer job when the weather's good. When it's bad it's a real pain. We've done it, like our fathers and grandfathers, all our lives. And let's face it, there's nothing else to do around here. No work except for the sea.'

Back in Pittenweem the crabs were nicked – the ligament to the claw cut – and all the crabs were put into keep pots and slung over the transom. The lobsters were carried ashore. I was gifted with fourteen crabs and the codling which friends and I feasted on that night. The harbour was quiet, the prawn boats making hay while the weather was good. After a week of gales the forecast was good. Fishing would be good over the days to come.

Two months later and I was out lobster creeling again, this time aboard the St Andrews creeler *Lena*, DE21, owned by Tom Meldrum. It was a bright Sunday afternoon as the two of us motored out past the old stone harbour wall, from the end of which we were shouted to by two young women. 'Give us a lift to Dundee,' they pleaded, waving and jumping up and down. 'We're going fishing,' we returned the shout. 'Oh, yes please,' they answered, but we smiled to each other and carried on.

Tom's boat is a Cygnus too, the 21ft version with a Saab engine which he'd had since 1964. He'd been creeling most of his life, he told me as we headed out to the first train. Yes, he was an all-year rounder, except during March and April when the boat came out of the water for an overhaul and his annual holiday to Crete. Then of course there was the constant repair to the creels. During the January storm he'd had fifty damaged or lost and another twenty or so the previous week. Consequently he'd only got seventy set – six or seven trains – so it would be a short day out.

These trains came up easily except one end pot that refused to be dislodged from the seabed. Plenty of undersize here, and one adult. To make matters worse, he'd only had one on the previous trip two days ago. And no crabs whatsoever, and no white fish for tea!

March is traditionally poor, progressively through the month as the cold water encourages the lobsters to stay put. The sea doesn't even begin to warm up until the end of May, hence the reason for a two-month break. Then, of course, the part-timers would begin their annual fishing.

We talked about the proposed shellfish licensing scheme and about the regulation code that Fife Council were hoping to introduce on the Shetland model. The trouble was nobody was answering the fishermen's queries, so, while the industry was facing collapse, nothing was getting implemented. And we talked about decommissioning, and how it's not helping the industry one iota. While the older, less efficient boats are decommissioned out of the whitefish sector, the owners then buy into other areas. In Aberdeen, Tom told me, they've been buying modern creel boats with their grant money, flooding the market with lobsters which has only served to drive down the price. How does this help the industry overall?

On the journey home we talked about the tiny shore landings between Kingsbarn and St Andrews. Just around the corner from our farthest train there's a small creek at Boarhills where I've a photograph of one small yawl pulled up clear. Close by, there's a salmon bothy on the shore, and a lifeboat house where the St Andrews lifeboat was sometimes launched from, after being hauled by horse from the town. Further west, at Kinkells, we motored close in by the Rock and Spindle, with sharp rocks protruding through the calm surface of the water. We imagined sailing ships creeping in at high tide, drying out to unload and what calamity would occur if a northeasterly gale sprang up. Such was the day of the sailing era that losses often went unnoticed and drowned seamen were as common as the wind that killed them.

Back in St Andrews the tide was very high – in fact so high that Tom said he'd never seen the water so far up the stonewall, lapping the grass at one point. It was the highest tide of the year, but still, far higher than before, and that without northwesterly winds to prevent the ebb from escaping the North Sea. Global warming. That the lobsters are affected by the minute rise in sea temperature is another observation that might account for their dearth. But the juveniles were by no means unusual and he recounted how four years ago, he'd lifted 600 from his full assembly of 240 pots.

So, we'd realised one half-kilo lobster, value about £7. Just about enough to cover the diesel and the bait. 'Folk think, when they see us landing three or four boxes that we're millionaires,' he said, 'but they forget the poor times like now.' He pointed to his stack of broken pots on the quay. 'And look at that lot that needs repairing, and some for sure throwing out … They don't see the other side, the upkeep of the boat, the bad days when the weather won't let us out.' But he loved the job, wouldn't change it for anything, the freedom, the sea, the danger, the sense of challenge, the solitude, the ups and downs. He smiled a wry grin, though, as he added, 'but I do still get a holiday or two in Crete'.

11

WAR AND PEACE

As Big Ben struck 11 p.m. on that night in August 1914, not only was Europe thrown into disarray but, for the fishing industry, it signalled a major change of direction that was to have an effect over the rest of that century.

The year 1913 was, as it turned out, the peak for the herring industry. From Shetland in the north, down to East Anglia in the south, and throughout the west coast of Scotland, the Irish Sea and parts of northern and western Ireland, herring were still King of the Sea. That year officially some 650,000 tons of herring were landed, among the 1.2 million tons of fish in general landed that year: a colossal amount. In Great Yarmouth and Lowestoft alone, in the fourteen weeks of the season there, 1,359,213 cran of herring was landed, an increase of about 20 per cent from the previous year. The official measure of a cran was a thousand fish but in reality in was closer to 1,300 fish. That year there were 1,165 Scottish drifters fishing the autumnal East Anglian fishery, 854 of which were steam-driven. A third of these came from the Moray Firth port of Buckie. Only Lowestoft had a higher number and the combined British fleet numbered more than 1,800 steam drifters. Each drifter was said to have given work to a hundred people, from the crews, the gutters, dock workers, tug crews, railwaymen, shipwrights, engineers, salesmen, curers, fishmongers, coalminers, coopers, rope-makers, net-makers, sail-makers and others.[1] The total catch for England and Wales was two million crans while in Scotland the summer herring produced 1,324,000 crans, a combined total of 3,324,000 crans which is approximately 606,000 tons. Add to this the catch for the west coast of Scotland, the Isle of Man and the smaller catches of Northern Ireland, Wales and north Devon (and some say it was over 700,000 tons). Lowestoft had, on one day, thirty-three drifters landing some 200 cran each, which was a large amount for the trade to cope with. Scotland, during the summer herring, landed 1,324,000 cran.[2] The total value of the British exports of salt-cured herring that year were almost ten million hundredweight (half a million tons), with a value of £5.9 million which would be over half a billion at today's rates.

A typical east coast of Scotland harbour scene, with boats drying their nets, this being St Monans in Fife.

Eighty per cent went to Russia and Germany. The value of the fresh herring sector was £4.5 million, some of which was exported as smoke-cured herring. Fishing, at times, employed a quarter of the working population.[3]

Rates of pay for that year were good too. A steam drifter earned an average of £795 while motor boats averaged £365 and sail boats £235. The average value of all fish landed was eight shillings a hundredweight. One estimate is that in total there were 6,500 million herrings landed that year.[4]

With the exports to Russia and Germany so high, it's hardly surprising that when Germany declared war on Russia on 1 August 1914, and then Britain declared war on Germany three days later, that the vast majority of that market collapsed immediately.

But what was the immediate impact of war? On that fateful day, 4 August 1914, there were hundreds of steam drifters, some sailing smacks and motorised vessels fishing as usual out in the North Sea. The order from the government, down via the Admiralty and the Board of Agriculture and Fisheries, and to the harbourmasters, was for all fishing boats to return to port by daylight the following morning. This message was to be passed on to all vessels with a wireless set and via other boats that didn't. For the sailing vessels, whether trawling or drifting, steamers were sent out to pass the message along. Furthermore, any vessel in port was to be prohibited from being allowed to sail. The North Sea was to be cleared to await the great naval battles that were to follow.[5]

Two German vessels were detained in Aberdeen. Ironically these boats, a drifter and a trawler, had come in to unload bumper catches. At the same time, four boxing fleets of steam trawlers – the Red Cross, the Great Northern, the Gamecock and the Hellyers – were working the various banks of the North Sea towards the German coast. These were fleeting boats in that smaller boats raced the catch back to port while the trawlers continued fishing and could stay out for a number of weeks. Most skippers and crew did not believe that Britain had declared war on Germany as it had previously been thought wholly unlikely, even if trouble was brewing in Europe. Nevertheless, the fleets eventually made it home.

The initial attitude of the Admiralty was to prohibit any fishing boat from going to fish in the North Sea though the various fishing grounds of the North Sea were by far the biggest contributor to the supplies of fish. When these dried up within days the Admiralty had to rethink their policy so that, by the end of August that year boats were once again fishing in restricted areas under heavy control of their movements. Steam trawlers had to remain within sight of the coast and be back in port by nightfall, whereas drifters were prohibited from entering ports at night. Both fished at their own risk. Part of the problem was the mining of areas and in late August fishing was restricted to west of a line drawn from the Hook of Holland to Sumburgh Head and in East Anglia south of the latitude of Lowestoft as there was a minefield off Southwold.[6] Another problem was that fishing boats were considered to be a convenient disguise for enemy agents to infiltrate ports and undertake acts of sabotage.

However, the reality of war soon hit home to the fishermen. Two Grimsby boats, *Capricornus* and *St Cuthbert*, were sunk by torpedo boats off Spurn Head that month. In early September, the trawler *Fittonia*, GY390, was sunk by a mine in the same area.[7] In the first year of the war, Grimsby lost a total of seventy-three vessels. Nevertheless, the boats continued to bring in the fish, with landings in 1914 of 907,000 tons, which had fallen to a not inconsiderable 390,000 in 1917. Prices had, though, risen on average by four and a half times that of those at the beginning.

Trawlers and drifters were open to attack anywhere by torpedo boats or submarines. But, after the Russian affair of 1910, some boats were accustomed it. Then the Russian Grand Fleet, on its way to Japan, came across the Gamecock fleet fishing some 200 miles west of Spurn Head. Having been warned of a Japanese surprise ambush, they opened fire on the trawlers and sank one, the *Crane*, killing the skipper and third hand, wounding several others and damaging two other vessels. After a national outcry and an international commission, Russia was eventually forced to pay £65,000 in damages. The Russian fleet was eventually destroyed by the Japanese.[8]

As well as boats fishing in coastal waters, trawlers continued to work in the northern latitudes, around Iceland, the White Sea and Greenland and, although some fishing continued, boats there were sunk by enemy action.

Throughout the conflict 1,467 trawlers and 1,502 drifters were requisitioned by the Admiralty for minesweeping and patrol duties. Some 394 of these were lost on naval duty during the war (246 trawlers, 130 drifters and eighteen Admiralty trawlers) and the majority of the 2,058 men lost on active duty were fishermen. As for those that remained fishing, 439 fishermen were killed while working, with 675 boats lost. Of these, 156 were trawlers and 270 drifters. Furthermore, 249 sailing smacks were sunk (127 in the North Sea, sixty-two in the Channel and sixty on the west coast) with the loss of fifty-three lives. Some 178 smacks were sunk by German U-boats surfacing, casting the crew adrift in their small boats and laying charges to scuttle the fishing boats. In the Firth of Forth, on one night in March 1917, a submarine sank eleven small herring boats in this way, leaving one small boat afloat for the crews.[9]

In the Channel it was the Dover Patrol that kept the vital routes between England and France open. John Dyson quotes thirteen million men, two million horses, half a million vehicles, twenty-five tons of ammunition and supplies and fifty-one million tons of coal as having crossed over to Dover. The drifters on patrol shot trains of nets made of thin galvanised steel that was intended to wrap around a submarine as it attempted to lay mines in front of troopships. Later they laid mines in a ladder fashion alongside the nets to prevent ingress of submarines. To stop German craft sneaking on the surface, patrols were made day and night which were largely successful in closing the Channel to them. In February 1918, German destroyers did attack at night when the drifters were lit up, and sank seven of them and two trawlers, killing seventy men and wounding hundreds.

Some trawlers gained recognition for outstanding service during the war. The *Gowanlea*, FR105, was one such vessel. She operated in the Mediterranean and saw active service in the Adriatic, ferrying troops to Corfu, until she was hit by enemy fire in 1916. However, holed and without a funnel, the vessel reached port for repairs, even though some of her crew had been killed. Credit was given to First Engineer William Noble who kept the vessel steaming at full speed under the most arduous conditions. The *Gowanlea* later gained repute the following year while standing up to the might of the Austrian navy by firing on a cruiser and escaping sinking, even though her crew had been instructed to abandon ship by the Austrians prior to their threat to sink the ship. She returned to Britain after the war and recommenced fishing, and was sold to Lossiemouth some years later.

Once the Armistice came on 11 November 1918, fishing began again in earnest though the numbers of vessels available was small compared to those fishing at the start of the conflict. One of the biggest tasks facing the country was to get the requisitioned fishing vessels back into use and this involved stripping out all their war equipment and installing fishing gear such as winches. By the end of June 1919, over a thousand vessels from English and Welsh ports had undergone refitting. On 30 August that year, the Admiralty allowed fishing to resume in all waters around the country except where mines and other dangers classified an area as closed.[10]

Such was the performance of these vessels that a building programme for a standardised boat was begun to replace those lost. These vessels became known as the Admiralty standard drifters. However, with the loss of the German markets because of the war and the Russian one after the revolution, the herring fishery never recovered to anything like its level of the beginning of the century. It is said that before the war 97 per cent of herring went for export.[11]

The Sprat Fishery

It wasn't just the herring trade that suffered from a loss of markets. Take the sprat fishery, for instance, of the estuary of the River Thames and the surrounding Essex rivers, and the offshore sandbanks and channels. These were fished by the fishermen using an ancient method that was at least 500 years old, called a stow-net. At first glance it appears to be a complicated system of a net suspended beneath a sailing smack at anchor. It extends from two baulks of timber, the lower one weighted, attached to ropes called handfleets which were attached to the boat's anchor chain. This was the mouth of the net which was attached to the baulks and flowed beneath the boat so that the cod-end was somewhere several boat-lengths astern of the boat in several fathoms of water. Using this method great supplies of sprats were caught which, like herrings, were pickled in barrels in towns such as Brightlingsea, which became the sprat centre. Some were sent straight to London or unloaded at ports such as Chatham, Leigh and Southend. In its heyday Brightlingsea firms could process 8,000 bushels a day, a bushel being the equivalent of eight imperial gallons. A barrel held three and half bushels. The pickle they used was a mixture of bay leaves, Spanish hops, cloves, sandalwood, pimento, sugar and salt, dissolved in brine.[12]

Before 1914 the boats worked in fleets with a bawley – a square-sterned sailing boat typical of the Thames (see Chapter 12) – carrying the catch to port. There were at least thirty working from Leigh and Southend and, though a little trade continued during the war, these numbers declined. In Brightlingsea it was a case of a growing trade with pickling yards opening. Canning factories also opened, including one in Colchester, and these survived until the 1930s when Brightlingsea's sprat fishery also declined. By the 1950s the stow-net had disappeared.

Motorisation

One of the biggest effects on the fishing industry had come into play during the few years before the war, though its impact perhaps wasn't as great as it otherwise would have been. This was, of course, the installation of engines into the sailing boats. Although steam drifters and trawlers continued fishing, the latter back in the northern Atlantic waters with a vengeance, motorisation at this stage only affected the smaller inshore craft.

The fitting of engines into these fishing boats seems to have originated in Denmark years before, in 1895, when a boat had a paraffin motor fitted, but it wasn't something that took on, probably because of the unreliability of the unit, the cost, the use of steam and the fact that many fishermen were afraid of change.

In Britain the first vessel to be engined was the 64ft drifter, *Pioneer* LT368, which came from the Lowestoft yard of Henry Reynolds in 1901. Built on smack lines with a normal rig, she had a 38hp four-cylinder Globe Marine Gasoline engine from Philadelphia, USA that itself cost £680. The overall price of the boat was £1,600 excluding her fishing gear. At first she was viewed with scepticism until she started realising startling results and, in 1905, she earned £788.

Another *Pioneer* arrived on the scene in 1905, built at Anstruther to Scottish Fisheries Board requirements and launched with a 20hp Dan engine. At 72ft between perpendiculars, she was a hefty boat and she retained her rig. The foremast alone weighed three tons. A 20hp was obviously not very powerful for such a big vessel though she did make 5 knots in calm conditions. However, the fishermen were not impressed as they could make more speed under sail. The vessel was sailed to the Thames, where various MPs came to inspect her. She returned north for more inspections in Aberdeen and the crew listed several objections with the capstan that didn't perform well at all. She later went to the East Anglian herring that autumn and fared well, grossing over £479 in almost eight weeks.[13] At the same time, other boats were being fitted with engines, such as the 35ft Sheringham whelk boat, *Reaper* YH34, that had a Gardner paraffin engine fitted. In Scotland, the first real successful conversion was the fitting of a 55hp Gardner engine into the 1901-built fifie, *Maggie Jane* BK146, from Eyemouth in 1907. On the west coast of Scotland, the Lochfyne skiff, *Brothers* CN97, was the first to have a Kelvin 7.9hp engine fitted in 1907, while on the Moray Firth it was two years later

Peterhead harbour with various fishing boats.

that the Zulu, the 42-ton *Mother's Joy*, was the first one motorised on the Firth, having a Fairbanks-Remington 60hp unit fitted.[14]

And so the process of motorisation continued, although, as we've seen, there was a flood of auxiliaries fitted between 1910 and 1914. However, that was exactly what the engines were considered – secondary units to help with the hauling of the nets and steaming in and out of the harbours. Reliability was still poor and all boats retained their rig although, in some cases, this was shortened. Figures for 1914 suggest that there were 694 motorised fishing vessels in Scotland that year, an increase of 171 over the previous year, and an overall increase of 613 since 1910.[15]

During the war there was a great increase in knowledge and expertise in these engines, mainly directed at the war effort but this enabled better and more reliable units to be manufactured and it is said that by 1919 there were 8,124 fishing vessels in Scotland, and of these, 1,844 were motor boats. But Britain was entering a time of austerity and depression, the herring fishery was not doing well and the fishing industry needed an injection of something to perk it up. Then, from across the North Sea, came another method of fishing that was to completely revolutionise the fishing industry.

The Danish Seine-Net

This, then, was the seine-net which, like motorisation, had its origins in Denmark and we will have to go back to 1848 understand it. Not only Britain, this was a mode of fishing that impacted on the fishing fleets all over the North Sea. This is generally recognised as being invented by fisherman Jens Laursen Vaever from Salling in Jutland. Like most of the farmer/fishermen from the Limfjord, after the sea broke through the western sea defences in 1825 allowing cod and plaice to invade, Vaever caught these fish using a *Kratvoddet*, a large beach seine-net run out from the shore using a small rowing boat and fixing one end of the net to a post. In the same way that the herring fishermen of Tarbert, Loch Fyne, experimented with beach seines to develop the ring-net in the 1830s, Vaever, in the late 1840s, experimented using a net in the same shape as the *Kratvoddet*, running it out as usual but then hauling the net back to another anchored boat. His first attempt was disastrous, much to the bemusement of the onlookers, although that changed to chagrin on the second attempt when Vaever landed 2,640 plaice. The fishermen working from the beach were happy to land forty or fifty fish, mainly plaice, a day. When Vaever landed 4,000 on his third attempt, there was a rush to follow his example. It is said that over his first two days of fishing he earned enough money for his wedding to Anna Marie Neilsdatter. Vaever was one of the great innovators in the fishing industry of the last 200 years, and in an industry slow to change, this was relatively rare.

Vaever's invention, which became known as the *snurrevod* (*snurre* being the rotating action around the anchor and boat and *vod* meaning net), spread to the east coast by 1870, to the northern fishing stations eight years later, Esbjerg by 1890, to the Bohusland coast of Sweden in 1894 and to Britain in 1920. This development was largely responsible for the 1880s boom in the Danish fisheries. Inshore fishing extended into deeper water and a fish manufacturing base grew up quickly around northern Denmark.

In Frederikshavn, originally the small fishing village of Fladstrand which gained a municipal charter in 1818 and changed its name and was the major fishing harbour for both the Kattegat and Skagerrak, the fishermen were one of the first to adopt the new method. However, as offshore fishing developed, it was soon clear that it was possible to fish the *snurrevod* in the open sea for which they brought in large so-called cutters. By the late 1870s these were 40–60 ton ketch-rigged fully decked vessels, some of which had been bought from England's east coast at a time the first steam trawlers were being introduced there. Others were built locally, modelled on similar lines, when the first shipwright called Buhl had commenced building. Many of these new vessels had wet wells incorporated into their hulls. Such a vessel was the *N.I. Laursen*, FN136, rigged as a gaff ketch.

Of course, it didn't take long for the other principal ports of Denmark to adopt the seine-net, which became known as anchor seining for obvious reasons. Esbjerg, which had its first harbour works started in 1869, had similar-sized cutters working from there by 1888 and within six years the method had spread to the west coast of Sweden. Larger boats used a small 20ft seine boat – a *snurrevodjolle* – with which to work the net out and around in a circle, before it was brought back to the cutter. A typical seine boat was modelled on traditional double-ended small boat lines and around 1903 the first engine to be fitted into a fishing boat was installed in one of these. The first engine was a Mollerup 2hp unit and the long-term effects of the petrol/paraffin internal combustion engine arrived. It didn't take long to catch on.

The Frederikshavn men built smaller cutters, oak on oak, with motors which obviated the need to use the *snurrevodjolle* to set the net, the first carvel-built example of which was the cutter *Gorm*, substantially smaller at just under 10m in overall length. A smaller rig was retained, and these boats had greater effectiveness and were easier to manoeuvre and became known as the *haj-cutters*, literally 'shark cutters'. Most of these retained the wet well and carried ice from the new ice houses. Shark cutters arrived in Esbjerg in 1910. However, some of the larger 50ft cutters – generally referred to as *kotters* today by many – continued being built, especially around Frederikshavn and other parts of northern Denmark, some of which have survived today and have been put back to a full sailing rig. Jens Vaever died in 1914 after being honoured by his countrymen.

After the First World War, the Danes began fishing the western side of the North Sea and consequently landed their catches into English ports. Some Grimsby fishermen observed them at work on the Dogger Bank and the same men then observed their gear in harbour and began using the same method upon their steam trawlers and drifters. In Scotland the first time the fishermen used the method was in 1921 and six years later the first Scottish seine-net vessel built specifically for the seine-net, the *Marigold*, was launched on fifie lines from the yard of William Wood & Sons in Lossiemouth.[16] In 1921 some 25,000 hundredweight of fish were landed using the seine-net while by 1955 this had risen to 1,500,000 cwt, such was the impact of this method on the Scottish fleet.[17]

Crewed by four men and a boy, the *Marigold* proved a successful boat. With a 36hp Gardner semi-diesel engine it was economical, whereas the steam drifters that fished, although superb for the job they were designed for, used tons of coal and just were not suitable. *Marigold* was similar to a motorised fifie but with a slightly sloping sternpost which shortened the keel, upon the length of which harbour dues were paid, and made the building into the sternpost of a propeller aperture relatively easy and efficient.

Anchor-dragging was the form of the seine-net used by the Danes. The Scots then developed their own variation called 'fly-dragging' which didn't involve the use of an anchor but they towed and hauled the net at the same time and found they caught more round fish such as cod and haddock. They also found it quicker to shift grounds.[18]

Over on the west coast of Scotland, ring-netting continued throughout the war years, although with severally depleted crews after many men had gone off to fight. Many of those that did remain fishing had made themselves comfortably off for the foreseeable future and numerous boats that had been lying idle throughout the war were in a sorry state. When men were demobbed, they came back to their villages to find no work available in the fisheries because of the lack of boats. The 1919 season was also a poor one which didn't suggest to many that they should invest in new boats. The Fishery Board then produced a plan of a 'model Lochfyne motor skiff' and invited tenders, indicating that the cost would be £1,100, a huge increase over the price of a skiff before the war.[19]

However, fisherman Robert Robertson of Campbeltown, described as one of the most innovative fishermen in Scotland and the first to install an engine into a Lochfyne skiff in 1907, ordered two new boats from the renowned boatbuilder James Miller & Sons of St Monans on the east coast, in 1921. The first of these, *Falcon*, arrived in Campbeltown the following year, seconded soon after by *Frigate Bird*. Based on craft Robertson had seen in Norway, and drawn up by Glasgow naval architect W.G. McBride, the boats were 50ft overall, had canoe sterns, were entirely decked over, incorporating wheelhouses and Gleniffer 18.22hp paraffin engines. They were a complete contrast from the sailing skiffs and, again, the other fishermen were sceptical. However, the boats performed well and soon became the accepted design for the Clyde and surrounding areas, albeit with some developments.

Meanwhile across the North Sea, the last development in the Danish anchor seiner was the adoption of the cruiser stern which appeared some time before the outbreak of war in 1939, and the subsequent invasion of the country by the Nazis. Although the canoe stern and variations of the cruiser stern appeared in the 1920s, the anchor seiners appear to have been content with their counter sterns until, presumably, engine power increased and the cruiser stern was deemed a better option. Thus the typical Danish seiner arrived, a boat that impressed the Grimsby men so much that they, too, adopted similar vessels and called them 'snibbies'.

In the 1930s the cruiser stern was also adopted by many of the seine-net boats in Scotland. The J. & G. Forbes-built *Cutty Sark* seems to have been the first in 1928 though she was an all-round boat, drifting, ring-netting, seine-netting and long-lining. Another of the first of these boats, *Harvester* BF132, was built by W.G. Stephens of Macduff and launched in 1935. She was 52ft in length, had a sloping keel, a straight vertical stem and rounded forefoot.[20] This type of vessel, bigger versions of which had been built for a number of years for the herring fishery, became the forerunner of what became widely known as the Scottish motor fishing vessel and was adopted by fishermen all over Britain.

However, once again, dark clouds were blowing in from Germany, and many were forecasting black days ahead, not just for British fishermen, but for Europe as a whole.

12

WORLD WAR TO COD WAR

To compete with the steam drifters, larger motor herring drifters were introduced with the building of one in Findochty in 1928, though it wasn't until the 1930s that these 80-odd-ft boats gained favour among the fishermen. J. & G. Forbes of Sandhaven, just outside Fraserburgh, built several. The *Efficient* started life there in 1931. She was a traditional herring drifter of the era, built of larch on oak with a straight stem, deep heel and cruiser stern. Her new owners were the Ritchie family of Rosehearty and she spent her first years drift-netting for herring alongside the steam drifters, some motor boats and the last of the sailing fifies and Zulus. Registered as FR242, and engined with a Petter Atomic diesel of 160hp, the unit was so advanced that her skipper was photographed standing alongside the engine and the resultant photograph being used in their advertising blurb.

William Stevenson & Sons of Newlyn bought the boat from the Ritchie family in 1937 when they realised the herring wasn't making enough to cover the boat, and she was taken to Cornwall to line and drift out of Newlyn. She even went to the Great Autumnal Herring Fishery off East Anglia for two years. In 1938 she was converted for trawling and fished until the outbreak of war in the closing months of the next year.

Efficient was then requisitioned in late 1940. It is thought that, after the German occupation of Norway in April of that year, she initially worked in ferrying men from Norway to Leith in Scotland. Boats had been sailing over from Norway since the spring of 1940, in what became known as the North Sea Traffic. Most of the Norwegians aboard their own boats were seeking to join the free Norwegian army that was being made ready to battle to liberate the country of the invaders. Over the period from the invasion to the end of 1941, 247 boats had sailed the North Sea, though the next year there were only seventeen due to the German awareness of the problem. The Germans increased their surveillance on the coast, scuttled or blew up some of the boats and threatened reprisals against those leaving. But sometimes escaped

The *Efficient* on the stocks on her launch day in 1931 at the yard of J. & G. Forbes of Sandhaven. (*Courtesy of Billy Stevenson*)

prisoners of war were also being channelled through Norway and picked up by boats. These were often British vessels until the surveillance was improved.

Against this background, the Special Operations Executive (SOE) set up the so-called Shetland Bus in which Norwegian skippers were given boats to sail back to Norway with agents whose job was to make contact with the resistance and to supply them with weapons, equipment and training where necessary. This was the beginning of the military phase of the North Sea Traffic and was run from Lerwick in Shetland, later from Lunna Voe and eventually from Scalloway in 1942. Losses were heavy for the Shetland Bus that year with seven boats lost, thirty-three men killed and the whole of the operation virtually shut down by the Germans. Tactics then changed in 1943 with the arrival of three submarine chasing boats – fast and armed – into Scalloway and these boats undertook missions in landing agents and taking off refugees. Not one boat or life was lost between their inception and the end of the German occupation.[1]

Among other exploits of various secretive missions, the *Efficient* ferried George VI while he was visiting the Scottish isles. Little else is known of her wartime work which appears to remain among many of the secrets still held from public knowledge from that period. One wonders what on earth she can have been involved in!

When war was declared in September 1939, most of the British distant-water fleet was either in port or on its way home, having been recalled a few days earlier when war seemed imminent.[2] The home fleet, too, stayed in port. Requisitioning of vessels began almost immediately. So what else did these fishing boats get up to during the Second World War? The answer is that most were requisitioned and ordered to join the trawler section of the Royal Naval Patrol Service, what had previously been known as the Royal Naval Reserve. Prior to the war, during the summer of 1939 when war seemed a distinct possibility, the Admiralty purchased sixty-seven vessels capable of trawling and ordered twenty more. These boats were to undertake minesweeping duties. Requisitioned boats were hired by a system known as Charter-Party, under which the government agreed to compensate owners for the loss of the vessel if it was sunk by enemy action. The Compensation (Defence) Act of 1939 stated how much a trawler or drifter was due if lost and, of course, this was a low rate, especially for the older drifters. For the newer motor boats the rate could be negotiated. At the same time the Fishery Board for Scotland was disbanded and all the Herring Industries powers suspended. The future of the herring was black indeed.

Most of the boats requisitioned in the Royal Naval Reserve were rust-stained, weather-beaten fishing boats that had been working for many years without much thought to a refit. Some 200 drifters were among those requisitioned. Such was the dilapidated state of some of the boats that they received the nickname 'Harry Tate's Navy'. Harry Tate was a music hall entertainer of the 1920s and 1930s who played the clumsy comic who could not understand modern gadgets and used to poke fun at the old boats of the navy. However, by the end of the war it was a worthy mark of courage. Out of the drifters in the 'kipper patrol' (as the defence of the British coast, especially the Channel, was termed), 146 were lost on active duty, which, given the state they were said to be in, isn't that surprising.[3]

These boats worked in many theatres of the war, from the Arctic to the Mediterranean, the Atlantic to the Far East, mainly in minesweeping and anti-submarine work. Their work in keeping the shipping lanes around Britain was vital for the ships of the Atlantic Convoys that were constantly resupplying the country with arms, equipment, fuel and other necessary supplies. In all, it is said that half the fleet was requisitioned at some time during the conflict. Few of these steamers survive today though the dual purpose trawler/drifter *Lydia Eva*, a superb example, can today be seen in Great Yarmouth or Lowestoft.

On the other hand, some boats did carry on fishing for the good of the country's food supply. However, fishing during this war was even more restrictive than in the last one. No passengers were allowed to be carried and the use of the radios and echo-sounders was restricted. The fishing grounds too were restricted and fishing was often confined to small areas. The fishing was limited to the Icelandic waters, the Irish Sea, off the west coast of Scotland and around parts of Ireland. Losses to fishing boats were great too as the Germans regarded fishing craft as legitimate targets and they were generally sunk by U-boats, German aircraft and mines. It had been said that the Germans had deliberately attempted to drive all fishing boats from the seas around Britain in the First World War and the general opinion was that was the case once again.[4]

Loss of life among the fishing fleets was once again high. In all, the Royal Naval Reserve lost 2,385 personnel and more than 400 trawlers, drifters and whalers. Some 1,243 British fishermen lost their lives, nearly half coming from Grimsby. In 1939 Hull had 191 trawlers and by VE Day, 96 had been lost.[5]

Once the war was over, owners were given a lump sum to cover the cost of the refit. Over the ensuing years, with a policy of scrapping drifters, various Acts of Parliament (Herring Act 1944; Inshore Fishing Act 1948; White Fish and Herring Industries Act 1948) made grants and loans available for the replacement of obsolete drifters and the purchase of new motor boats.

At the same time Admiralty boats became available. During the war the Admiralty built a series of boats which were designed for use as fishing vessels after the war. These became known as the Admiralty MFVs and came in four different keel sizes: 45ft, 61.5ft, 75ft and 90ft. They were offered to the fishermen under the grant and loan system – some called it the 'Grunt and Groan

Scheme' and Scottish fishermen took eighty-five by 1948. The herring stocks had recovered during the non-fishing years of the war and now abundant supplies were encouraging fishermen to start drifting once more. In 1950 the Scottish fleet consisted of 5,222 vessels, 3,843 of which were motor boats and 967 still registered as sailing vessels. Of the rest, most were steam trawlers, drifters or liners.[6]

We've mentioned both steam trawlers and drifters but several steamers were built specifically for lining and worked in the waters around the Northern Isles, Faroe and as far away as Iceland and Greenland waters. These 'great liners', as they were called, fished the grounds that the trawlers were unable to trawl over, the rocky deep waters. They set many fleets of lines, each up to 500 fathoms long with up to a 150 hooks fixed to snoods. During the war little great lining took place as single boats were not keen to venture out alone. For a comparison, in 1943 great liners landed 4.1 per cent of the total Scottish white fish catch, while seiners landed 31 per cent and trawlers 56.2 per cent, but within a few years there was a great revival after no fishing for several years. By 1948 there were twenty-two steam liners working out of Aberdeen and the percentage share of fish more than doubled. Two years later steam liners had swollen to thirty-four vessels while there were by this time another six motor liners.

Numbers then decreased over the next few years. It was said that foreign boats were fishing some of the traditional grounds, bait was costly, as were the boats to run, and the crews preferred other forms of fishing which was largely due to the nature of lining. It's a long and tedious job with the baiting of the lines and most boats operated on a share system in which the men had to produce their own gear, whereas the trawler crews were being paid a set wage and had no gear to buy.[7]

Anstruther, on the East Neuk of Fife, built four new motor liners in the 1950s: *Verbena*, KY97; *Silver Chord*, KY124; *Brighter Hope*, KY37; and *Radiation*, A115. The latter, at 97ft in length, was the largest liner built in Britain and was, ironically, launched from the Smith and Hutton yard in Anstruther on 31 January 1957 in a force 10 storm. She was powered by a Mirrlees National TLSGMR6 engine. Built in wood, as it was regarded that steel would double her cost, she principally fished for cod, skate, ling and halibut. She set forty-two fleets of lines, each 300 fathoms long with 100 hooks fixed to snoods on each. She fished throughout the 1960s when most remaining liners were either laid up or converted to trawling and only finished fishing in 1978, after which she went into museum ownership.[8]

On 1 September 1958, the Icelandic government expanded its territorial waters from 4 miles to 12 and the British government declared almost at once that British trawlers would continue fishing under the protection of the

Steam trawlers leaving Lowestoft. Often these boats would be at sea for two weeks or more, returning to unload for only a short period in which the crew were able to spend with their families.

Royal Navy in three areas. Various confrontations between Icelandic gunboats and British trawlers ensued though British warships came to the rescue. In one particular case in November 1958, an Icelandic patrol vessel encountered the trawler *Hackness* which had not stowed its nets legally. *Hackness* did not stop until the Icelandic vessel had fired two blanks and one live shell off its bow. HMS *Russell* came to the rescue and its captain ordered the Icelandic captain to leave the trawler alone as it was not within the 4-mile limit recognised by the British government. The Icelandic captain refused to do so, and ordered his men to approach the trawler with the gun manned. In response, the *Russell* threatened to sink the Icelandic boat if it so much as fired one shot at the *Hackness*. More British ships then arrived and the *Hackness* retreated. However, an agreement was settled later that month which stipulated that any future disagreement between Iceland and Britain as to where Britain could fish would be sent to the International Court of Justice. In total, the First Cod War saw a total of thirty-seven Royal Navy ships and 7,000 sailors protecting the fishing fleet from six Icelandic gunboats and their 100 coastguards.

During the late 1940s the design of the distant-water fleet altered drastically, due to the adoption of diesel engines. The very first of these 'oil burners' retained the old pipestalkie tall funnels and wheelhouse though within a couple of years a more modest funnel and redesigned wheelhouse was adopted, giving the boat a more modern feel, although the mizzen steadying sail continued to be part of the standard gear. Such a boat was the one 178ft 1949-built *Cape Cleveland*, H61, owned by Hudson Brothers Trawlers Ltd. Built by John Lewis & Sons Ltd of Aberdeen, her name was changed in 1965 to *Ross Cleveland* when Hudson's were taken over by the Ross Group. The hull form of these boats was considered to be the best for the Arctic trawling:

> … deep, low and magnificent in the water, with high flared bows to thrust breaking water aside, throwing it away from the ship instead of back board or digging it up by the hundred-ton to fill her working decks. Minimum rigging reached aloft to hold high ice up there – the radio aerials and their spreaders, one stumpy, sturdy mast: the small stack stood abaft the compact, instrument-filled bridge. Could she ice up and fall over? Dodge to her death, overwhelmed at last in the murdering sea? Or capsize in shrieking squall of hurricane force under assault by some swift-moving mountain of wind-maddened water coming in at change of tide or over foul ground, sweeping over the bulwarks and remaining there, pinning the ship down? For high-flared bows can blow off, too, when the ship lies-to and, having driven her across the sea's trough, hold her there. And that could also be fatal.[9]

The *Ross Cleveland* was 'dodging' during the northeast storm that was blowing right into the Isafjordur on 5 February 1968. In the preceding month two trawlers – *St Romanus* and *Kingston Peridot* – had been lost, the first it is believed on 11 January and the second on the 26 or 27 January. Dodging means steaming ahead very slowly, heading into the gale as anchoring would have been impossible. In force 11 winds the conditions are just as awful as can be imagined: screaming wind, the sea throwing all it can, freezing temperatures and a motion without any pattern. Ice build up above threatens the very boat as the waves turn her around. The *Ross Cleveland* did just that, and another wave pushed her down, the sea filling her decks and she was wounded. Unable to fight, another wave hit her, the mortal blow that took her over on her port side. The skipper in the wheelhouse on his radio, speaking in a quiet voice was heard by another skipper who, too, was fighting for his ship's survival. 'Help us, Len. Help us, she's going over, she's laying over. Give my love and the crew's love to the wives and families,' Phil Gay said. And then quiet. Skipper Len Whurr recalled seeing her lights on and suddenly they went out. One crew member did survive in a life raft which fetched up ashore, though two others in it had died from exposure. Mate Harry Eddom, aged 26, had been chipping ice from the radar apparatus and was dressed in full oilskins which saved him. 'When she began to go she went in six seconds,' he said. 'It wasn't the ice. It was the wind and the sea.' For Hull it was the worst tragedy, made worse by the loss of the single-screw side motor trawler *Notts County*, GY643, which went ashore the same night, and another Icelandic trawler that was lost with all hands.[10]

When the news filtered back home about the first two boats, it was a devastating blow to the tight-knit fishing community in Hull and the trawlermen's wives began a safety campaign, meeting with trawler owners and government ministers. Some wives picketed the dock to ensure all departing ships carried radio operators, attracting much national media attention. As the wives' deputation arrived at the dock in front of TV cameras and journalists on 5 February 1968 for the meeting with the trawler owners, news broke of the loss of *Ross Cleveland*. The following day the women travelled to London, again with massive media coverage, and met ministers to discuss a variety of reforms to the fishing industry. The same day, trawler owners were instructed to implement new safety arrangements based on the outcome of the meeting, with immediate effect.

The Holland-Martin Report of 1969 followed from these tragedies. In the report it was calculated that trawlermen had a mortality rate seventeen times that for the male population and that those fishermen aged from 15 to 44 were twenty times more likely to die as a result of an accident at work. Fifty-seven men were lost in a matter of weeks after the three losses above and the report also found that in the ten years preceding that 208 trawlermen had lost their lives. The report told the world just how dangerous fishing was, especially in the distant-water fishing.[11]

The Second Cod War, as these wars became known, started when Iceland increased its fishing limits to 50 miles. Again the British refused to recognise this. Numerous British and West German trawlers continued fishing within the new zone on the first day. The Icelandic leftist coalition which governed at the time ignored the treaty that stipulated the involvement of the International Court of Justice. It said that it wasn't bound by agreements made by the previous centre-right government, with Lúdvik Jósepsson, the fisheries minister, stating that 'the basis for our independence is economic independence'.

During this war, the Icelandic Coast Guard started to use net-cutters to cut the trawling lines of non-Icelandic vessels fishing within the new exclusion zone. On 18 January 1973, the nets of eighteen trawlers were cut. This forced the British seamen to threaten to leave the Icelandic fishery zone unless they had the protection of the Royal Navy. Then, on 17 May, the British trawlers left the Icelandic waters, only to return two days later with British warships. Various altercations followed between boats until, after a series of talks within NATO, British warships were recalled on 3 October. An agreement was signed on 8 November which limited British fishing activities to certain areas inside the 50-mile limit, resolving the dispute that time. The resolution was based on the premise that British trawlers would limit their annual catch to no more than 130,000 tons. This agreement expired in November 1975.

Then, of course, the Third Cod War began when Iceland declared a 200-mile limit and the British government again refused to recognise this. The conflict, which was the most hard-fought of the Cod Wars, saw British fishing trawlers have their nets cut by the Icelandic Coast Guard, and there were several incidents of ramming by Icelandic ships and British trawlers, frigates and tugboats. Over the course of three months various incidents were reported in the press. Britain deployed a total of twenty-two frigates and seven supply ships, nine tug-boats, and three support ships to protect its fishing trawlers, although only six to nine of these vessels were on deployment at any one time. Iceland deployed four patrol vessels and two armed trawlers. The Icelandic government tried to acquire US Asheville class gunboats, and when denied by the American government they tried to get Soviet Mirka class frigates. A more serious turn of events came when Iceland threatened closure of the NATO base at Keflavík, which would have severely impaired NATO's ability to defend the Atlantic Ocean from the Soviet Union. As a result, the British government, under pressure from the Americans, agreed to have its fishermen stay outside Iceland's 200-nautical mile (370km) exclusion zone without a specific agreement. That, then, was the end of distant-water trawling and a series loss to Britain's fish consumption requirements.[12]

On the other side of Britain, in and around the northern Irish Sea, the Clyde and parts of western Scotland, the ring-net fishing was booming. Some say the 1950s was the peak of that fishery with the so-called modern developments in the method having perfected it. Boats had become bigger because of the need for more deck space after the use of deeper nets brought on by introduction of winches and bigger boats had larger engines which needed

Ullapool in the 1950s, at the peak of Scottish west coast fishery in the twentieth century. The boat is *Crimond*, BCK118, built as a herring drifter.

greater buoyancy aft. Thus the cruiser stern was incorporated into the ringer, a transition from the canoe. Angus Martin tells us that, as a general rule, pre-war ringers were of the canoe-stern design and the post-war vessels of the cruiser-stern design.[13] Other innovations in the process of ring-netting since the early part of the century included additions to the net, the feeling-wire, brailers, echo-sounders and pursing rings. With a decline in the herring in the Clyde in the post-war years, more concentration was played upon fishing the Minches. At the same time many of the fishers increasingly adopted seine-netting and some bottom-trawling for prawns, which was to become almost the only profitable fishing in the late twentieth and early twenty-first centuries. Dual purpose boats with power-blocks for mid-water trawling, larger wheelhouses for all the electronic equipment for navigation and fish-finding needs and powerful engines of 200hp became the norm. By the 1970s more boats were trawling than ring-netting and, with eventual closure of the herring fishing after the collapse due to the vast amounts being fished with the purse-seine, herring fishing in and around Loch Fyne almost came to an abrupt halt.

It was, of course, the fisheries policy of the European Union (what we then knew as the Common Market) that ordered the closure of the herring fishery as stocks were close to an absolute collapse. Britain entered the European Economic Community on 1 January 1973 after Prime Minister Edward Heath had negotiated entry and part of the agreement was the acceding of the British territorial fishing limits into a joint pan-EEC fishing area. When it was first decided upon in 1970, it was agreed that fishermen from all countries within the Community should have access to all waters. Britain – whose territorial waters contained 65 per cent of Europe's rich fishing grounds – had to accept this otherwise membership would be denied. Some say it was Charles de Gaulle of France who insisted upon this. In 1976 the EU extended its fishing waters from 12 to 200 miles (22.2km to 370.4km) from the coast, in line with other international changes. This required additional controls and the Common Fisheries Policy (CFP) as such was created in 1983. This now had four areas of activity: conservation of stocks, vessels and installations, market controls, and external agreements with other nations.

Meanwhile, down in the southwest of England, fishing was also undergoing huge change. The pilchards had long gone, mackerel was unpopular and while Brixham boats were engaged mainly in beam trawling, the Newlyn boats, those that weren't trawling, were gill-netting out in the Western Approaches, off the south coast of Ireland.

Going back to beginning of this chapter, the *Efficient* was renamed *Excellent* after the sailing lugger owned by William Stevenson until 1888, and re-registered with her present letters and numbers which, too, were those of the original boat, PZ513. Over the next forty years she remained the backbone of the Stevenson fleet. As the fleet expanded, *Excellent* always managed to compete favourably with the new craft. In 1962 she was re-engined for the second time, receiving a naturally aspirated Lister Blackstone ERMGR5 – 280hp at 750rpm – which she still has today. She continued to trawl up to the 1990s.

In 1998 I joined her for ten days fishing in the Western Approaches. On the first morning of fishing, while I'd been slumbering in my coffin berth, the crew had already shot the nets, each tier consisting of about twenty nets, with anchors and floats at each end. *Excellent* had six tiers of these nets, each net being 120 yards long by 3 fathoms deep, set about 18 inches above the seabed, so in total amounting to over 8 miles of netting with a mesh of 4 inches.

A complete net with sole, foot and head rope cost about £160, the sheet of net alone costing some £70. As the nets are often broken, their upkeep is costly. Once the nets have all been shot over the stern, they are left for twenty-four hours or so and the vessel tediously steams up and down the 8 miles, taking over an hour in each direction.

That night I was put to work, assuming watches as normal as any other vessel. I can still recall watching the other Newlyn boats patrolling. Gill-netters show the normal red over white lights, but to differentiate them from other fishing boats operating static gear – i.e. not trawling – they also display a flashing yellow light. These vessels all marched up and down their gear, like soldiers on guard. Not hovercrafts, as the book on lights will tell you, but fishermen guarding their livelihood from the dangers of marauding Spanish trawlers! That night I also saw the loom of the Fastnet light low on the horizon.

We hauled at first light, using the hydraulic winch, one crew-member scanning the net all the while for hake, at which point a shout of 'Hake-o' alerts the winch operator in the wheelhouse to slow up and the fish untangled. Two other crew feed the net back into the pound, while the fourth guts the fish. In calm conditions they work fast, perhaps an hour a tier. Rough conditions, or with a glut of fish, can triple the time. On that first haul we brought aboard about 15 stone of hake and 10 of cod, haddock, ling and monkfish. Not a good haul, so we motored south for about 50 miles and by midnight the nets had been shot again. After that, business adjourned to the galley for roast pork (or curly-tails as pigs are referred to through superstition) washed down with tea – all the boats are generally 'dry' at sea.

April Fools' Day brought sunshine, and a sense of excitement: the lure of the kill. Hauling began at 3 p.m., and the excitement was short-lived. Mack – or mackerel – filled the net. Mackerel, like herring, perishes quickly and has to be landed immediately unless you have the huge refrigerated salt water tanks to keep it fresh. We didn't, and since we were 180 miles from Newlyn, it was obvious that we weren't going to be able to land it, so it had to be cleared from the net and chucked over the side. Adding insult to injury, the hake was scarce.

That afternoon I took over from Joe in the wheelhouse, while he helped on deck with the clearing and the gutting of what fish there were. I was amazed how quickly time went, concentrating as I was on the hauler, another winch that fed the net aft and the engine controls to keep the vessel's head upwind along the line of the net – although the crew probably didn't agree as they were stung by jellyfish and soaked by the spray. More importantly, my wages weren't dependent on the fish caught.

The whole operation of hauling a tier, steaming back again to shoot it in the same place, and then proceeding with the next ones in turn, took twelve hours. As the fish came aboard, they were gutted and packed in the plastic fish boxes, and immediately these went down into the fish room to be layered with ice.

We had taken aboard six tons of ice at £15 a ton before departure, and it's amazing just how long ice does remain in a mass when packed tightly into the hold. On a subsequent voyage aboard *Excellent*, I found ice in the hold that had been there for over two weeks and it was still able to cool food and beer. On this occasion the ice was shovelled into the fish boxes before these were stacked. Hake went to port, white fish to starboard, although the catch of hake was poor and there was a disappointing imbalance in the number of boxes on either side. Once this was all below, we could eat and sleep, although even after an exhausting day, we all had to suffer another two hours on watch.

I recall thinking one night on watch about the Common Fisheries Policy and how its resentment by Cornish fishermen is caused by the insult of French craft fishing within sight of the north Cornish coast with ten times more cod quota than they have. When Britain sold out its fishermen through equal access to a common resource at the negotiations for British entry to the EEC, some say Cornwall lost out more than any other part of the UK because of their proximity to the Western Approaches with its rich pickings. Possibly the Scots will disagree, but there's no doubt that the Southwest has seen a tumble in trade as many of the fleet have packed up through decommissioning and retirement. It seems that now the coastal fishermen – some call them artisan fishermen – are expendable to politicians who consider it justifiable for them to lose their livelihoods so that the industry can be controlled by the few big players. Fishing, then, is to be taken down the same road as coalmining, shipbuilding and the cotton industry, handed piecemeal to ever more powerful businessmen who direct operations from some sun-soaked tax haven by telephone, while those that have lived through fishing all their lives are unjustly discarded into a sea of despair, just like all those fish that are thrown back through the impractical mechanics of the Common Fisheries Policy. Basically fishing will disappear from the British traditional way of life.

Anyway, by the Thursday it was obvious that we weren't going to be blessed with a good catch, even if others were. That, in a nutshell, is fishing. The boat alongside you can be getting stone after stone of good fish, while you hardly get anything. The next time, though, it will be you getting the catches while they do not. The word on the radio, however, was that there was no hake around. Added to this, the wind increased from the northwest and Joe told us tales of how winds of force 10 could suddenly appear from this direction completely unannounced.

It was definitely time to go. We hauled in for the last time, again taking about ten hours in the freshening seas, even though the nets weren't being shot again. The mackerel was basketed this time, although we found on our return that it was not saleable. By midnight we were steaming eastwards at 10 knots, following a dotted yellow line on the Shipmate plotter. We clocked up 11 knots rounding the Runnelstone buoy just south of Lands End. We entered Newlyn on the Friday evening, and jostled for space alongside the quay. The others in our group arrived about half an hour later. We unloaded and weighed the boxes in: 170 stone of hake and 70 stone of white fish. The others, who had told us that their catches were poor, had over 800 stone. Oh, the lies fishermen tell over the radio!

With the boat cleaned and damaged nets cleared out, the crew returned ashore, while I borrowed the skipper's berth for the night. I didn't fancy manoeuvring into mine for the last time. When morning came, I visited the market as the remnants of the catch were being sold. Ours had gone. However, prices were low.

When I caught up with the crew later on after they had picked up their cheques, I was disappointed to learn that they had each earned just £225. This was a full share, calculated thus: the value of the catch (the hake was selling at £25 a stone), less £200 for the boat, the expenses of the trip (fuel, food, ice and oil – probably about £800), which leaves the profit. This is divided by eleven to determine the value of a share. The owners get five and half shares (they pay for the nets, boat upkeep, navigational gear, paperwork, surveys, etc.), the skipper gets one and a half share and the crew one each.

So that day our crew got £225 for a hard week's graft – and that's every two weeks. The big catches probably raise over £1,000 per share. Why do they do it? Some say it's in the blood. Generations of Newlyn families have gone to sea. On land, life appears as an intrusion – cars, traffic wardens, newspapers, telephone. At sea they're forgotten. It's the same for the nomadic sailor, of course, but his life doesn't really touch reality; fishing somehow does. It's a job on the one hand, and a way of life on the other. Who, though, would do it for £225 every two weeks?

13

FISHING BOAT DESIGN OVER TIME

To the fisher, the fishing boat is their most important tool, the one they rely upon. It is their working platform, safety net, workshop, net store and fish hold all in one. They rely on it to take them to work, to keep them secure at work and then to get them back to port safely. Although many of today's such vessels are often smelly, oily, dirty vessels, beneath the grit and grime of toil lie seaworthy, well-fettled and proudly owned craft. Annual paint jobs, constant engine maintenance, safety checks and updated electronics all ensure that vessels continue to safeguard life aboard as much as possible, catch fish to a maximum and operate under the strict rules that today's European Common Fisheries Policy enforce.

Things, though, were different in the old days. In the days when men were men, and fishing boats worked under sail and their crews fought the waves with sheer strength of mind, their boats meant more: they might have been platforms of terror and discomfort at sea, but when they journeyed safely home they were really well looked after. They were scrubbed and scraped, painted or varnished and the sails tanned in various mixtures (as we shall discuss later) to protect them from the rotting effect of seawater. Often, they were keenly raced in annual regattas that many fishing fleets became renowned for. Indeed, because of their expertise in sail operation, fishermen were often crew aboard the large Victorian yachts that were often built just to race. In the parts of Britain that became centres of yachting in the nineteenth century – the Thames, the Clyde, the Solent – it was fishermen who were central in providing the manpower able to sail these picturesque craft.

It is generally regarded that early boatbuilding was influenced from various directions. In northern Britain it was a German/Scandinavian (Saxon/Viking) influence that led to the use of open clinker-built craft, while a Dutch influence gave some of the keel boats seen on parts of the east coast. Powerful French three-masters often were seen closer to the southern English coast and resulted in similar three-masters being adopted for fishing which in turn led to the Cornish luggers and many other southern types. And back beyond that, skin boats had been in use ever since mankind took to the sea and their development is somewhat more unclear.

Britain has had a most diverse collection of fishing craft. To describe them in full would take up far more pages than are available here and readers are directed to the author's book *Traditional Fishing Boats of Britain & Ireland* (Shrewsbury 1999). Nevertheless, it would be an omission not to give an overall appreciation of them.

To many a layman it is Scotland that is renowned for its quality of boatbuilding, although this is in blatant disregard for many class-quality boatbuilders around the UK. Two reasons that Scotland has such a reputation might be a) their proximity to good supplies of boatbuilding timber such as oak, larch and Douglas fir; and b) the fact that documented details of Scottish boats go back to the mid-nineteenth century whereas for craft south of the border the evidence is not so forthcoming.

In the Scottish case it was Captain John Washington who was summoned by the government to enquire into the aftermath of a gale on the north-east coast in August 1848 when some 124 boats were wrecked and at least 100 fishermen's lives lost. Of course, this wasn't the first storm to cause such damage on the fishing fleets of the whole country, but it was the first time that people began to wonder why such losses of life went by without question. Part of Washington's remit was to consider the design of boats in use on that coast and to compare these with others around the coast.

In his resultant report, released the following year and running to many pages, he produced plans and/or details of craft from both sides of Scotland, from the Isle of Man, St Ives, Penzance, Kinsale, Galway, Hastings, Deal, Yarmouth and Scarborough. Of those on the east coast of Scotland, he gives details of boats from Wick, Buckie, Fraserburgh, Peterhead, Newhaven and Dunbar, all of which were double-ended, which has given modern-day historians an insight in the vessels the fishing fleets were using. However, as to their suitability of purpose, he was not impressed. Among his recommendations – and he added drafts of four proposed fishing boats drawn up by renowned naval architect James Peake of the Royal Dockyard in Woolwich – were that boats should be decked over, harbours should be improved upon to allow access at all stages of the tide, crews should not be engaged from landsfolk and fishermen should not be paid by the fish curers in whisky. Decked boats, in the views of many of the fisherfolk, were unnecessary as it was believed they took up space and that this meant less fish could be carried. The obvious advantage of decking boats was they would have been able to stay at sea longer in the extreme sea conditions and survived, whereas the small, not particularly seaworthy boats headed straight for home when the weather turned, most being wrecked when they were unable to enter harbour at low water.

Of those Scottish boats the report gives drafts of, it was only the Fraserburgh type that had any suggestion of a foredeck. Between this one and that from nearby Peterhead, there is influence of more upright stems (the front bit) and sternposts (the back bit) in what is considered to be Dutch, and it is widely thought that this emerged after many Dutch fishers moved to Fife in the seventeenth century when their countrymen were masters of the North Sea herring fishery. However, it must be said that the similarities end there as many Dutch vessels of that era were bluff-bowed, flat-bottomed craft. Nevertheless, Washington's drawings appear to be the earliest of the type that became known as the *fifie*. In time these vessels became up to 70ft in length sporting two huge dipping lugsails on masts, the fore of which was so big that a man had difficulty stretching his arms around.

To the north, in the Moray Firth and up to the north coast, the favoured boat was more Viking in shape and was obviously influenced by Scandinavian boats, which isn't surprising since the country's proximity to the countries across the North Sea. The double-ended *scaffie*, as they have since become known, had steeply raking sternposts and cutaway forefeet on upright but slightly rounded stems.

In the Northern Isles the Norse influence was even more obvious. With Shetland being part of the Norse empire until 1469 and being geographically nearer to Norway than to, say, Aberdeen, as discussed in Chapter 3, and having a dire lack of trees, boats were imported from Norway aboard ships. At first these were rigged with one squaresail though the lug-rig was adopted in the eighteenth century. The boats often came in kit form and were pieced together by Shetland boatbuilders until they simply imported the timber and cut the patterns themselves to build boats with subtle changes to suit local conditions. Boats came in various sizes depending on the type of fishing and all were eventually lug-rigged so that we have *sixareens* (six-oared deep sea boats), *fourereens* (four-oared inshore craft), and various *yoals* (*yols* from the Norse '*jol*' meaning small boat, a term used in various parts of eastern Britain). In Orkney we have 'yoles', both from the north and the south of the islands. All these craft are double-ended. In Orkney the main difference between the boats was that those to the south – the South Isles yoles – were sprit-rigged as against the lug-rigged northern versions, with some differences in hull shape. The southern boats were the largest and were almost identical to the Stroma yoles from that tiny island in the Pentland Firth close by Duncansby Head, and which worked further along the inhospitable northern coast.

Then, in the very late 1870s, one of the most effective and lovely of British sailing fishing boats was built as a hybrid between fifie and scaffie, taking the most salient points of both to combine into one boat which became known

Two small Orkney yoles and a fifie, *Rose* K365, on the beach at St Mary's in the very southeast of mainland Orkney, where boats were once built. (*Orkney Library Archive*)

as the *Zulu*: with the loss of life of Scottish soldiers on the battlefields of South Africa, the ensuing public outcry caught the attention of fisherfolk who somehow used the name for their new vessels. Whether this was for one particular vessel at first, or the whole type, is not clear but evidence does support the first supposition. The Zulu had the upright bow of the fifie and the sloping sternpost of the scaffie although at a more acute angle which gave it a huge overhang at the back end. Like the fifie, the Zulu had two large lugsails and the largest, the *Laverack*, BF787, built in 1902, was 84ft in length excluding bowsprit and bumpkin on a 54ft keel length. With many Scottish harbours charging harbour dues based on keel length, these were kept as short as possible.

On the west coast of Scotland, although various small boats (*bata* in Gaelic) display Viking influences, it was the Lochfyne skiffs that have been called the prettiest of all British workboats. These were double-enders again in the Scandinavian style and had one standing lugsail. They developed purely out of setting ring-nets as discussed in Chapter 2 from earlier line skiffs that worked drift-nets in and around the loch. On the eastern side of the Clyde similarly shaped vessels, with one standing lug each, were called *nabbies*. Indeed, evidence supports the belief that the lugsail was introduced into Loch Fyne by the Ayrshire fishermen who, in turn, had imported the lug from Fraserburgh district. Thus, as is expected, this is proof that fishermen themselves were largely responsible for introducing innovative ideas into inherited traditions in the fishing fleets.

In the Outer Hebrides the *sgoth Niseach* (Ness skiffs) have been described in Chapter 3, while the small lobster and line boats of the southern isles (Barra, the Uists, Grimsay and Eriskay) were introduced from the Oban area of the mainland.

Moving down the west coast, we've already explained the influences behind the Isle of Man nickeys and nobbies in Chapter 6. Similar craft worked from Northern Irish harbours such as Kilkeel, Ardglass and Portavogie, while smaller boats such as the *drontheims*, which worked along the Irish shoreline between Dublin and around the north coast to Donegal, were Scandinavian in influence and bore many similarities to western Scottish boats. Many of these, especially on the east coast, are called yawls.

The Lancashire nobbies, on the other hand, bear no relation to the Manx craft except in name. Various explanations have been given for the term 'nobby'. Dictionaries refer to a nobby as a 'rich, influential man' or 'nob', coming from the Scots 'knab' which itself was shortened to 'nab' to produce 'nabby'. This seems justifiable as the Clyde nabbies were in existence prior to the first Manx nobby arriving, mirroring the Clyde boats, but this doesn't explain its adoption in Morecambe Bay. Yet there is a belief that the early Morecambe boats evolved from Solway Firth boats so it is possible the name might have been loosely applied in that way. Another possibility is that 'nobby' refers to 'smallness' in various walks of life, and thus is to differentiate between small cutters and large vessels.[1]

Nevertheless, the Lancashire nobby – variously called a Morecambe Bay nobby, prawner or sprawner – developed into a fine working boat after the intervention of naval architect William Stoba who singlehandedly altered the design to produce what we now identify as a boat of 35ft in length on average, rigged with gaffsail on single mast with topsail and foresails. A long counter stern enhances what is a boat of low freeboard, necessary when working nets and trawls over the side from the cockpit. Some boats had a small cuddy, while smaller boats worked shrimp trawls in Morecambe Bay and larger boats worked out in the Irish Sea. Indeed, the design gained favour with fishermen from the Solway Firth right down to Aberystwyth in Cardigan Bay.

Cornwall's luggers are world renowned and, as for the Lancashire nobbies, many are still sailing today. Generally there are two types, split by the infamous Lizard peninsula. To the west are the double-enders of Mounts Bay and St Ives while to the east are the transom-sterned luggers of Falmouth, Mevagissey and Looe. However, of course, nothing is ever as simple as that and Porthleven, to the west of the Lizard, was home to several lugger builders who launched many transom-sterned versions. To the west there were two distinct variations, the fuller shape of St Ives and Mousehole where boats had to dry out on the tidal harbour sands and the later models in Mounts Bay that were able to stay afloat in the harbours of Newlyn, Penzance and Porthleven after their construction and development in the mid part of the nineteenth century. To the extreme east of the county, at Polperro, they preferred the gaff rig on their 'Polperro gaffers' as did the Plymouth fishers on their 'Plymouth hookers'.

The smaller crab boats of Cornwall were all transom-sterned to work pots over the square stern where buoyancy was greater. From Sennen Cove in the west to Cadgwith, Gorran Haven, boats were similar in hull shape though the latter were sprit-rigged. Across the border in Devon, crab boats worked around the South Hams peninsula though they were, too, sprit-rigged. Other Cornish boats worthy of mention are the pilchard seine boats and the Falmouth Working Boats that dredge for oysters wholly under sail and are mentioned in Chapter 9.

Likewise the powerful Brixham trawlers have been mentioned in Chapter 7. These ketch-rigged vessels really were powerful out of the necessity of dragging beam trawls along the seabed. Similar trawlers worked out of Plymouth and Dartmouth in the southwest and Yarmouth, Lowestoft and Scarborough on the east coast. The main builders were in Brixham, Galmpton, Rye, Lowestoft and Grimsby, though building was not exclusively confined to these ports. Once motorisation gained a foothold in the early twentieth century, many of these trawlers were sold to Scandinavia where they worked well into the second half of that century and have since been restored to, or at least near to, their original state. Names like *Leader*, *Pilgrim*, *Vigilance* (all from Brixham), *Keewaydin* (Rye), *Excelsior* (Lowestoft) and *City of Edinburgh* (ex-*William McCann*, Grimsby) have become household names among traditional boat enthusiasts.

The English coast of the Channel is home to numerous small beach-based craft such as the Beer luggers, the Chesil Beach lerrets, Poole fishing boats, Itchen ferries from the Solent, Portsmouth seiners, Selsey crabbers, Bognor lobster boats and a variety of Sussex beach craft, the best known perhaps being those of Hastings where an active beach-based fishing industry still survives (these boats were briefly discussed in Chapter 4). Folkestone was known for preferring to have their craft built in Cornwall and many such luggers have been based there. Smaller beaches employed small lug-rigged craft such as at St Margaret's Bay, east of Dover. The one thing all the south coast boats have is that they have evolved through influences from across the Channel and even today the traditional boats of both sides display a common heritage.

The Thames estuary is home to an array of bawleys and smacks, both big and small. Bawleys were River Thames boats, said to have evolved from the cutter-rigged 'Peter boats' that worked the river. Bawley is probably a corruption of 'boiler', denoting the way of boiling shrimps while at sea. They were transom-sterned vessels with little sheer and a shallow draft for working the shoal waters over the sandbanks of the estuary. They were common around

Margate, Faversham, Chatham, Strood, Gravesend, Leigh-on-Sea and Southend. They were instantly recognisable for having a short mast, tall topmast and long gaff on the loose-footed mainsail. Many, it seems, were built by Aldous of Brightlingsea, famous for their smacks, although there were, of course, builders such as Gill & Son of Rochester, E. Lemon at Strood, Fiddle of Gravesend and Stone of Erith in Kent, Heywood at Southend and Cann at Harwich.

Smacks of Essex are renowned for their speed, their voracious fishing of, especially, oysters and the fact that many have survived and continue sailing today. These days they seem to be everywhere in the Essex rivers and backwaters, though some have now got free in their retirement from fishing and gone looking, sailing to other quarters around the coast. There are a few in Cornwall that, over the years, have migrated from perches upon muddy creeks to a more resplendent place among the other traditional craft of that county. Some say the West Country folk don't restore them in the same way as the Essex folk but I wouldn't want to comment on that.

The oldest, *Boadicea*, CK213, was built in 1808 and has stayed true to her birth-county, staying much of her life in the hands of the family of her original owner. She was built as a clinker-built boat, though in 1890 during a refit, she was rebuilt in carvel planking. She retains a transom which is how the early boats were, though around the middle of the nineteenth century lute sterns were added onto the transoms and, by 1860, counter sterns had been generally adopted by builders. Nineteenth-century smacks came in three sizes and were mostly registered at Colchester (CK) or Maldon (MN). The smallest were under 35ft and worked oyster dredges and trawls. The mid size were up to 50ft and generally spratted with a stow-net, dredged for oysters or trawled while the largest dredged for oysters away from home, as far away as Luce Bay, North and South Wales, the Firth of Forth and closer to home off Shoreham and the Norfolk coast. Some went to the Dutch island of Terschelling and obtained the nickname 'skillingers'.

Further north, cod smacks were built at Harwich specifically for the Icelandic fishery as described in Chapter 8. Many were used to fish the North Sea in winter. Numerous other small types of boats worked this coast – *dobles* were the Kent equivalents to the Peter boats, the *bumkins* were small open oyster dredgers at West Mersea, double-ended whelk boats worked the Kent coast, modelled on Cromer crabbers and *winkle-brigs* were small winkling boats.

Herring, of course, was king in East Anglia, and large lug-rigged drifters worked out of Yarmouth and Lowestoft, as did the trawlers already mentioned. Some drifters even adopted the gaff rig. Beach boats were transom-sterned, small, two-masted punts which drifted for herring and sprats, trawled and potted. At Yarmouth, a particular type of shrimper evolved, of which there were eighty boats at one time. These were half-deckers and did not boil the catch aboard but took it home, often to sell outside their houses to promenading holiday-makers. Double-ended beach yawls worked the northern part of the coast, between Cromer and Aldeburgh, attending to shipping in the Yarmouth roads and up towards the Haisborough lightship. Some of these fished when not otherwise busy, and sometimes carried herring ashore from the larger drifters. All these beach craft sometimes took trippers out during the summer season.

The Cromer crab boats have been discussed, as have the cobles and keel boats of Yorkshire and Northumberland. King's Lynn was home to the *Lynn yoll*, a cockle and mussel collecting boat that worked the Wash, while King's Lynn also had its own smacks, the smaller of which fished for shrimps and the larger dredging for oysters and fishing for whelks. Many were built by the well-known builder Worfolk Bros, while nearby Boston had its own small fleet of smacks built by local builder Gostelow. We've also seen that Grimsby and Hull were bases to the deep-sea fleet and trawlers from the North Sea. Shrimpers also worked out of Paull. (See Chapter 4)

Of course, numerous types of boats fished rivers and some such as the stop-net and compass-net boats, the coracles and the long-net punts, have already been mentioned. In Ireland a host of small boats worked the rivers and inshore fisheries such as the Cheekpoint prongs, the Ballyhack yawls, the Towelsail lobster boats and mackerel yawls of Roaringwater Bay, the Achill yawls, the Shannon gandelows, as well as the well-known skin boats of which there are various types.[2] Clovelly picarooners worked from that harbour.

The advent of the steam era, in comparison to industry and the railways, had a late impact on the fisheries. Steam trawling, although initial experiments occurred in the 1850s, didn't really get going until the 1880s and for the herring fishery not until the turn of the century. However, once that initial impact was made, the fishing fleets soon absorbed the innovation and built steamers and we've seen in an earlier chapter their effect on the fisheries.

In the same way, there were many in the fisheries who didn't take to the idea of the internal combustion engine. A few did and one such pioneer was skipper, Robert Robertson, of Campbeltown. He was the first to fit an engine into a Lochfyne skiff, his being the *Brothers*, CN97, in 1907.[3] This was a Kelvin 7.9hp unit made by the Bergius Launch & Engine Company of Glasgow, in the early days of the Kelvin company that became world renowned for its engines. Indeed, there were few fishermen on the west coast of Scotland that didn't have a Kelvin engine. Others went for Gardner of Manchester, Thornycroft, later of Southampton, the Ailsa Craig Motor Co. of London or Gleniffer of Anniesland, Glasgow. There were, by the outbreak of war in 1914, some fifty companies that had fitted engines into British fishing vessels over the previous decade or so.[4]

Robert Robertson was at the forefront in modernising the fishing fleet and in the early 1920s visited Scandinavia and was impressed with their design of vessel. When he returned he commissioned the Glasgow naval architect W.G. McBride to design a boat based on the craft he had seen in Norway. The resultant boat was a canoe-sterned vessel of approximately 50ft in length and he showed this to William Miller of renowned Scottish boatbuilder J.G. Miller & Sons of St Monans and placed an order for two boats. The first, *Falcon*, arrived in Campbeltown in April 1922 and the second, *Frigate Bird*, a month later. Both had Gleniffer engines and the total cost of both boats was £1,277 14*s*, excluding nets and gear. These boats were totally unlike the Lochfyne skiffs.[5]

Although at first not entirely successful at the ring-net, they soon proved the opposite though the rest of the fleet remained sceptical. Four years later, Robertson ordered another boat from the same yard – all his successive boats were built by Millers – but this one being smaller at almost 42ft. It was deemed that the freeboard was lower for lifting baskets aboard the *Crimson Arrow*. Two years later he ordered a larger 46ft boat – the *Nil Desperandum* – which had a forward wheelhouse and a ring-netting winch aft. By this time other fishermen had been convinced as to the sense in building similar boats and several arrived from the yards of Walter Reekie of St Monans and William Weatherhead of Cockenzie. By the 1930s, with more vessels being built, the true canoe-sterned ring-netter had arrived in and around the Clyde, many based on the Ayrshire coast. Robertson himself, with his eyesight failing, retired from fishing in the late 1930s and died in January 1940 at the age of 59. Nevertheless, he goes down in history through his technological expertise that brought so much to the development of the ring-net; he will be remembered for his pre-eminence among the ring-net fishermen and undoubtedly among the few who can be regarded as the most innovative of British fishermen.

Meanwhile, on the east coast, the cruiser-sterned fishing boat was gaining ascendancy after the adoption of the Danish seine-net. The design spread rapidly throughout Britain so that cruiser-sterned boats were being built as far away as Cornwall and by several yards in Ireland through grants from the BIM (Bord Iascaigh Mhara), the Irish Sea Fisheries Board. Previously to the BIM's establishment in 1952, the Congested Districts Board (CDB) had promoted fishing by buying in Scottish fifies and Zulus in the late nineteenth century and which fished the west coast. Tyrrell's of Arklow had launched the first motorised fishing boat in Ireland – the *Avoca* – in 1908 and this set off a chain of events that resulted in the BIM designing several standard boats for the Irish fisheries. The best known of these was perhaps the BIM fifty-footers, eighty-eight of which were built between the mid-1950s and late 1960s.[6]

Pretty ring-net boats lined up at Carradale, north of Campbeltown on the Kintyre peninsula. Always varnished, these boats were built both on the Scottish east coast and by Nobles of Girvan on the west.

In conclusion, British and Irish boatbuilders have undoubtedly produced some of the finest fishing boats the world has seen. I was reminded of the great days of Scottish boatbuilding by a clip of a film I saw recently. This was the Gosling fifteen-minute short, *Build Me Straight*, well worth watching. It begins with the naval architect – complete with his Senior Service fags of course – putting the finishing touches to one of his drawings of a boat, the type of which is given away by the model of a fishing boat on his desk. The scene changes abruptly to the sections being fared on the mould loft floor before it switches again to the felling of an oak tree. Then the building of the vessel gets underway, starting with the keel and sternpost. The date is 1963 and the yard William Weatherhead's of Cockenzie. The film then highlights the building of the vessel from fixing frames and steaming and nailing the planking, to laying the deck and caulking. This is in the days before disposable saws and electric planers and there's plenty of adze work for the workforce. Once the structure is completed the tanks are manhandled in and the smart new pill-box wheelhouse craned aboard with a man crouched on the roof. The eight-cylinder engine – looks like a Gardner to me – is also craned in and suddenly the hull is varnished and the local sign-writer has arrived to paint on the registration – BA208. The game is given away and we realise we have just watched the birth of the renowned Sloan family ringer-netter *Wistaria* which, as many Clyde fishermen will tell you, was a good boat, neighbouring with the *Watchful*, BA124, at the ring-net. She slides down the ways into the water and sits proud and high in the water before being fitted out. Then she's towed over to the quay in preparation and, as the lines are thrown ashore, we are given a profile view of her. How pretty she is with her extreme sheer line, especially in the upturned stern. Suddenly the continuity of the film is lost and we are aboard the ringer, *Maryeared* TT57, built for the McAlpine family of Tarbert, as she heads out to sea for her trials. Both boats look wonderful in their varnished elegance. *Maryeared* is, as far as I know, still afloat, in Brixham, I'm told, though I had a look while recently there and couldn't see her.

It's one of those moments where the viewer is taken back to the heyday of wooden fishing boatbuilding, when health and safety was only a figment of someone's imagination, when phone numbers were just four figures before STD codes, before hard hats replaced flat caps, when people could smoke to help them concentrate on the job at hand and when wooden ladders were homemade. An era, that is, that many yearn back to – judging by some boat-builders, some still adhere to the same rules!

Wooden boats continued to be built into the very last decade of the twentieth century, this one at Macduff Shipyards in about 1998. (*Courtesy of Bodie's of Banff*)

14

FISHERMEN AND FAMILY

There's no doubt that fishermen the world over were once a unique and remarkable band of men tied together by the sea, the common bond. Sadly, that has somewhat changed today because of technology though there still remains a very large contingent that still work under the impression that theirs is a livelihood worth cherishing and that their methods and attitudes alone will ensure its survival. Some fishers, who are in the minority of course, are damaging both the marine environment and the fish stocks with their persistence in building and operating vessels that have little concern for what they leave behind, only interested in what they can catch to maximise profit and so ensure continuity in the economic world of today. Ever-increasing efficiency through bigger engines, more electronic screens to stare at, more sophisticated mechanisation in deck gear, hotel-standard accommodation to stay at sea longer – what hope is there for the rest of the world because of those that abuse the sea to appease the bankers and financial institutions that already have much to answer for.

With around 95 per cent of fishers working on what is considered to be a small scale, they are the vast majority who adhere to certain traditions, not for any sentimental reasons but because they have respect for the past and stick to their superstitious prejudices. In Britain the percentage was approximately 78 per cent in 2010.[1] That respect itself is in their genes, nurtured through childhood. It is for the same reason that many of them go into fishing in the first place. Even today there are some that fish because they say it's in the blood: their ancestors did it therefore they do. However, this percentage is now rapidly decreasing as the traditional fishing communities are displaced by the advance of second homes. Where in the past it was local councils who frowned upon the conditions that fishermen lived in, and in some cases transplanted these people onto the periphery of their town or village, nowadays it is those with the money that can afford to have a home in the city and weekend retreat in the country. 'Country' so often means in the middle of a seaside town – and this is most obvious in Cornwall, west Wales, Yorkshire and north Norfolk.

So what exactly is a fishing community? In the same way as, for example, a mining community lived in close-knit quarters, so did fishers. In towns they would generally be housed in one quarter and various examples remain, though perhaps the best is in Aberdeen. Here the fishing quarter was based in Footdee – locally called Fittie – an area of land at the eastern end of the River Dee. It is widely assumed that the name came from 'foot of the Dee' though in actuality it comes as a dedication to St Fothan. The planned housing development was set out in 1809 by the then Superintendent of the town's public works, John Smith, to re-house the fisherfolk from what were considered to be the hovels they were living in previously. These original fishermen of Aberdeen were said to have been a race apart, coming from Scandinavia.[2] The village, when it was built, consisted of two-storey cottages set out originally in two squares of twenty-eight dwellings although various additions were made during the nineteenth century. Furthermore, some of the houses were added to due to the influx of fishermen from outside the town.

In 1885 Footdee was described as a quaint suburb of Aberdeen and at the time had some one hundred families in residence and the writer regarded it, like all others of fisherfolk, as being peculiar, though differing from those of other working people:

> In many things the Footdee people are like the gipsies. They rarely marry except with their own class; and those born in a community of fishers seldom leave it, and very seldom engage in any other avocation than that of their fathers. The squares of houses at Footdee are peculiarly constructed. There are neither doors nor windows in the outside walls, although these look to all points of the compass; and none live within the square but the fishermen and their families, so that they are as completely isolated and secluded from public gaze as a regiment of soldiers within the dead walls of a barrack ... the total population of the two squares was 584 – giving about nine inmates for each of the two-roomed houses. But the case is even worse than the average indicates. 'In the South Square only eight of the houses are occupied by single families; and in the North Square only three, the others being occupied by at least two families each – one room apiece – and four single rooms in the North Square contain two families each! There are thirty-six married couples and nineteen widows in the twenty-eight houses; and the number of district families in them is fifty-four.' The Fittie men seem poorer than the generality of their brethren. They purchase the crazy old boats of other fishermen, and with these, except on very fine weather, they dare not venture very far from 'the seething harbour-bar;' and

the moment they come home with a quantity of fish the men consider their labours over, the duty of turning the fish into cash devolving, as in all other fishing communities, on the women. The young girls or 'queans,' as they are called in Fittie, carry the fish to market, and the women sit there and sell them; and it is thought that it is the officious desire of their wives to be the treasurers of their earnings, that keeps the fishermen from being more enterprising. The women enslave the men to their will, and keep them chained under petticoat government. Did the women remain at home in their domestic sphere, looking after the children and their husbands' comforts, the men would then pluck up spirit and exert themselves to make money in order to keep their families at home comfortable and respectable. Just now there are many fishermen who will not go to sea as long as they imagine their wives have got a penny left from the last hawking excursion.[3]

Bertram doesn't speak too highly of the Footdee fishers but he did also quote a local journalist who countered the claim that they were 'a dirtily-inclined and degraded people' by writing that he found their houses 'clean, sweet and wholesome' on inspection. The walls were whitewashed, the furniture well-rubbed, the bedding clean and the floors freshly sanded though one might wonder why he was looking into the bedding, and why the floors were freshly sanded. Presumably well-rubbed furniture suggests it was dusted and polished. Nevertheless, the unnamed journalist presented a picture of tidiness and order not normally associated with fishers and suggested that this picture was seldom seen in the classes of the population on a higher social scale. The mention of nineteen widows brings to life the horror of fishing when women are left alone by tragedies among the fisherfolk, something mentioned in earlier chapters and which again hammers home the dangerous reality of this occupation.

Whereas Footdee was part of a much larger city, the coast of Britain is littered with small fishing communities that have existed just on their own, out on a limb so to speak. A fine example of a planned fishing settlement is Low Newton-by-the-Sea, mentioned in Chapter 4. Nestling on the very edge of the Northumberland coast, some half way between the harbours of Beadnell and Craster which are some six miles apart, there's a terrace of houses on three sides of a square with the open side facing the sea. Situated at the northern end of Low Newton Bay, the top of the beach is almost at the point where the last house ends, so close to it are the cottages. These were built as fishermen's cottages in the eighteenth century although it is certain that some form of housing for fishermen existed prior to this as the fishing is said to date back at least to the fourteenth century and probably beyond. Originally called Newton Seahouses, to distinguish it from North Sunderland Seahouses (later to become just Seahouses) the Square, as it is known, has since been added to and the cottages are all rented out as holiday homes, although the Ship Inn, formerly the Smack Inn, occupies the northwest corner and is said to be older than the cottages themselves. Now belonging to the National Trust, the settlement formerly belonged to Newton Hall. The coastguard cottages were added about 1829. The Square exists as only one of two sets of 'Seahouses' left in Northumberland. Craster, the home of the famous Craster kipper, was once Craster Seahouses, where new houses were built in about 1780 for fishing families on a vacant plot of land by the sea on the south side of the stream that runs into Craster Haven.[4]

However, of course, many fishermen lived in communities that were planned for that purpose. The British Fisheries Society, as mentioned in an earlier chapter, financed the building of several herring stations in Scotland. Apart from Pultneytown, Wick, on the northeast tip of Scotland, which flourished as Europe's herring capital in the mid-nineteenth century, the only other settlement of success was Ullapool, on Loch Broom. Here today the orderliness of the housing is obvious – long straight roads parallel to the shore and each other, with crossing roads at right angles. Aberaeron, in west Wales, is today a well laid out Georgian town dating from the early nineteenth century with a harbour and warehouses and, it is said, a fleet of sixty herring boats. However, it would seem that the town could not support a year-round herring fishery and that the fishing was supplemented by shipbuilding and the export of grain and lead ore.[5]

Fishermen always needed space to store gear, whether sails, nets or pots. On the Moray Firth, a typical fisherman's house of the mid-nineteenth century had two or three rooms (as at Footdee) with lean-to sheds. New houses had tiled or slate roofs though the older ones still had turf on the roof. Larger houses had part, or all, of the upper floor given over to a spacious loft area where gear could be stored and nets mended. These lofts would have a separate entrance by an outside staircase and, even in the twentieth century, houses where the upper floor was confined to storage were being built in some ports and fishing stations. But, as standardisation became the norm, the postwar fishermen had to do with the same type of house as other workers, be they bakers, butchers, candlestick makers or any other labouring workers.[6]

Fishing, as has been shown, was always a family affair though it was the wife that literally knitted the family together, she being the catalyst for the marital bond. Or at least this was the case before the days of the second half of the twentieth century – postwar Britain really – transformed Britain into something unrecognisable a century before. In those older times it was the wife who was in control and, as Bertram saw, it was she that ran the family income, looked after the home and brought up the children. It was she that induced

The net sheds of Hastings, recently restored using Heritage Lottery funding.

BRIGHTON. - The Fish Market

Brighton fish market under the Arches. Selling the catch at market was usually the domain of the wife, much in the same way as the women hawked around the countryside in rural fishing communities.

the early sense of tradition in the children to play their part so that their contribution was widely recognised. The wife, herself coming from a fishing family, knew too well the future that lay ahead for her offspring and that there was no escape. Thus the children helped out in various ways – picking mussels or whelks or whatever shellfish was needed for bait, to dig for worms in some cases, to bait the long-lines, to repair nets, bark them, repair the boat and even going out to sea at a tender age.

Furthermore, in the great days of the Scottish herring fishery, it was young women (both wives and daughters) that did the curing, working for the fish curers around the country: we shall learn of these girls, and the stout women they turned into, in the next chapter. In Morecambe Bay, the women, both young and old, worked in the local shrimp factory, shelling the shrimps because it was considered that this tedious job after the boiling was only women's work.

Women in fishing communities had many roles apart from the immediate ones within the home. Various photographs available today show women of a particular build carrying their menfolk out to their boat, thus ensuring at least that they set out to sea in a state of dryness although they probably wouldn't remain so for long. Although they seldom sailed out aboard the boat – superstition wouldn't allow women aboard – their fishing work didn't stop once their husbands had sailed off. They might pick shellfish for bait or to sell, check the finances, buy and cook food, do the weekly washing, repair clothes, knit ganseys (the traditional jerseys of most fishers) or simply keep the home tidy. On top of that they bore children, and that in itself, when added to the general debilitating effect of the hard work upon their bodies, increased the danger of premature death.

Peter Frank uses the example of Maud, the eldest daughter of Jane Harland, who unwittingly came into the role as fisherman's wife when her mother died after giving birth to her tenth child who was twenty-one years Maud's junior. Maud had vowed not to marry into fishing since childhood, prompted, probably by her parents who shared the same belief that the life was too hard. She saw her father get up at 2 a.m. to check the weather and then he'd come back and rouse the family. Maud used to wish that 't'cobles wouldn't get off today'. Once her father had gone she'd start work on the mussels. Until she married five years later a bricklayer, she started every day thus and the worst was when the mussels were frozen in winter, 'You got bad fingers with them.' It was work of the sheer 'wearying, unremitting repetitiveness' type indeed.[7]

In many parts of Britain we come across colourful fishwives: Newhaven, Edinburgh and Llangwm, Pembrokeshire being two examples many miles apart. In Cullercoats, Northumberland, there's a good description of their work from 1838:

> The duties performed by the wives and daughters of the Cullercoats fishermen are very laborious. They search for bait – sometimes digging sand-worms in the muddy sand at the mouth of the Coble-dean, at the head of North Shields; gathering muscles [sic] on the Scalp, near Clifford's Fort; or gathering limpets and dog crabs among the rocks near Tynemouth; – they also assist in baiting the hooks. They carry the fish which are caught to North Shields, in large wicker baskets called creels, and they also sit in the market there to sell them. When fish are scarce, they not infrequently carry a load on their shoulders, weighing between three and four stone, to Newcastle, which is about ten miles distant from Cullercoats, in the hope of meeting with a better market.[8]

The Yorkshire photographer Fisher of Filey made various studio portraits of fisherwoman in their so-called 'traditional dress', this being the costume of their work. It was intended to be warm for working on the shore, and consisted of woollen jerseys worn under bodices, shawls, cloaks, bonnets, aprons, thick woollen socks and strong shoes.[9] The fisherwomen of the Penclawdd cockle fishery commonly walked to the market at Swansea, carrying a basket in each hand and another on their head. They walked the first seven miles to Olchfa barefoot before donning boots after washing their feet in the stream.

A typical fish wife from Llangwm in Pembrokeshire. These women walked miles hawking the day's catch around the locality.

On the return journey, after hopefully selling the catch, they filled their baskets with provisions for the family.[10] Similarly the women of Llangwm, a small community on the western shore of the River Cleddau, were well known for hawking herring, salmon, oysters, shrimps and cockles around the locality. These women controlled all aspects of the fishery and no merchants were ever employed. Their clothing was equally well known and recognisable by their colourful tweed dresses, aprons and black felt hats, and they for speaking their own dialect of Welsh. One woman, Dolly Palmer, was known for her strength and beauty and was even interviewed by the *Daily Mail*.[11]

For the majority of fishwives, when the husband was out sailing, there was always one thing in the back of her mind. The constant worry was that he might never return, and many a woman might keep one eye checking on the clouds from time to time. A Mrs Harrison gave an apt description of how a woman did feel when her husband was out in rough weather. This was in the 1960s:

I know my boy goes to sea and he's got a dangerous job working off the Shetlands, but when he goes I expect him to come back. My husband had some very narrow escapes during the war and he's been overboard about three times but I don't expect him to go and drown either, I think that's the only way you can look at it unless you're going to worry yourself sick all the time. I've been very worried once – though that wasn't until after it occurred. It was ten or twelve years ago when he was out herring catching with his younger brother off Caister. October or November, and the net must have fouled the cork that bungs the bottom of the boat. They had seven cran of herring on board and their boat sank under it. Fortunately the corks on the herring nets just kept her buoyant so she was level with the top of the water. They burned their shirts, burnt everything they could but nobody saw her, not even the coastguards, until at last a fishermen did notice and took them into Caister. I can always remember – he must have gone up to the Caister lifeboat house and rung me at about two o'clock in the morning. He said, 'Well thank God I can hear your voice, thank God I can still talk to you.' I thought what on earth has happened, does he want me there? But he said 'Somebody is going to bring us home, will you be prepared to get up early in the morning to go to Caister and help salvage anything we can?' It's strange because we had every faith in this boat, she's still being used down at Sheringham. After that I was sort of sick for a fortnight. But he had two boats. He couldn't use that one because the engine had got water in it, so that was a big set-back, but he'd had the other built. He came home, got the mechanic to make sure the engine was all right, pushed it down and went off the next night. Just like that, because he had to go again.[12]

Belgian fisherwomen with their shrimp nets which they push through the shallow water over sand. Others work on horseback with trawls, similar to the Morecambe fishers who didn't ride the horse but worked from a cart.

In some parts of the world the women were fishers. In Britain this was mostly confined to cockle picking on the sands of Morecambe Bay or around the Bury Inlet and River Towy in South Wales. Good examples of these robust women also once worked in Belgium and France picking shellfish from the beaches as well as picking crabs from rocks and using nets in the shallow water to catch shrimps. As in Britain, the French women who sold the catch wore colourful traditional dress and, in one instance in 1908, the President M. Fallieres met a band of these women to pay homage to their work at Dunkirk.[13]

These fishing communities were, to a great extent, self-sufficient. They had no need for outside help as the jobs within the community stayed within. The fishermen themselves were either perfect examples of God-fearing men, taking their religious beliefs seriously or, in some cases, they were the exact opposite, regarding their contemporaries as pious fools. Much has been written about these religious attitudes.

The only things they imported were their boats and its gear, although some communities had their own boatbuilder, sometimes an itinerant jobbing boatbuilder who would build to order on the local beach or field. Hemp first, then cotton, netting was bought in although the job of setting up a drift-net or whatever was done by the fishermen. Nets were barked periodically to prevent their rot in seawater until manmade materials arrived in the twentieth century. To do this, a tannin-strong solution was made up. Oak bark was used extensively and records of Welsh trade show huge amounts being brought in from Ireland while some was also exported from South Wales. The solution was made by boiling up the bark in water in a huge vat. Often such a container, with a fire below, was set up in a harbour so that all the fishermen could use it, and often they worked cooperatively, helping each other in the work. The net would be dropped in using an A-frame to hoist it, and then left for sometime before being hauled out and hung to dry of the net poles. All harbours had net poles as the old nets were often hung up to dry after each use at sea. Sometimes they were hauled up the mast of a boat to dry in the same way.

Cutch – or catechu to give it its proper name – was adopted in the late nineteenth century and is a preservative made from the acacia tree of the Indian subcontinent. It arrived in Britain as a brittle rectangular lump in a wooden box, packed around with large leaves, the box measuring about 18in by 12in by 8in. It was made in India by boiling the wood and bark of the acacia – especially the species *Acacia catechu* – in water and then evaporating the resultant brew. The fishermen then broke up the lump which was not unlike treacle toffee in brittleness, and added it to boiling water before immersing their nets. Cutch was also used in the dying and leather industries, and thus was used by the fishermen to tan their sails. Other additives were included when tanning sails to help preserve them, among which were unsavoury substances such as rancid butter, dog faeces and other compounds that are there to generally fix the dye. Nowadays powders such as quebracho are used with dyes and other modern fixing agents. But, there again, no fisherman these days tans his sails: that's left to the enthusiast with his restored traditional boat!

It's a strange thing but some boats used to tan their sails red while the majority of fishermen coloured theirs brown. Red, you see, is a colour that was regarded unlucky in many quarters, as was green. 'Red and green should not be seen, except upon a Derby Queen' goes the saying, though how the fact that some fishing boats were painted green (and red) equates to this is unknown. Superstitions, after all, are negotiable, in that they differ from port to port. Some were sacrosanct throughout the fleets: no red-haired women aboard, don't whistle up the wind, etc. Many animals could not be mentioned aboard: rabbits, pigs, rats, monkeys, ferrets and salmon were variously referred to as 'moppies', 'curly tails', 'long tails', 'hairy faces', 'futtrets' and 'red fish' though even here there were regional differences. In and around

Campbeltown rabbits were 'bunnies', salmon 'billies' and pigs 'doorkies'. The custom of speaking these words was so imprinted on the minds of fishermen and their families that Angus Martin relates a story told by George Newlands of Campbeltown of how a young fisherman's son Willie insisted in saying 'P-i-g ... doorkie' instead of 'P-i-g ... pig' in lessons because 'My daddy'll no let me say that', referring to the actual word 'pig'![14] Just why are these particular animals taboo? It has been pointed out that pigs, unlike most farmed animals, are bred only to eat while others such as hens, cows and sheep have a dual purpose though whether this makes any difference is unknown. Rabbits are pests and game as well as pets in some cases. There's an instance of a fisherman hunting and hanging dead rabbits in his fish hold only to find the night's fishing so abundant that the hold was full of herring. So you can shoot them, eat them, bait your creels with them and hang them in the hold to bring luck: but don't mention them in word! But that's the point about superstition; they are completely contradictory and often seem whimsical to outsiders.[15]

Martin also tells us of various other superstitions from around the Clyde. Stones were used in the ballast of the Lochfyne skiffs as they were in many other areas. White stones were considered unlucky in both Kintyre and Ayrshire, these being referred to as 'chuckies' in that they were thrown overboard. A white handled knife was another no-no. But over on the east coast of Scotland it was deemed lucky to have a few white and red stones in the ballast as these were supposed to possess magical properties.[16] In some communities it was bad luck to take ballast stones from one boat and put them into a new boat.

Swan Vesta matches were deemed unlucky to have aboard by some simply by association with swans because they were neither sea birds nor land birds. When the swans were rarely encountered, the superstition was transferred just to the matches and there's a tale of how a boy was sent off for matches to the local Dunure shop and when he came back the skipper saw that they were the taboo matches and threw them over the side.[17]

Simply journeying to work and meeting certain people can result in fishermen turning round and going back home, refusing to set out to sea. Confront a priest or man of the cloth, a cat or certain women, especially those with red hair or physical deformities, and many fishermen would first attempt not to cross their path on the way to the boat and if they did, delay – or even postpone – their trip out. Martin mentions one fisherman passing a tramp and if seen or greeted would return home, sprinkle salt over his shoulder before setting out once more. Catherine Czerkawska recalls the Girvan chimney sweep Hughie Clark, who some regarded as blighting their day and notes that chimney sweeps generally tend to be blackened as ministers are dressed in black, which might explain their taboo given that the extremes of black and white have great significance in superstitious contexts.[18]

The skipper is often the most superstitious aboard and he alone can delay the day's fishing. Starting out on Friday is deemed unlucky, especially if the weather has delayed the fishing until then. 'Crows don't build on Friday' they say.[19] Neither should new boats be launched on a Friday. Mondays were bad days to some, as was the thirteenth of the month, although the peril of Friday the thirteenth is recognised throughout society. Don't borrow things on a Monday either, though it has been said that fishing on a 'bad' day would often bring you a good catch if you dared venture out.[20] A boat should never be turned against the sun when fishing, steaming or manoeuvring. Hatch boards should never be turned upside-down, as shouldn't baskets, boxes and pond boards, as otherwise the boat itself might capsize. Eggshells should be crushed when throwing overboard or otherwise they will float along, following as 'witches boats'. Another 'witch' superstition or ritual is the 'burning out of the witch' when fishing is bad. This involves lighting an oily rag and wafting it around all the nooks and crannies in the boat and shouting at the same time, chasing the witch and her bad luck away.

Superstitions were also real for those left ashore. Women would not comb their hair at night when the menfolk were at sea for fear that they would be drowned with their feet entangled in it. Neither would they allow their men to wear clothes dyed with *crotal*, a lichen, because the belief was that crotal would go back to the rock from whence it had come.[21]

Superstitions survived the end of the working life of a boat. In Llangwm, in southwest Wales, a fisherman there refused to part with one of the last small compass-net boats when the author asked about it, although it was already in a derelict state. He wanted it to rot away where it was. Martin recalls a story told by Donald MacVicar of Kames, where a fisherman left a perfectly good boat on the shore to rot rather than selling it and one explanation is that the fishermen believed they would live until the boat they have abandoned began to fall apart.[22] When researching the history of the Lochfyne skiffs, the author remembers Neil MacDougall of Carradale telling him how one skiff his father built, the *Clan Matheson*, was scuttled off Plockton as the owner did not want to sell her on. Another MacDougall boat, the *Clan MacDougall*, CN9, was allowed to rot away on Port Righ beach, Carradale, a similar fate awaiting the *Maggie MacDougall*, CN65.[23] This is one reason that few Lochfyne skiffs survived into the late twentieth century, although their light construction might have exacerbated the situation.

Few superstitions involve luck and this is thought to be because fishing itself is basically insecure and dangerous and thus bad luck is more likely than the good variety. On the other hand, you'd be forgiven for thinking that, just because it is a dangerous job, they would be in need of more good luck. A coin under a mast was always a good omen and a John Dory left on top of the wheelhouse is considered lucky, though maybe not for the fish!

Holiday-makers coming ashore after a short trip around the bay. Fishermen often made more money from this work than from fishing in the peak of the holiday season.

Two things fishermen do learn are about the weather and local knowledge. Haloes around the moon are a sure sign of wind and various colourings in the clouds foretell of bad weather. However, as we've seen, they weren't always right when recognising approaching bad weather. It is said that the fishermen of the haaf fishery in Shetland, and those from the north of Lewis, could interpret the weather by watching waves and how the mother wave came at them. Being out in a small open boat many miles from the sight of land meant they learned quick. Barometers were placed in various harbours in the nineteenth century so that these could contribute to warnings of gales to come.

But it was their knowledge of the local area, gleaned from years of experience from fishing around the small coves and rocky reefs that was so useful. Many fishermen joined the local lifeboat crew after the introduction of lifesaving boats in the early nineteenth century, both for this local knowledge and their seamanship qualities. This remains so even today when many a longshore fisherman is a member of the RNLI's crew.

We've already seen that fishing was never an occupation with set annual earnings, unlike other labouring jobs. This, too, remains the case today. The share system has been around for a long time even if some fishers did not benefit, as in the case of the truck system in outlying parts of Scotland. Seldom did a crew get a fixed wage even through a particular fishing season. Occasionally a hand might get an advance to join a crew but the share system ensured that the boat and its gear were paid for before the crew, and that the skipper received more than the boy at the bottom of the ladder (literally when redding the header rope!). Nevertheless, skippers and boat owners were able to earn huge amounts when the fishing was good and prices high. Areas of the country abound with grand houses that were built upon the backs of fish, and especially from the herring.

There's a belief among many parts of society that fishermen are huge drinkers of alcohol. It has been said that the vice of drunkenness is a stumbling block which fishermen are liable to fall over.[24] These probably stem from the days when some were said to have been paid in whisky but are wholly exaggerated. Captain John Washington did find that the fishers of the east coast of Scotland did receive whisky but not in total payment, and he advocated this practice was ended. Others profess that they drink when the fishing is good from the profit and then, when it is bad, drink to drown their sorrows. Surely this is the case in many professions when the pay is erratic – princely at times of plenty and impoverishment at times of emptiness.

However, having said that, the drink was obtainable in the days of trawling the North Sea under sail. Grog-ships, called 'copers' from the Dutch *koper*, to barter, were old fishing smacks coming from continental ports selling cheap liquor and tobacco. The fishermen were attracted to them with the promise of one drink to relieve the boredom and hard labour of fishing. But the liquor was often raw spirits and fishermen were sometimes poisoned by it, others acting in a violent way or even becoming demented. A ration of rum might be served in the Royal Navy, but the rum served here was called by the fishermen 'chain lightning' such was its effect. It was also one reason for the great loss of life.[25]

In 1893 the North Sea Fishing Act made it illegal to sell alcohol to fishermen at sea, and for them to purchase it. The copers simply went elsewhere, though a few still worked around the North Sea. This fact alone encouraged the young missionary Ebenezer Mather to raise money to buy and fit out an old smack for trawling, and crew her with evangelists to spread the Christian word among the deep-sea fishermen. His ultimate aim was to have such a vessel among all the fishing fleets, which would be a floating church, a dispensary, library and temperance hall, according to James Dyson, and which Mather himself described as 'a veritable anti-coper'. Thus the *Ensign*, his first vessel, set sail from Yarmouth on 7 July 1882 to the scorn of fishermen. But, contrary to those sceptical fishermen, Mather's movement gathered pace when he bought duty-free tobacco at Ostend and sold it to the fishermen at the same price, under-cutting the copers. The fishermen were given a cup of tea aboard, clothing was supplied, first aid given out, songs sung and prayers said. Within two years the Mission to Deep-Sea Fishermen was born and by 1890 there were eleven vessels, the so-called Bethel Ships – preaching the message of God. Many fishermen, as we've seen, were God-fearing folk and it seems they didn't need too much persuasion in some parts. Thus today's Royal National Mission to Deep-Sea Fishermen evolved, an established institution that remains in the forefront of helping fishermen and their families at difficult times. Not only do they provide shelter, but on a daily basis they open their doors so that fishermen can meet, eat and shower at many venues dotted around British fishing ports. As a charity, they are financed wholly by donations, and make a massive contribution to the fortunes of fishermen everywhere.[26]

Much of their work involves working with the bereaved families of missing fishermen. When a boat is lost and crew members die, the local branch of the RNMDSF comes to the rescue. A colleague volunteers to help and sometimes tells me about the work he does. A family needs comfort in many different ways – from purely financial to emotional help, from form-filling to dealing with funerals. Injured fishermen receive help in different ways though they are just as needy. A fisherman recently lost fingers in the winch and my colleague spent many an hour helping him to readjust to life ashore. The State doesn't recognise urgency and sometimes it can take ages for restitution to occur. The Mission steps in as a buffer. Fishing, as we've seen, is a dangerous occupation and it is not always death that destroys a man's earning capability.

Nevertheless, fishermen do still drink though rarely at sea. Often, when back from several days or weeks at sea, and armed with a bunch of wages, he'll hit the shore hard, pubs in fishing ports being renowned for their often rowdy behaviour. But who wouldn't relax after spending hard days afloat without much except the monotonous routine that fishing can be. Look at the figures again for 1909 and we see that seventeen fishermen were killed returning to their vessel while another eight fell into the dock and most were presumably under the influence. This represents some 11 per cent of the total deaths of fishermen. This is almost double the percentage of deaths attributed to drink of the crews of seagoing trading vessels.[27]

Fishermen have always been able to earn good wages at certain times (while at others they are awful). So, with good wages, they play hard, though dependency on drugs – especially class As – has become a major problem in some communities, just as they have in towns up and down Britain which are totally unattached to the stresses of fishing. That's the nature of today's modern world where fishermen have lost much of their former identity and as likely a fisherman can come from an inland town, attracted by the call of the sea, even though there's no history there. Traditions linger through sentiment in many cases and these are fading very quickly, to the ultimate detriment of us all.

15

WOMEN IN FISHING

In 1861 there were 42,571 fishermen and boys engaged in the herring fishery in Scotland and that part of England over which the Scottish Fishery Board had jurisdiction. Something like 900 million herrings were caught that year and much of this fish was landed into Wick. All these herrings were either salt-cured or smoked, and for this an army of herring lassies was employed to gut the millions of fish.

Drawn mostly from the coastal villages of Scotland, women and girls alike flocked to the towns and villages where the fishing boats were landing their vast amounts of the fish. In 1862 it is said that there were 3,500 herring lassies – as they became known – gutting 50 million herring over a two-day period and more than 800,000 barrels were cured in total that year in Scotland.[1]

These girls, leaving their districts probably for the first time, followed the fleets down the coast, from the spring and early summer fishery off northeast Scotland, perhaps up to Shetland to begin with, and gradually down the east coast to the autumnal fishery off East Anglia. Some went west, travelling to the west coast, the Outer Hebrides and over to Ireland. For example, Annie Watt, born in Peterhead, worked at Ardglass for seven weeks and arrived in Gorleston, near Great Yarmouth in 1908 for the first time. Often she then returned to Ireland for the winter fishery after maybe a few days at home over Christmas. Like many of these Scots girls, she eventually married and settled in Yarmouth.[2]

Many young herring lassies came from Stornoway in the Outer Hebrides where work was hard to come by. Mrs Mary Keating was one such woman who travelled south from there in the 1920s and worked various herring fisheries until she arrived in Passage East, in County Waterford, working at the Fish House built by Arthur C. Miller in 1901. Mary eventually settled in Passage East and married, her daughter Peggy O'Neill (née Keating) living in nearby Dunmore East.[3]

Others went over to the Isle of Man and parts of Wales. In 1912, the year before the peak of the herring fishery, there were some 10,800 women and girls on the move from Scotland, mostly from the Highlands of Scotland but not exclusively so. 1913 saw 854 million herring being landed into East Anglia in just fourteen weeks, almost all of which was gutted by the herring lassies, though it is impossible to estimate how many lassies were working in Yarmouth and Lowestoft. The nearest estimate is that 2,400 girls worked the Shetland season that year and that 1,600 of these later travelled to these two towns, although there were most likely to have been other girls coming from other directions.[4] However you look at it, this annual migration of this female workforce lasted for almost a century and is unique in British history on such a scale. The 1960s seemed to have brought the phenomenon to an end, when, in 1962, it was reported that only a handful of girls – less than a dozen – were still at work and by 1968 there were none.

So how did the system work? It was down to the curers to find their own workforce and many of the new girls were recruited by agents of the different curers who travelled around the fishing villages before the season started. These agents tended to recruit whole crews, each crew consisting of two gutters and one packer and on signing up for the season's work each girl would receive an initial payment – the so-called 'arles' from the Gaelic *a earlais* – which was around ten shillings at the turn of the century. By the 1920s this was three pounds and it guaranteed that the crew would stay with that curer for the whole of that season. Most of the girls were young and some started at the tender age of fourteen, though by the time war had ended in 1945 the average age of the women was much higher.

Once the arles was paid and the job confirmed, each girl would then pack everything she needed for a period away from home that could last several months. In went workwear, her Sunday best, bedding, the tools of the job (knives and sharpening stone), knitting needles and wool, toiletries, a plate, mug and cutlery and, finally, a bible into a wooden trunk or chest often called a 'kist'. Travel was arranged by the curer or his agent who would supply train or boat tickets. Some even chartered special trains just for their lassies down to East Anglia, these departing from towns such as Fraserburgh, Oban, Mallaig, Kyle of Lochalsh and Aberdeen.[5] Sometimes the luggage went by lorry. George Davidson who worked for A. Bruce & Co., fish curers of Fraserburgh in the 1930s, recalled that the kists went down to Yarmouth on the back of the company's Austin lorry at 40mph while the gutting crews went by train.[6]

Once the crews had arrived at the fishing port they would be allotted lodging with a family or in a boarding house at best, though in the more outlying fishing stations such as in Orkney and Shetland, or on the west coast of Scotland, they were often housed in wooden huts built for the purpose. These were usually very basic accommodation and the girls would have a small stove to cook on. In the bigger ports the landlady would often cook the food provided by the girls as part of the service. Up to the First World War, lodging cost somewhere in the region of 3s 6d a week. Such was the constant stink of fish about the girls that most landladies removed the carpets before the start of the season, replacing these with straw mats which could be thrown out at the season's end. It was not uncommon for three girls to share one bed. Tradition has it that they were often woken up at five o'clock in the morning with a bang on their door and the cry 'Get up and tie your fingers', a reference to the 'cloots' or bandages with which they wrapped their fingers, tied on with bits of old rag, to protect them from cuts and the salt. They dressed in warm clothes to counter the often cold windy spaces they worked in and their outerwear consisted of rubber boots and oilskin aprons.

Work started early in the morning when the first boats came in, though Trevor Lummis notes that sometimes they worked through the night, 'from 10 am to 4 o'clock the next morning'.[7] The herring was carried from the boat by the labourers and placed into the long trough called a 'farlane' where it was roused in salt by the coopers who would otherwise be busy making barrels. The girls stood at the farlane and gutted – or 'gypped' – the herring at great speed, using their small, sharp knife. In one easy movement they inserted the knife into the belly, and with a quick twist, the guts and gills came out and dropped into a basket. The herring was then thrown into one of five tubs which, when full, were neatly packed into more barrels in a very neat way, the herring dark side up on the bottom layer, and alternatively afterwards, each layer being roused in salt, until the top layer with the silver belly up. The barrel was sealed and left for several days before being opened and the brine poured off. By this time the herring would have shrunk as its moisture was removed, and the barrel was topped up from another cured barrel, before being resealed and the brine added through a bung hole. It was eventually branded under the eye of the Fisheries Officer using a brass stencil and the various Scottish Crown brands were recognised throughout Europe as guarantees of quality.

Many of the best girls gutted at the rate of one a second, i.e. sixty a minute or 3,600 an hour. Thus a crew of two gutters working up to twelve hours a day could rack up a total of over 85,000 a day, though in reality the figure was probably nearer 60,000, taking into account the time to move the baskets to the barrels and breaks. With a barrel holding between 700 and 1,000 fish, this meant that some seventy-five barrels could, in theory, be filled a day, though it would be difficult to maintain this over a long period. However, one report does state that one crew produced 288 barrels in four working days of twelve hours each when the fishing was 'big' and the crew 'good'.[8]

Wages were generally paid hourly rate with extra barrel money and a living allowance paid on top. Gracie Stewart was 19 when she was photographed topping up a barrel at Lowestoft in 1904. She was from Buckie on the Moray

Herring lassies at work at the farlane. The number of barrels in the background shows the massiveness of the industry. Barrel-making – or cooperage – was itself a huge business.

Gracie Stewart filling herring barrels with brine. This is one of the most enduring photos of the curing process and contrasts the young woman's beauty and radiance with the smell, the grime and the gloupy liquid of the job at hand.

Firth and she later married and settled in Lowestoft and had two sons and a daughter. However, at the time of the photograph her granddaughter estimated she was earning a halfpenny an hour and received another ten shillings at the end of the season. Contemporary evidence suggests a weekly wage of between 8s and 17s 6d and an extra hourly rate for topping up the barrels of between 3 and 6d. Before 1914 the average take-home pay was in the region of ten shillings which had risen to one pound ten years later. The arles was in addition to these figures and it is said that the girl responsible for packing the barrels negotiated with the curer over the rates of pay and other engagement terms.[9]

Sunday was never worked and the previous Saturday night was for dancing or going to the pictures and work finished early so that they could get back to their lodgings to get ready. A night at the pictures cost fourpence, according to Annie Watt.[10] Any spare time in between was spent knitting. Sunday were reserved for religious observance and Sunday schools, and a visit to the Fishermen's Mission at four o'clock to listen to the weekly fishermen's singing. Their best dresses, carefully kept in their kists for the occasion, were brought out while their working clothes were hung out to dry after a morning's washing.

The annual report of the Chief Inspector of factories and workshops of 1901 was severely critical of the working conditions of the herring lassies. Miss Adelaid Anderson reported that 3,000 women in Fraserburgh the previous year were housed in unfurnished sheds where barrels were stored during the winter. They would, according to her, 'bring everything – bedding, cooking utensils, and any furniture they need. In this room they eat, sleep, entertain friends, and perform their domestic duties, with what I can only consider marvellous harmony.' In Yarmouth they worked on unpaved, undrained, uncovered plots of land where the soil was awash with decaying fish.

Not surprisingly, then, strikes were common. When the rates of pay shrank after the First World War when markets disappeared and some curers went bankrupt, the women downed their knives until the curers re-established reasonable rates. Rest rooms, canteens and first aid stations, as well as maximum working hours, were negotiated between the curers and the factory inspectorate after that war. Rest rooms were for use when work was slack and canteens ensured meals could be taken within the time allowed. Previously 'diet time' was not allowed and they had to eat on the hoof, grabbing a watery cup of tea and a few biscuits if they were lucky during the day. First aid points about the curing yard also provided cures for splinters from barrels and salt sores. In 1931 they went on strike again to insist on a minimum weekly wage and, in Yarmouth, agreed to fifteen shillings. Five years later, 4,000 lassies, led by Maria Gott of Rosehearty, went on strike again to regain a shilling for each barrel packed after the rate had been reduced to 10*d* two years previously.[11] They timed the strike to coincide with the busiest time of the season, stopping work for three days before their demands were met. Even though they were not members of any union, and lacked organisational skills, the way the ringleaders moved from yard to yard, spreading the word, was testament to their determination. The curers stopped buying fish so that the fishermen couldn't sell their catch and within hours the industry ground to a halt and was totally paralysed. The amazing thing is that it took three days for the curers to capitulate.[12]

The herring lassie phenomenon has perhaps attracted more nostalgia than any other aspect of the herring fishing trade, more so than the boats and fishermen themselves. The idea of roving hordes of what were on more than one occasion described as 'buxom' women (quite unfairly in this author's opinion as some were extremely beautiful women as in the case of Gracie Stewart), coming from the coastal and highland regions of Scotland, was unheard of at the time, and the air of pride with which they undertook their arduous task has not failed to impress historians and writers alike. Often it is said how they would sing while at work, and when they were not working, they clustered in groups and the only sound heard was the rattle of knitting needles accompanied by the occasional laughter. That they were an unusual band of folk is accounted for by the fact that they invariably came from fishing communities which, as we've seen, were already set apart from the rest of society. Yet they were generally a lively bunch, dancing often while singing when not working.[13] Annie Watt also tells us how they would sing and dance while travelling down from Scotland on the train.[14]

In conclusion, the term 'fisher lassies' is worth noting because it wasn't just the herring that these young women worked at, even if this was where the majority were. Take canning, for instance: Morton's canning factory in Lowestoft employed dozens of girls in the 1920s. Although much of what they pickled was Dutch vegetables out of the herring season, the company had come down from Aberdeen in 1901 to cure and can herrings. A year later the plant was the probably largest canning factory in Britain. Herring lassies worked on a separate pickling plot barrelling fish while on the main site some 20 million herrings were canned. Girls worked in teams in a range of buildings on the site which were devoted to canning. These contained presses, formers, seamers and a lacquering shed where cans of all shapes and sizes were manufactured.[15] Arthur Collins worked there after the Second World War:

> Yes, we had rows o' girls packin' cauliflower, gherkins and silverskin onions in the jars. We had our own pickle boats come over from Holland with cauliflowers and cucumbers and onions, and they used to land on our own

quay ... as soon as the Home Fishing started, everything went over to her-rins. The drifters used to come up-through-bridge and land on our quay and we also had lorries bring stuff up from the fish market ...When the herrins arrived at the factory, they would go to the knobbing machines which cut off the heads and squeezed the guts out. Then they were put into vats, washed around in brine, left in for so long, and eventually taken out and sent to the packing lines ...We did rows [*sic*] as well. They were packed into seven ounce tins, either as hard or soft, and we had quite a good trade in them. See, we used to tin kippers for export, Australia and New Zealand and places, and we had splitting machines to get the herrins ready for curin'. There was a number o' smokehouses there at the factory and then, in the end, the management got a smokin' machine to speed up the job. That was like a great big oven and it cut down the time needed for the smokin' side. Back before the war Morton's used to do a lot o' red herrins and they had their own underground pits where they used to store the fish before they were cured ... Oh yes, we had six or seven lines battin' out the tins. Sometimes we used to get in extra supplies down from Scotland, but the Home Fishing was the main season. When that died away, o' course, canning herrins died away with it, so the firm had to go into other things. We used to do a fish paste, which was mostly made out of whiting, and then there were all the other various products. O' course the factory was originally built for herrins, just like Maconochie's. There was a lot o' herrins done at that place as well when it became the Co-op.[16]

Morton's eventually stopped dealing in herrings in 1956 because of the collapse of the fishery although the company carried on until 1988 canning all number of other products, the last can being one of Redcurrant & Raspberry Fruit Filling.

It was the same in the net-making industry where Minnie Pitcher started working for Stuart & Jacks of Lowestoft in 1919 for 7*s* 6*d* a week. Alongside her, girls were employed as beatsters and braiders, keeping the fleets served with fishing nets. As far as she was concerned, the sons in a family were given a trade whereas the daughters 'went to work to help keep the boys'. In her case her brother got 2*s* 6*d* a week in his apprenticeship while her father, as a coalman, earned eighteen shillings a week. Thus her contribution was regarded as vital to the family's finances and goes some way to explaining why the daughters of fishing families chose to be a fisher lassie, if not a herring lassie![17]

16

MODERN FISHING, THE EU AND LEGISLATION

Ships always seem to have an air of dignity, or so I believed when I was young. This idea, I assume, was nurtured from visits to Liverpool Docks, armed with paper and pencil where I used to go to draw the images of smoky funnels, ocean tramping and the days before the jet engine completely transformed global travel. Later my ship interest waned while I developed a healthy appetite for traditional working boats and the folk that sailed them. Fishing boats became an obvious extension, and later an emphasis. With this came almost a hatred of the larger fishing craft as a result of both their sheer ugliness and their ravishing of the sea. These 'vacuum-cleaners' swept up all within their sights, without any attention to conservation and protectionism. They were simply mechanical monster ships built to rape, or so I thought.

It was with this in mind that, back in about the late 1990s, I caught a train to Aberdeen. I'd decided it was time to experience at first hand this pillaging. Perhaps I was lucky to find anyone to have me aboard for a few days, so vehement had I been in my opposition to their use, especially in inshore waters. From Aberdeen a bus took me to Fraserburgh, so that by ten o'clock that evening I was searching the quayside after my quarry among the numerous boats of all descriptions, big and small.

Daystar, BF250, belonged then to Alec West, and was skippered by his son Alexander, who, judging by the way he reversed and turned her in a dock that was hardly longer than the boat as we departed that evening, knew his boat. At a mere 49.28m in overall length, *Daystar* was by no means the largest of the pelagic purser/trawlers. The 1994-launched Norway-built *Altaire*, LK429, was 243ft (74.06m) long, had a 4331kW (5805hp) engine and could carry, at the maximum, something like an awe-inspiring two and a half thousand tons of fish. Not surprisingly, then, she was at that time the largest tank ship in the UK fleet.

Daystar, though, was perfect for me to learn about the way these fellows caught their herring. She had a 1990kW (2668hp) Caterpillar main engine, and could carry only 300 tons of herring in her tanks, which is pumped from the net through an 18-inch diameter pipe into refrigerated sea water (RSW) tanks.

I quickly did some mental calculations, in awe of these quantities of fish. Imagine an open herring boat of around the end of the last century, say a scaffie from Wick for example. Twenty crans of herring would be deemed an average catch, not brilliant, but neither disastrous. This weighs about three tons, so it follows that one thousand boats would catch 3,000 tons, a thousand boats being something like the number working out of Wick in about 1870, before steam drifters joined in with the fishing. So ten *Daystars* or, would you believe it, one and a bit *Altaire* can catch the same amount as the whole fleet in Wick might catch in one night, give or take a few fish. One thousand boats employed, say, 4,000 fishermen, and probably the same amount again on shore. *Daystar* has up to twelve crew, and perhaps the same are employed ashore. Four thousand jobs for, say, a 150, or much less in the case of the biggest boats. No wonder the conception of modern-day fishing has gone all haywire.

I mulled all this around in my mind as we sped north towards Orkney. After all, the same fate has befallen agriculture, as has most of Europe's industry. Or what is left of it. But, like everything else, it's a question of balance: the advantages of technology versus the old ways of full employment and conservation. And it's pretty obvious that there are at least some advantages in these bigger boats.

Like the increased safety and comfort aboard. No cramped coffin-like bunks here, but double cabins. Mine, which I had to myself, even had a television and video upon the table. There are two flush toilets, a shower and a washing machine. Up above there's a huge mess-room with seating for sixteen people, a galley with fridges, large cooker and washing-up machine and a communal TV. All the comforts of home, in fact. Well nearly! And atop the superstructure there's the bridge, all 20ft by 20ft of it, bristling with sonar screens, fish finders, radars and radio equipment, as well as the normal navigation gear and engine and winch controls. Technological wizardry with state of the art computers that, given a few more years, will completely oversee the fishing procedure. These are what many people believe to be the final death knells to the industry, and there's no stopping it. Progress marches on in its inevitability, and we all have to join the bandwagon to keep in competition, or so we're told. The only debatable point is the stage at which you choose to jump aboard or over the side, as your way of thinking leads. For this still remains a personal choice – just. Although, I must add, these scientific advances do produce positive improvements. Such as the split-beam sonars that can measure the size of fish about to be hoovered into the net. Shoals with a high density of immature fish can technically be avoided. Not that many signs show an improvement in selectability from the fishes' point of view!

Once past Orkney, the job of the ship was to locate the shoals. For us, the only appearances were those on the sonar screen. The lore of the natural appearances is of no consequence to these vessels. Alexander spent his time gazing into this screen and that, moving the range and angle controls of the sonar, altering course to chase a possible hit, and then to consider the viability of the shoal as the fish finder picked it up. Sometimes big red bubbles burst onto the screen, lingering above the seabed. I was instantly reminded of those speech bubbles we all used to read at one time in comics. These were herring, he assured me, but they were few and far between. Mostly the red bubbles hid on the seabed, in the troughs of the rocky uneven ground. For this is where these super-trawlers don't have it all their own way. To set the net over this rough seabed would be likely to result in the loss of the gear, and at £28,000 a time this is deemed a risk too far. We steamed north to Foula, described by one crew-member as the 'arse hole of the world' such was its exposure from the North Atlantic. Still no fish, and then our neighbour boat, another pelagic trawler, the 1974-built *Convallaria*, BF58, developed steering problems. We altered course for Lerwick, on Shetland's east coast.

Bressay Sound, the piece of water that brushes Lerwick's harbour, was once the centre of a vibrant herring fishery. In the days that the Dutch commanded the North Sea fishery, hundreds of their boats would be anchored here. It has been said that there were up to 2,000 Dutch craft here once, although many believe this figure to be exaggerated and 800 is considered more likely. It seems rather irrelevant perhaps, the important factor being the sheer strength of Holland's grip upon the herring fishery. De Caux tells us that, in 1603, their catch was valued at £396,583 from 5,000 vessels, and that 200,000 people were involved in the taking of this fish. This seems a vast sum, and he himself does add that these figures should be taken with a large grain of salt.[1]

After a brief interlude at Lerwick – a chance to look around was an added bonus – we sailed in the early morning at about three o'clock. As darkness fell at about one o'clock, a visible dawn appeared almost immediately. By three it was nearly daylight. A wonderful experience, and, although I'd experienced the same midnight sun in Finland, somehow here, especially off the west of Shetland, it was more memorable.

We did eventually shoot the net, although I've forgotten which day it was on. They all seem to merge into one long day and short night, such was the routine. The only thing that was like clockwork was the feeding of the hungry stomachs, and each morning, anywhere between about ten and twelve o'clock, there was a call over the intercom of 'right boys, breakfast is served in the dining room!' As the normal cook had had to stay at home to go to his mother's funeral, each crew took his turn at the galley. Somehow, though, I managed to avoid this duty, thankfully. The same call came in the evening for the main meal of the day. In between, cups of coffee and a smoke in the drying room.

The first time we shot the net was at night. I remember it well, because the process involved the throwing of a line between the two boats. As it was our net that was to go over the side, *Convallaria* had to come close to us to receive the line, which then had one end of the net attached. Unfortunately, their skipper overestimated his run in, so that, as I gazed out from the side of the bridge, all I could see to my horror was the brightly lit ship poised about ten feet away from our side. Alexander shouted over the radio, and thankfully, *Convallaria* regressed into the darkness, but the episode was a stark reminder about the dangers of securing lines between the vessels to enable pair-trawling to take place. His second run was better, and, after several attempts, the line was across the heaving ocean and passed around their winch. Both ends of the net were cast, and the head ropes let out. This then gave me my first view of the complete net on the sonar screen, where the bottom of the net was clearly visible above the seabed. This height between ground and net was controlled by the winches, and, in theory, the net was streamed so that the green bubbles of herring (they were green on this screen, yet red on the fish finder) were swallowed by the open mouth, just like that infernal 'Pac-man' computer game that whizzes around a screen gulping up a score as it goes. But I was excited, as a constant stream of these bubbles was passing into the net and I anticipated tons and tons of herring. We trawled for a couple of hours before one of the sonic 'eggs' fired off, alerting us to the fact the net was filling. There were four of these eggs on the net, and once all four had fired the net was deemed full. We began hauling even though only one had gone off, yet I still imagined tons and tons of herring. Yet disappointingly there was only seven or eight tons, which wasn't deemed enough to bother starting the pump, so it was discarded so that it just floated away across the sea: dead fish – seven tons of it at somewhere between £150 and £200 a ton? I didn't begin to fathom the sense of this.

Unfortunately, the net became all tangled up during this trawl, caused by problems in the winch mechanism aboard *Convallaria*. However, after a couple of hours, suitable repairs were made, so that we again commenced a trawl, this time using their net. The process of setting the net proceeded, with them passing their end of the net over the stern and sending the line over to us, it being then attached to our winch, and the other end of the net being cast off. The trawl was run out and we steamed along at about four knots. This time I couldn't watch the action on the screen as this is only seen on the sonar set on the one boat whose net was in use. After a similar period as before, we hauled in, passing a line back to *Convallaria* to enable the net to be brought alongside the boat. Unfortunately, our skipper decided to head straight off to Lerwick once more, to disentangle the net ashore, such was the extent of the rat's tail of entanglement. We passed through Bressay Sound once more, with its ghosts of the herring boats lurking beneath the surface. I took an instantaneous decision to catch the ferry back to Aberdeen, such was my uneasiness at taunts of being a Jonah. Yes, for certain, there was most definitely a dearth in herring, but, as Alexander pointed out, we had been fishing two weeks earlier than they had last year. And was I responsible for gear failure aboard *Convallaria*? But it wasn't just that, as I realised I was weary. Not weary of tiredness, but weary of trying to convince myself that what was happening around me was somehow justified in the greater sense of fishing. Deep inside, I felt stirrings of dissatisfaction, a belief that I was party to a plundering process, and approving of it. I wasn't, although I recognised that I didn't have an alternative to offer. I've always believed that criticism is unjustified without the proffering of other options. It really was not a matter of returning to the old ways, no re-rigging our fishing boats with lugsails and single-cylinder petrol/paraffin engines! No turning back, but there must be some change of emphasis to ensure that tons and tons of perfectly good fish aren't just thrown back into the sea. And is it acceptable to send hundreds of tons of fresh fish into fish meal and industrial uses? With a slightly heavy heart I said my farewells and caught the ferry, an expensive and disappointing experience, given poor food and a seemingly antiquated service aboard. Still, that's another story for someone else.

As I munched through the insubstantial fare I considered the statistics. Britain had a fleet of over 40,000 boats in the 1870s, and the boats over 40ft in length had fallen to 17,000 by 1920. This progressively shrunk until there were only 12,500 by 1950. Landings of herring also fell from a peak in 1913 when over half a million tons were landed that year. By 1950 only 176,300 tons were landed, 90 per cent of which went through Peterhead. By 1959 the total annual Lowestoft and Yarmouth landings equalled what would have arrived in one night. It seems that the English herring heyday, that had existed for centuries since Cerdick landed, was over.

The next decade saw the introduction of the purse-seine-net from Norway as the last of the drift-net boats disappeared. The introduction of this aggressive method had by far the greatest impact upon herring stocks than any other single innovation. A continuous net up to 2,000m long is set in deep water around a suspected shoal, and the bottom rope is progressively tightened to form a pond with the fish inside. Once this is so tight that the fish are just a seething mass, the herring is pumped into the tanks. Catches of 1,000 tons were reported in one catch. Not surprisingly this had a drastic effect upon the

North Sea herring stock. In 1965 it was reported that 259 Norwegian pursers caught 615,000 tons off Shetland when the entire British landings were only 100,000 tons. Total landings that year rose to 1.2 million tons, nearly double its average for the previous decade. Over the next ten years catches fell dramatically until it was estimated that 70 per cent of the entire stock was being removed year on year. With landings down to 200,000 tons in 1975 political pressure finally brought about a response, as, two years later, the North Sea herring was closed. The west coast of Scotland followed suit the following year. The excesses of some fishermen returned to haunt everyone.

A partial recovery was reported in 1981, when it was reopened. Landings rose once more to 800,000 tons, but has fallen back a considerable amount in recent years. Purse-seines have waned in favour of the mid-water trawl. 1998 quotas for Britain were: North Sea 38,910 tons; Clyde 1,000 tons and west coast 46,360 tons. Ironically, 1999 saw a world glut with the landings up 157 per cent as a result of the Russian and Asian financial collapses. Herring that was a few years earlier selling at £450 a tonne was down to £105. It took a few years to stabilise but, in 2013, herring stocks were labelled as being healthy in most parts though the west of Scotland, and Ireland and the Irish Sea are at a level where they are overfished but still open for fishing. The 2013 Total Allowable Catch (TAC) for North and Norwegian Seas herring was 478,000 tons, of which the UK quota was 70,965 tons.

But what went wrong with fishing when entry into the Common Fisheries Policy was meant to protect stocks on the advice of scientists from ICES, the International Council for the Exploration of the Seas, the oldest intergovernmental organisation in the world concerned with marine and fisheries advice.

First, let's explain the basic system. TACs are set by the European Commission and their politicians on advice from fishermen and scientists. Take herring, for example, in 2013. The main UK catch was in the North Sea as mentioned above. However, the total TAC for herring was 1,387,538 tons, of which the EU fleet had 753,982 tons. This was split between the countries of the EU. Denmark has the highest total quota of 145,133 tons, Finland 104,897 tons and the UK 100,837 tons, and so on. The UK quota was again split up and allocated to various companies and boats in line with the size of the boat, the fishing capability and other factors such as the amount of money they paid for access to quota. Sounds a nightmare – it is. For each stock the same applies and the annual allocation at the Council of Ministers in December has become a horse-trading affair and, let's admits it, a farce. The problem is the Common Fisheries Policy. Whereas Norway and Iceland have healthy fisheries, Europe does not.

Why not then? In the author's opinion it is simply down to the massive scale that the Common Fisheries Policy attempts to regulate over. Is it right that 78 per cent of the British fleet receive such a small percentage of the quota as in the case of the small 'under tens' fleet? On average their share of the quota is 4 per cent, down to 1.2 per cent in the North Sea (ICES area IV) and 7 per cent in the English Channel, Western Approaches, Celtic Sea and Irish Sea (ICES area VII). How can that be justified for fishers from coastal communities who have relied upon the fisheries for generations?[2]

Whereas Norway and Iceland have an almost complete control over their own fisheries over an area adjacent to their coasts, the European Union attempts to direct and regulate over what is in fact a huge area of contrasts, individual customs and cultural traditions. From the Mediterranean, along the Atlantic seaboard and through the Bay of Biscay, the Western Approaches, Western Ireland and Scotland, the Irish and North Seas, English Channel, throughout the whole of the Baltic and over parts of the northern Atlantic, this body of bureaucrats exercises various tools that assume to encompass all the different cultures that share this huge expanse of sea. This they call the common access which, in reality, is an excuse for a common plundering. Norway, although it has many agreements with the EU over some areas such as the North Sea, has been much more forward over the last twenty years in bringing in legislation to make some inroads into the problem of overfishing.

The EU has relied upon the ill-fated quota system to maintain stocks over the last thirty years and has failed miserably. To this they have added a 'days at sea' policy, thus reducing the amount of time fishers can fish and have introduced 'selective gear' whereby technology improves net design. Then they have decommissioned fishing boats to reduce the fishing fleet with the result being that, although the numbers of fishing boats have gone down, public money has been used to produce a fishing fleet that is much more efficient and therefore capable of taking the same amount of fish from the sea as it did with a higher number of more inefficient fishing vessels. And, as a consequence of an enforced scrapping policy, this has seen many of the older, some historically sensitive, fishing boats disappearing altogether. Alongside all these measures, the fleet has been 'discarding' thousands of tons of fish while at sea when they have landed too much of a particular species. The law-makers in the EU have known about this for thirty years yet have, until very recently, been unwilling to actually do anything about it. Over those years hundreds of thousands, probably millions, of tons of good fish have been discarded, to pollute as the vast majority do not survive.

Norway, on the other hand, implemented a different approach to the discards of fish, banning it in 1987. However, this ban was part of a comprehensive package of policies to minimise discards even if they believed it would be almost impossible to eradicate them completely. They adopted a process of 'closed areas' while also bringing measures to counter 'high grad-

A fishing boat lies rotting away at Applecross, on Scotland's west coast, perhaps a pointer for times to come as fish stocks are wiped out by corporate greed.

ing', by which vessels discard smaller, legally sized fish when they catch larger fish that fetch higher rates at market. Although no one measure can solve the problem of overfishing, a mixture of obliging fishermen to move grounds when they have exceeded allowable by-catches or found undersized fish, closing areas and making fishermen themselves responsible for informing the authorities if they believe an area is being overfished, can help. Surveillance of the boats contributes but one measure that encourages fishermen in the white fish sector is the compensation scheme for fishermen who land fish caught unintentionally in contravention of the regulations. Instead of the State receiving the economic value of fish caught in this way, in order to show loyalty to fishermen, 20 per cent of the value is retained by them if it is established that the illegal catch was taken unintentionally. Other measures exist to avoid over-quota fish in the pelagic sector.[3]

Iceland, too, uses various control measures as well as enforcement to maintain the responsible management of its fisheries. As in Norway, discards are banned and all catches must be landed. Extensive provisions are made for the temporary closures of fishing areas to protect spawning fish from all fishing and well as areas of other vulnerable habitats. Some of the closures are permanent – as off the north and northwest coasts where fishing by bottom trawl, mid-water trawl and the Danish seine is not permitted within 12 miles of the coast and around other parts of the coast where trawling is restricted to smaller vessels within the 12 miles – while other closures are temporary and even seasonal. Furthermore, Iceland has one of the most sophisticated enforcement regimes in the world, in particular regarding port control and the weighing of all catches. Ever since the 1970s when Iceland extended its 200-mile limit (the same limit as Norway), its fisheries have been closely monitored. Before the extension, foreign boats were catching over 100,000 tons of fish a year in these waters from Icelandic stock, and this was estimated to be about a third of its cod stock, a quarter of its haddock stock, and half of the total catches of saithe and redfish.[4] No wonder they wrested control over these waters, otherwise the foreign, mostly European, vessels would have wiped out the complete stock. However, these days, both Norway and Iceland have managed to create sustainable fisheries around their coasts while the European Union, and its Common Fisheries Policy, continues to fail. Europe simply would be unable to efficiently enforce similar effort controls with any hope of success because of the areas of sea involved. It tries, poor thing, but the will-power just is not there.

And so, while the fisheries in its waters around its shores continue to decline, the European Union vessels fish further afield. Today's European Commissioner for Maritime Affairs and Fisheries, Maria Damanaki, has recently made the announcement that, 'We will not fish in any other waters in a way that we will not fish in our own waters.' Judging by the way the EU has acted over the last thirty years, they look to be about to continue the absolute plundering of fishing grounds around the globe and that, added to the antics of other countries worldwide (Russia, China and Japan for a start), does not bode well for fish stocks around the planet in the coming decades!

NOTES

Introduction

1   The Washington Report 1849. For a succinct article on the report by Adrian Osler, see *Maritime Life and Traditions*, issue no. 3, June 1999.
2   The best report on this is from the Manx Society vol. XVI with a personal account taken from A *Tour through the Isle of Man* by David Robertson (1794) who witnessed the disaster.
3   See Peter Aitchison, *The Children of the Sea*, East Linton, 2001.
4   See Marie Feeney, *The Cleggan Bay Disaster*, Glencolumbkille, 2001. The author is a granddaughter of one of the survivors.

1 Early Fishers

1   F. Dakronia and P. Kounouklas, 'Fishing Technology: The Kynos Contribution', unpublished report.
2   William Radcliffe, *Fishing from the Earliest Times*, London, 1921.
3   See Mike Smylie, 'Octopus Pots', *Maritime Life & Traditions* no. 31, 2006.
4   See D.J. Brewer and R.F. Friedman, *Fish and Fishing in Ancient Egypt*, Warminster, 1989.
5   A. von Brandt, in *Fish Catching Methods of the World*, London, 1972, gives a thorough account of these more unusual forms of fishing.
6   L. Pedersen, '7000 Years of Fishing: Stationary Fishing Structures in the Mesolithic and Afterwards', in A. Fischer (ed.), *Man and Sea in the Mesolithic*, Oxford, 1995.
7   See M. Bell, 'The Goldcliff Late-Mesolithic Site 5400–4000 Cal BC', CBA report 120, 2000.
8   F.M. Davis, *An Account of the Fishing Gear of England and Wales*, London, HMSO, 1936.
9   D. MacDonald, *Lewis, A History of the Island*, Edinburgh, 1978.
10 Mike Smylie, *Anglesey and its Coastal Tradition*, Llanrwst, 2000.
11 E.E. Evans, *Mourne County*, 1951. Perhaps the best classification of these weirs has been put forward by N.V.C. Bannerman in *The Bronze Age Coast Project – Ancient Fish Trap Types*, 2000.
12 See R.J. Slack-Smith, *Fishing with Traps and Pots*, Rome, 2001. Also 'Fishing Baskets of Asia Pacific', a pamphlet of an exhibition of fish traps held in Canada in 1997–98.
13 Various authors have written on the fishing techniques of the River Severn, including the present author. For a brief look, see John Neufville Taylor, *Fishing on the Lower Severn*, Gloucester, 1974.
14 J. Bickerdyke, *Sea Fishing, The Badminton Library of Sports and Pastimes*, London 1895.
15 Oppian of Corycus, *Halieutica*, LOEB, Cambridge, MA, Harvard University Press, 1928 (translated by A.W. Mair). This was his poem of fishing (Halieutica) of some 3,500 lines, which he wrote in the second half of the second century.

2 The Growth of the Herring Fishery

1   See Mike Smylie, *Herring: A History of the Silver Darlings*, Stroud, 2004.
2   Arthur Michael Samuel, *The Herring; Its Effect on the History of Britain*, London, 1918.
3   John Haywood, *Dark Age Naval Power*, Hockwold-cum-Wilton, 1999.
4   Samuel, *op. cit.*, 1918.
5   For a detailed account of the Dutch herring fishery, see Anthony Beaujon, *The History of the Dutch Sea Fisheries*, London, 1884.
6   Smylie, *op. cit.*, 2004.
7   John Dyson, *Business in Great Waters*, London, 1977, tells this story among others.

8   Samuel, *op. cit.*, 1918.
9   The Commissioners and Trustees for Improving Fisheries and Manufactures in Scotland, *His Majesty's Patent for Improving Fisheries and Manufactures in Scotland*, Edinburgh, 1727.
10 Jean Dunlop, *The British Fisheries Society 1786–1893*, Edinburgh, 1978.
11 Malcolm Gray, *The Fishing Industries of Scotland 1790–1914*, Aberdeen, 1978.
12 Smylie, *op. cit.*, 2004.
13 See the *Manx Sea Fishing 1600–1990s* educational pack published by the Manx Heritage Foundation, 1991.
14 Angus Martin, *The Ring-Net Fishermen*, Edinburgh, 1981.
15 Angus Martin, 'The Campbeltown Fishing Industry', in *The Campbeltown Book*, Kintyre Civic Society, 2003.
16 As quoted by Martin, *op. cit.*, 1981.
17 Angus Martin, *The North Herring Fishing*, Isle of Colonsay, 2001, recounts stories of fishermen berthing there in the 1950s.
18 Martin, *op. cit.*, 1981.
19 See Mike Smylie, *The Slopemasts, a History of the Lochfyne Skiffs*, Stroud, 2008, for a history of these craft.

3 The Crofter-Fishermen of Scotland

1   James R. Coull, 'Crofter-Fishermen', in J.R. Coull *et al.* (eds), *Scottish Life and Society – Boats, Fishing and the Sea*, Edinburgh, 2008.
2   R. Stuart Bruce, 'The Haaf Fishing and Shetland Trading', in *The Mariner's Mirror*, vol. 8, no. 2, 1922.
3   HMSO, *Second Report to the Commissioners Appointed to Inquire into the Truck System (Shetland)*, Edinburgh, 1872.
4   A.D. Cameron, *Go Listen to the Crofters – The Napier Commission and Crofting a Century Ago*, Stornoway, 1986.
5   James R. Coull, *The Sea Fisheries of Scotland*, Edinburgh, 1996.
6   J.R. Nicolson, *Shetland's Fishing Vessels*, Lerwick, 1981.
7   Coull, *op. cit.*, 2008.
8   Mike Smylie, *Traditional Fishing Boats of Britain & Ireland*, Shrewsbury, 1999.
9   James Anderson, *An Account of the Present State of the Hebrides and Western Coasts of Scotland*, Edinburgh, 1785.
10 Coull, *op. cit.*, 2008.
11 Cameron, *op. cit.*, 1986.
12 *Shetland Times*, 1881.
13 James Hogg, *Highland Journeys*, Edinburgh, 2008.
14 Donald Macdonald, *Lewis: A History of the Island*, Edinburgh, 1990.
15 Cameron, *op. cit.*, 1986.
16 Dean Munro, *Description of the Western Isles of Scotland*, Edinburgh, 1774.
17 Calum Ferguson, *Children of the Black House*, Edinburgh, 2003.
18 Cameron, *op. cit.*, 1986.
19 *Ibid.*
20 Angus Duncan, *Hebridean Island – Memories of Scarp*, East Linton, 1995.
21 Angus Edward MacInnes, *Eriskay Where I Was Born*, Edinburgh, 1997.
22 As quoted in Paul Thompson, *Living the Fishing*, London, 1983.

4 Longshoremen of England

1   Personal communication in 2012.
2   See Robb Robinson, 'Inshore and Local Fisheries, c1530 to 1880', in David J. Starkey *et al.* (eds), *England's Sea Fisheries*, London, 2000.
3   See Gloria Wilson, 'The English North Sea Coast', in Julian Mannering (ed.), *The Chatham Directory of Inshore Craft*, London, 1997.
4   Peter Frank, *Yorkshire Fisherfolk*, Chichester, 2002.
5   Mike Smylie, *Traditional Fishing Boats of Britain & Ireland*, Shrewsbury, 1999.
6   Gloria Wilson, *Freshening Breezes – Fishing Boats of Cleveland and North Yorkshire*, Stroud, 2013.

7   John Dyson, *Business in Great Waters*, London, 1977.
8   David Brandon, *Along the Yorkshire Coast*, Stroud, 2010.
9   See Barrie Farnill, *A History of Robin Hood's Bay*, Helmsley, 1966.
10 Fran Weatherhead, *North Norfolk Fishermen*, Stroud, 2011.
11 Daniel Defoe, *A Tour thro' the whole Island of Great Britain*, London, 1725 [1927].
12 Peter Stibbons, Katherine Lee and Martin Warren, *Crabs and Shannocks*, Cromer, 1983.
13 Frank Buckland, *The Fisheries in Norfolk – especially Crabs. Lobsters, Herrings and the Broads*, HMSO, 1875.
14 Michael M. Marshall, *Fishing – the Coastal Tradition*, London, 1987.
15 Robert Simper, *Beach Boats of Britain*, Woodbridge, 1984.
16 Smylie, *op. cit.*, 1999.
17 See Edward Cooke, *Shipping & Craft*, London, 1970 (facsimile edition).
18 Marshall, *op. cit.*, 1987.
19 F.M. Davis, *An Account of the Fishing Gear of England & Wales*, London, 1937.
20 E.W.H. Holdsworth, *Deep-Sea Fishing and Fishing Boats*, London, 1874.
21 See Steve Peak, *Fishermen of Hastings*, St Leonards-on-Sea, 1985, for a full history.

5 West Country Pilchard Fishing

1   Keith Harris, *Hevva! Cornish Fishing in the Days of Sail*, Redruth, 1983.
2   Cyril Noall, *Cornish Seines and Seiners*, Truro, 1972. Noall has a complete history of the pilchard industry.
3   John Dyson, *Business in Great Waters*, London, 1977.
4   Richard Carew, *The Survey of Cornwall 1602*, Redruth, 2000.
5   Richard Fenton, *A Historical Tour through Pembrokeshire*, London, 1811.
6   Mike Smylie, *Working the Welsh Coast*, Stroud, 2005.
7   George Owen of Henllys, *The Description of Pembrokeshire* (1603), Llandysul, 1994.
8   Daniel Defoe, *A Tour thro' the whole Island of Great Britain*, London, 1725 [1927].
9   Richard Carew, *The Survey of Cornwall 1602*, London, 1602.
10 Mike Smylie, *Traditional Fishing Boats of Britain & Ireland*, Shrewsbury, 1999.
11 Cyril Hart, *Cornish Oasis … A Biographical Chronicle of the Fishing Village of Coverack, Cornwall*, Mullion, 1990.
12 Defoe, *op. cit.*, 1725.
13 Noall, *op. cit.*, 1972.
14 John Sampson Courtney, *A Guide to Penzance and Its Neighbourhood*, Penzance/London, 1845.
15 William Daniell, *A Voyage round Great Britain, volume VIII*, London, 1825.
16 Noall, *op. cit.*, 1972.
17 *Ibid.*
18 Captain William Roberts, *Perranporth Cornwall (North Coast): Reminiscences of Perranporth from the Year 1833*, Truro, 1939.
19 Noall, *op. cit.*, 1972.
20 *Ibid.*
21 *Ibid.*

6 Fishing the Irish Sea

1   See the resource booklet *Manx Sea Fishing 1600–1990s* published by the Manx Heritage Foundation, 1991.
2   W.C. Smith, *A Short History of the Irish Sea Herring Fisheries*, Liverpool/London, 1923.
3   *Manx Sea Fishing*, *op. cit.*, 1991.
4   William Blundell, *A History of the Isle of Man (1871)*, 2008.
5   George Owen of Henllys, *The Description of Pembrokeshire* (1603), Llandysul, 1994.
6   Guillaume Rondelet, *Libri de Piscibus Marinis, in quibus Piscium expressæ sunt. Quæ in tota Piscium historia contineantur, indicat Elenchus pagina nona et decimal*. This was the first French work ever published on fish in 1554.
7   Mike Smylie, *The Herring Fishers of Wales*, Llanwrst, 1998.
8   Colin Matheson, *Wales and the Sea Fisheries*, Cardiff, 1929.

9   E.A. Lewis, *The Welsh Port Books 1550–1603*, London, 1927.

10 R. Warner, *A Walk through Wales in August, 1797*, London, 1798.

11 Thomas Westcote, *A View of Devonshire in MDCXXX*, Exeter, 1845.

12 Mike Smylie, *Herring – A History of the Silver Darlings*, Stroud, 2004.

13 Charles Harper, *The North Devon Coast*, London, 1908.

14 Smith, *op. cit.*, 1923.

15 Mike Smylie, *Traditional Fishing Boats of Britain & Ireland*, Shrewsbury, 1999.

16 Mike Smylie, *Fishing Boats of Cornwall*, Stroud, 2009.

17 See Angus Martin, *The Ring-Net Fishermen*, Edinburgh, 1981, for the full story.

18 Mike Smylie, *The Slopemasts – A History of the Lochfyne Skiffs*, Stroud, 2008.

19 Sam Henderson and Peter Drummond, *Built by Nobles of Girvan*, Stroud, 2010.

20 Robb Robinson, *Trawling, the Rise and Fall of the British Trawl Fishery*, Exeter, 1996.

21 British Parliamentary Papers, *Report from Committees on the State of the British Herring Fisheries*, 1798.

7 Trawling the Silver Pits

1   Robb Robinson, *The Rise and Fall of the British Trawl Fisheries*, Exeter, 1996.

2   Michael Graham, *The Fish Gate*, London, 1943.

3   Walter Wood, *North Sea Fishers and Fighters*, London, 1911.

4   Hervey Benham, *The Codbangers*, Colchester, 1979.

5   John Dyson, *Business in Great Waters*, London, 1977.

6   Daniel Defoe, *A Tour Thro' the whole Island of Great Britain*, London, 1927.

7   Dyson, *op. cit.*, 1977.

8   Mike Smylie, *Traditional Fishing Boats of Britain & Ireland*, Shrewsbury, 1999.

9   Graham, *op. cit.*, 1943.

10 Dyson, *op. cit.*, 1977.

11 Ibid.

12 Robinson, *op. cit.*, 1996.

13 J.M. Bellany, 'Pioneers of the Hull Trawl Fishing Industry', *The Mariner's Mirror*, no. 51, 1965.

14 Edgar March, *Sailing Trawlers*, London, 1953.

15 Robinson, *op. cit.*, 1996.

16 *Ibid.*

17 Wood, *op. cit.*, 1911.

18 Robinson, *op. cit.*, 1996.

8 Fishing beyond the Continental Shelf

1   M.G. Dickinson (ed.), *A Living from the Sea – Devon's Fishing Industry and its Fishermen*, Exeter, 1987.

2   Evan Jones, 'England's Icelandic Fishery in the Early Modern Period', in D.J. Starkey *et al.* (eds), *England's Sea Fisheries*, London, 2000.

3   John Dyson, *Business in Great Waters*, London, 1977.

4   *Ibid.*

5   Jones, *op. cit.*, 2000.

6   Robb Robinson, *The Rise and Trawl of the British Trawl Fishery*, Exeter, 1996.

7   Mike Smylie, *Fishing Around Morecambe Bay*, Stroud, 2010.

8   John Knox, *View of the British Empire, more especially Scotland, with some proposals for the Improvement of that country, the extension of the fisheries and the relief of the People*, London, 1784.

9   Charles MacLean, *The Fringe of Gold*, Edinburgh, 1985.

10 Dyson, *op. cit.*, 1977.

11 Michael Graham, *The Fish Gate*, London, 1943.

12 Dyson, *op. cit.*, 1977.

13 Mike Smylie, *Traditional Fishing Boats of Britain & Ireland*, Shrewsbury, 1999.

14 Dyson, *op. cit.*, 1977.

15 *Ibid.*

16 Excerpt from *Toilers of the Deep* (1893) as quoted by John Dyson, *op. cit.*, 1977. The piece was entitled 'The Black Monday Gale' and occurred in December 1883.

17 HMSO, *Return of the Deaths of Seamen and Fishermen reported to the Board of Trade in the Year ended 30th June 1909*, London, 1910.

9 Cockles, Mussels, Oysters and Scallops

1 Angus Martin, *Fishing and Whaling*, Edinburgh, 1995.

2 J.T. Jenkins, *The Sea Fisheries*, London, 1920. Jenkins was superintendent of the Lancashire and Western Sea Fisheries at around the turn of the twentieth century.

3 F.M. Davis, *An Account of the Fishing Gear of England and Wales*, London, 1937.

4 Eija Kennerley, *The Old Fishing Community of Poulton-le-Sands*, Lancaster, undated.

5 A.M. Wakefield, 'Cockling at Morecambe Bay', in *The Pall Mall Magazine*, edited by Lord Frederic Hamilton, vol. XVI, London, 1898.

6 J.H. Orton and H. Paynter, 'The Lancashire Sea Fisheries', in *Scientific Survey of Blackpool and District*, 1936. For more details on this fishery, see 'The Fisheries of Morecambe Bay' by Andrew Scott, in *Morecambe, Lancaster and District: Souvenir of the Conference of the National Union of Teachers, Easter 1908*, published by OUP/Hodder, 1909.

7 J. Geraint Evans, *Cockles & Mussels: Aspects of Shellfish Gathering in Wales*, Cardiff, 1977, and *Inshore Fishermen of Wales*, Cardiff, 1991.

8 See www.msc.org for more information on the MSC.

9 George Owen, *The Description of Pembrokeshire*, Llandysul, 1994.

10 See *The Transactions of the Liverpool National Eisteddfod 1884*, Liverpool, 1885.

11 Colin Matheson, *Wales and the Sea Fisheries*, Cardiff, 1929.

12 J.O. Halliwell, *Notes of Family Excursions in North Wales*, London, 1860.

13 Matheson, *op. cit.*, 1929.

14 A. Franklin, G.D. Pickett and P.M. Connor, 'The Scallop and Its Fishery in England and Wales', Lowestoft, 1980 – a laboratory leaflet from the Ministry of Agriculture, Fisheries and Food.

15 See the resource booklet *Manx Sea Fishing 1600–1990s* published by the Manx Heritage Foundation, 1991.

10 Lobsters and Crabs

1 Daniel Defoe, *A Tour thro' the whole Island of Great Britain*, London, 1725 [1927].

2 William A. Bingley, *A Tour around North Wales Performed in the Summer of 1798*, London, 1800.

3 J.T. Jenkins, *The Sea Fisheries*, London, 1920.

4 E.W.H. Holdsworth, *Deep-Sea Fishing and Fishing Boats*, London, 1874.

5 Peter Stibbons, Katherine Lee and Martin Warren, *Crabs and Shannocks*, Cromer, 1983.

6 J. Sinclair, *The Statistical Account of Scotland*, (OSA), Edinburgh, 1791–9.

11 War and Peace

1 Mike Smylie, *Herring – A History of the Silver Darlings*, Stroud, 2004.

2 Christopher Unsworth, *The British Herring Industry*, Stroud, 2013.

3 Neal Green, *Fisheries of the North Sea*, London, 1918, gives slightly different figures.

4 Arthur M. Samuel, *The Herring; its Effect on the History of Britain*, London, 1918.

5 Douglas d'Enno, *Fishermen against the Kaiser*, vol. 1, Barnsley, 2010.

6 *Ibid.*

7 Robb Robinson, *The Rise and Fall of the British Trawl Fishery*, Exeter, 1996.

8 Walter Wood, *North Sea Fishers and Fighters*, London, 1911.

9 John Dyson, *Business in Great Waters*, London, 1977.

10 Robinson, *op. cit.*, 1996.

11 Christopher Unsworth, *The British Herring Industry*, Stroud, 2013.

12 Hervey Benham, *The Stowboaters*, Colchester, 1977.

13 L.W. Hawkins, *Early Motor Fishing Boats*, Norwich, 1984.

14 Mike Smylie, *Traditional Fishing Boats of Britain & Ireland*, Shrewsbury, 1999.

15 Hawkins, *op. cit.*, 1984.

16 Mike Smylie, *Traditional Fishing Boats of Europe*, Stroud, 2013.
17 A. Ritchie, *The Scottish Seine Net Fishery 1921–1957* (Marine Research No. 3), HMSO, 1960.
18 David Thomson, *The Seine Net*, London, 1969.
19 Angus Martin, *The Ring-Net Fishermen*, Edinburgh, 1981.
20 Gloria Wilson, *Scottish Fishing Craft*, London, 1965.

12 World War to Cod War

1 Trygve Sørvaag, *Shetland Bus*, Lerwick, 2002. David Howarth's *The Shetland Bus* (1951) also tells the story.
2 Robb Robinson, *The Rise and Fall of the British Trawl Fishery*, Exeter, 1996.
3 See Paul Lund and Harry Ludham, *Trawlers Go to War*, 1971, which specifically examines Harry Tate's Navy.
4 Walter Wood, *Fishermen in War Time*, London, 1911.
5 Robinson, *op. cit.*, 1996.
6 Iain Sutherland, *From Herring to Seine Net Fishing*, Wick, 1985.
7 Gloria Wilson, *More Scottish Fishing Craft*, London, 1968.
8 Mike Smylie (ed.), *Fishing Boats* (the magazine of the 40+ Fishing Boat Association), issue 4, Spring 1996, has a brief description of the boat.
9 Alan Villiers, *The Deep Sea Fishermen*, London, 1970.
10 John Nicklin and Patricia O'Driscoll, *Trawler Disasters 1946–1975*, Stroud, 2010. The book details all losses and wrecking from Aberdeen, Fleetwood, Hull and Grimsby.
11 Austin Mitchell and Anne Tate, *Fishermen – the Rise and Fall of Deep Water Trawling*, Beverley, 1997.
12 Andrew Welch, *Royal Navy in the Cod Wars: Britain and Iceland in Conflict 1958–1976*, Liskeard, 2006.
13 Angus Martin, *The Ring-Net Fishermen*, Edinburgh, 1981, as quoted in a letter from W.P. Miller.

13 Fishing Boat Design over Time

1 Nick Miller, *The Lancashire Nobby*, Stroud, 2009.
2 See Criostoir MacCarthaigh (ed.), *Traditional Boats of Ireland*, Cork, 2008, for a fantastic description of Irish craft.
3 Mike Smylie, *The Slopemasts – A History of the Lochfyne Skiffs*, Stroud, 2008.
4 L.W. Hawkins, *Early Motor Fishing Boats*, Norwich, 1984.
5 Angus Martin, *The Ring-Net Fishermen*, Edinburgh, 1981.
6 See Pat Nolan, *Sea Change, The Rise of the BIM 50-footer and its Impact on Coastal Ireland*, Dublin, 2008.

14 Fishermen and Family

1 Emma Cardwell, 'Invisible Fishermen, The Rise and Fall of the British Small Boat Fleet', in Thomas Højrup and Klaus Schriewer (eds), *European Fisheries at Tipping Point*, Murcia, Spain, 2012.
2 Peter Anson, *Fishing Boats and Fisher Folk on the East Coast of Scotland*, London, 1930.
3 James G. Bertram, *The Harvest of the Sea*, London/Paisley, 1885.
4 Stafford Linsley, *Ports and Harbours of Northumberland*, Stroud, 2005.
5 Mike Smylie, *Working the Welsh Coast*, Stroud, 2005.
6 Peter Anson, *Scots Fisherfolk*, Macduff, 1950.
7 As quoted in Peter Frank, *Yorkshire Fisherfolk*, Chichester, 2002.
8 William and Edward Finden, *Ports and Harbours*, London, 1838.
9 Frank, *op. cit.*, 2002.
10 Smylie, *op. cit.*, 2005.
11 Mike Smylie, *The Herring Fishers of Wales*, Llanrwst, 1998.
12 As quoted by Sally Festing, *Fishermen, a Community Living from the Sea*, Newton Abbot, 1977.
13 Nelson Cazeils and Fanny Fennec, *Il y a un siècle … Les Femmes et la Mer*, Rennes, 2003. The book, although in French, has gorgeous illustrations and photographs of these women.

14 Angus Martin, *The Ring-Net Fishermen*, Edinburgh, 1981.

15 Catherine Lucy Czerkawska, *Fisher-folk of Carrick*, Glasgow, 1975.

16 Walter Gregor, *Notes on the Folk-lore of North-East Scotland*, vol. 7 of Folklore Society Publications, 1881.

17 Czerkawska, *op. cit.*, 1975.

18 Ibid.

19 William Innes, 'Superstitions', in *Fishing Boats*, the magazine of the 40+ Fishing Boat Association, no. 11, 1998.

20 Czerkawska, *op. cit.*, 1975.

21 Angus Martin, *Fishing and Whaling*, Edinburgh, 1995.

22 Martin, *op. cit.*, 1995.

23 Personal comminucation.

24 'Fisher-Folks', in *The Highland Magazine*, Oban, no. 7, September 1885.

25 John Dyson, *Business in Great Waters*, London, 1977.

26 Dyson gives a full account of the Bethel ships and the Mission to Deep-Sea Fishermen.

27 HMSO, *Return of the Deaths of Seaman and Fishermen reported to the Board of Trade in the Year ended 30th June 1909*, London, 1910.

15 Women in Fishing

1 Mike Smylie, *Herring – A History of the Silver Darlings*, Stroud, 2004.

2 David Butcher, *Following the Fishing*, Newton Abbot, 1987.

3 Arthur E. Neiland, *The Fish House – Passage East*, self-published, 2012.

4 Christopher Unsworth, *The British Herring Industry*, Stroud, 2013.

5 *Ibid.*

6 Smylie, *op. cit.*, 2004.

7 Trevor Lummis, *Occupation & Society – the East Anglian Fishermen 1880–1914*, Cambridge, 1985.

8 Butcher, *op. cit.*, 1987.

9 Smylie, *op. cit.*, 2004.

10 Butcher, *op. cit.*, 1987.

11 Smylie, *op. cit.*, 2004.

12 Unsworth, *op. cit.*, 2013.

13 Smylie, *op. cit.*, 2004.

14 Butcher, *op. cit.*, 1987.

15 A.R Charlesworth, *The Morton's Story*, self-published, 1995.

16 *Ibid.*

17 *Ibid.*

16 Modern Fishing, the EU and Legislation

1 De Caux, J.W., *The Herring and the Herring Fishery*, with chapters on 'Fishes and Fishing' and 'Our Sea Fisheries in the Future', London 1881

2 Emma Cardwell, 'Invisible Fishermen, The Rise and Fall of the British Small Boat Fleet', in Thomas Højrup and Klaus Schriewer (eds), *European Fisheries at Tipping Point*, Murcia, Spain, 2012.

3 www.fisheries.no/resource_management

4 www.fisheries.is/management/fisheries-management

Visit our website and discover thousands of
other History Press books.

www.thehistorypress.co.uk